1980

University of St. Fran...
GEN 850.9 P...

W9-ACF-359

3 0301 00090735 8

Writers in The Italian Renaissance

ABOUT THE BOOK

A comprehensive exquisitely written and constructed history of the literature of the Italian Renaissance, the cradle of modern civilization.

Humanist writers succeeded in creating the profession of writer with all its now familiar social and economic power. Prince Rospigliosi shows that it was these pioneer professional writers who created the Renaissance, and not, as is often supposed, it that produced them. They dealt lethal blows to rigid hierarchical medieval authoritarianism, thereby creating modern society.

Prince Rospigliosi has elaborated a colourful tapestry about the rich and extraordinary lives led by the precursors and guiding spirits of the Italian Renaissance. Dante, Petrarch, Boccaccio, Pius II, Lorenzo de Medici and Poliziano were not only original geniuses, but also great individual characters, who come to life throughout this refreshingly lively history. This is an indispensable book for both layman and scholar.

ABOUT THE AUTHOR

Prince William Rospigliosi is descended from the Tuscan family to which Pope Clement IX and the great Rospigliosi cardinals belonged. During the Renaissance, his ancestors were notaries in Pistoia and themselves contributed to humanist literature. Educated at Cambridge University, he spent much of his early career in broadcasting and journalism. He was Vatican correspondent for *Time* and *Life* for fourteen years and for Roman newspapers another fifteen years, while contributing regularly to Italian newspapers and magazines. He has written a number of outstanding stories, including *A Clock for Fiumiciono* (subsequently made into a film), and a book about his experiences in Rhodesia.

WRITERS IN THE ITALIAN RENAISSANCE

BY WILLIAM ROSPIGLIOSI

Gordon & Cremonesi

LIBRARY
College of St. Franci
JOLIET. ILL.

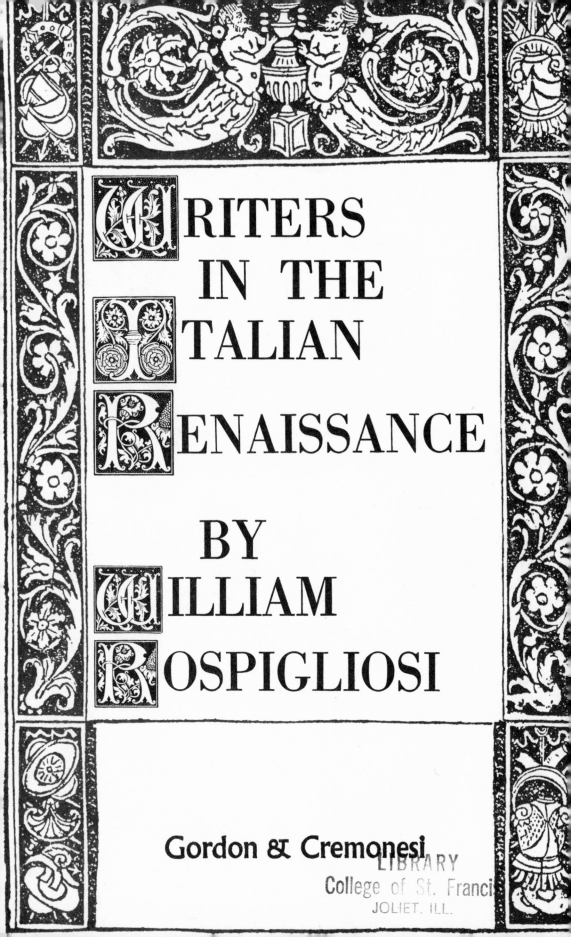

© William Rospigliosi, 1978

All rights reserved. No part of this publication
may be reproduced, stored in a retrieval system, or
transmitted in any form or by any means, electronic,
mechanical, photocopying, recording or otherwise,
without permission in writing from the publishers.

Designed by Heather Gordon
Set in 11 on 13 pt Bodoni
by Input Typesetting Ltd., London
and printed in Great Britain
by The Pitman Press, Bath

British Library Cataloguing in Publication Data
Rospigliosi, William
    Writers in the Italian Renaissance.
    1. Italian literature – To 1400 – History
    and criticism 2. Italian literature – 15th
    century – History and criticism 3. Italian
    literature – 16th century – History and criticism
    1. Title
    850′.9   PQ4075   78–40400
LCCN: 78–040400
ISBN: 0–86033–072–9

Gordon & Cremonesi Publishers
London and New York
New River House
34 Seymour Road
London N8 OBE

850.9
R822

To Susan

89059

Contents

Foreword

This book has been written as an introduction for students of the Renaissance and for others aroused by curiosity in that constructive and joyful period. I have therefore taken care that it may be picked up and read at random, not only from the beginning to the end. The reader may choose to follow the order of the book and step into the Renaissance at its highest moment and then read on to the motives that brought it about. If he prefers, he may start with the last chapters, and work back to the Era at its climax. With a little knowledge of the times, it may be hoped that the reader, when familiar with the people of the epoch, may pick up the book at any point as a manual in which to check his recollections, re-live his first impressions or just dwell pleasantly for some moments in the life of a bygone age.

The main subject of the book is how and to what extent the Writers of the Renaissance influenced the society of their time. Society did not influence them, except providing them with the opportunity to develop their art. It was they who influenced those around them perhaps more than writers do today and the result was magnificent.

Gratitude goes first of all to Paul Tabori, who read and corrected the early chapters until death caught him one night, when, as always, he was working for others, chiefly the P.E.N. club the international organization of Poets, Playwrights, Editors, Essayists and Novelists and the writers in prison in countries that await their freedom. My heartfelt, grateful thanks are due to Peter Elstob of P.E.N., to the Vatican Library, the Angelica Library in Rome, the American Academy and the British Council, the Laurenziana in Florence, the University Library in Basle, the National Library in Zürich, the beautifully appointed and courteous Cantonal Library of the Ticino with its courteous staff and, last but certainly not least, the Library of Locarno, which, with limited funds and unlimited difficulties, is an Institution worthy of the highest respect particularly because of the sense of duty and dedication of its attendants. But the greatest and warmest thanks of all are due to Doctor Ruth Liepman of Zürich for her smiling encouragement and factual help without which this book would never have been published. Grateful thanks to Ms Herta Ryder of Hughes and Massie Ltd. and to Heather Gordon and Gilles Cremonesi for their assistance and guidance.

This study of the Writer's influence on society in the Italian Renaissance of the XIVth and XVth Centuries is yet another of the thousand reasons for the Author to be grateful to Susan, without whom this book would never have been started or, if begun, would never have been finished.

The Author
Locarno (Ticino) 1978
Switzerland

PART I

THE

LAURENTIAN

ERA

195. BERNARDINO CORIO. Woodcut from his
Milanese Chronicle, 1503 (detail).

CHAPTER ONE

Civic Pride in Renaissance Florence

ECENT research has thrown fresh light on many aspects of the Renaissance which had escaped our notice until now. The reason is not far to seek. There is no period of history that so closely resembles our own as the Italian Renaissance of the fourteenth and fifteenth centuries.

It was an epoch when, just as is happening today, all set values were abruptly overthrown. Trusting faith and blind obedience ceased of a sudden to provide spiritual and mental peace and man realized he was witnessing the sunset—as it happens, a glorious sunset—of previously held notions and found himself faced with the responsibility for making the world more livable not by following a pre-arranged and well-directed order, but through an effort of his own imagination and his will.

The miracle of the Renaissance is that—at this juncture—man, undismayed by the sight of a familiar world collapsing all around him—feeling suddenly unfettered from civil and ecclesiastical systems that had left the individual no initiative—yet marvellously found within himself the power to build a Golden Age, that many believe has not since been surpassed.

This glorious period was not reached without anguish and distress, not wholly dissimilar to the torment that besets men's minds today, so that, going over and meditating on the events and thoughts of that time of renewal, we are sometimes able to catch a glimpse of possible solutions to problems that threaten us now and our preoccupations become less formidable.

We come to realise that the Copernican discovery that the Earth was not, after all, a fixed centre with all stars revolving round it, was a revelation far more upsetting to the man of the Renaissance than any flight to the moon or beyond can be to anyone of us today. We grow to appreciate that the sudden realization that the Church was not the sole "Keeper of the keys to Heaven"—that one no longer need feel terrorised by demons or crushed by superstition nor by the power of Emperor and Pope, changed man's vision of the structure of society as it had existed for long dark centuries.

Naturally this realisation grew by stages and its penetration into all levels of society was gradual and much was retained of what was good in established orderly government and divinely inspired Church leadership. But as Horsburg tells us in his book on Lorenzo de'Medici[1] "Medieval dogmatism and ecclesiastical authority had thrown fetters around the mind of man, compelling it to move within a narrow and confined circle of ideas ... there is about medieval Schoolmen the pathos which attaches to a chained giant. Endowed with vast intellectual powers, they were without adequate scope for exercising them fully and freely."

The spirit which animated the medieval world was that of submission to authority. The inspiring certainty of the Renaissance was that of "free enquiry", the use of individual judgement, the worth and dignity of conviction freely reached.

So we have Lorenzo de'Medici on his deathbed (or so the story goes) humbly asking absolution and pardon from the friar and erstwhile friend, Girolamo Savonarola. The monk enjoined him to repent sincerely of any massacre or injustice he might have been guilty of or might have prevented and Lorenzo readily complied. But then Savonarola said that one of the conditions of his granting absolution was that Lorenzo, from his bed, restore to Florence the government of guilds and corporations. Though threatened with the terror of Hell, Lorenzo turned to the wall. Medieval man would have given way to fear and obeyed a Church convinced she was infallible in all any one of her confessors asserted. Lorenzo de' Medici, true man of the Renaissance, clearly discerned even in the throes of mortal sickness, the difference between the spiritual world in which he acknowledged the Church as leader and the political sphere into which the Church has no infallible right to enter. In this sphere, he felt his loyalty was due to the people of Florence, whom he had led to unequalled heights, and not to the friar however authoritative his garb and rank.

It is not certain that the episode actually took place, but the story—if story it is—lights up the difference between the subservient man of the Dark Ages and the free individual of the Renaissance. A long and difficult climb had led to this freedom of mind and judgement. There is a long period of history when the old ideas and inveterate terrors are interwoven with the fortitude of those who thought of man as more important than hierarchical structures, be they civil or ecclesiastical.

But one event stands out as having brought the idea of individual freedom to the collectivity: the armed resistance of the City of Florence to the Milanese Gian Galeazzo Visconti's attempt to bring under his tyranny the whole of Central Italy from the Alps to the Papal States.

We read in Leon Battista Alberti's Treatise on the Family (Book IV) that one of his relations—Piero Alberti—exiled from Florence, was received by the Duke of Milan, who, thinking to find an ally in someone who had been banished by the Florentines, said to him: "It seems to me both honest and manly to conquer (Florence) by force of arms since it is the custom of Princes to use force and I would not like to be judged less brave than others of my rank."

To this, Piero Alberti replied: "It is no less honest for those who have tasted freedom to defend it with their lives .... It is my duty to advise my Motherland with love and diligence and faith in her future. This is my duty, like that of any other citizen, even if the Alberti are persecuted by the present government of Florence. It would not be right to attempt anything against one's country because of harm suffered through the lack of virtue of its leaders."[2]

How different this concept from that of medieval man, whose allegiance was to his feudal Lord, or at most to his Comune and its allies, but never to his Country. Piero and Leon Battista Alberti's conviction was certainly shared by most Florentines as their desperate resistance and final victory on the City walls proved conclusively.

Dante believed and wrote that "The Emperor [he meant the German Emperor of the Holy Roman Empire] having all things, will desire nothing and will ensure justice to all men." The individualistic Florentines of the Renaissance entertained no such illusions. They saw in Dante as Vittorio Branca writes[3] "One of the greatest geniuses of anachronism—a faithful follower of medieval interpretation against the tastes of his own time. He was blindly convinced of the sacred attributes of the aristocrat as against the bubbling search for progress of the citizens of a Free City. He was an upholder of feudalism against the rising and victorious middle class, artisan and merchant."

Paradoxically, what makes Dante really great is neither his political opinion to which he clung so fervently nor his theology. His chief merit lies in having shown that the vernacular could vie successfully with Latin and reach poetic heights undreamed of. It is because of this that Dante became the inspiration whereby culture ceased to be confined to a limited number of scholars and reached the large masses of the people.

Dante suffered for his attachment to the vernacular. Many very important scholars of undoubted fame held him in contempt for it. Petrarch—the great Master of the musicality of the Tuscan tongue—openly despised Alighieri for having written the Divine Comedy in Italian and not in Latin. He wrote in a letter: "I too have played with this language in my youth as a way to rest the mind from literary endeavour. But I will not stoop to seek the applause of the raucous tavern-keeper and such."

By contrast, the extrovert, gregarious, self-reliant Florentines of the days of Lorenzo de'Medici in the following century, were literally bursting to share all they knew with others, with as many men, women and nations as possible. They wanted knowledge and the joy of possessing it to spread far and wide and they saw in the vernacular the language best suited to divulge notions and perceptions and express the essence of what they knew and felt.[4]

To Lorenzo and the Florentines, literature and poetry were a way of life and an expression of political realism. They were the instruments whereby Florence, hemmed in as she was between the powerful and grasping Papal States, the Duchy of Milan,—defeated but still dreaming of conquest,—the crafty, scheming Kings of Naples, could rise to be—despite all enemies—the foremost city in Europe, the one to spread the light of art and literature of our modern Era. Through excellence in the arts, adroitness in diplomacy, ability in banking, judgement and imagination in trade, Florence was destined to achieve a rank that others would envy, despite their own superior military might and political power.

Because of the importance the Florentines gave to exactness and clarity of expression, it is no wonder that literary men held the most important positions in Medicean Florence and were eagerly sought after in every activity. The writer, who merely wrote and sought a publisher and public simply did not exist in Florence. The clarity or agreeableness of his tongue were used not so much as an end in themselves, as to convey a precise and nuanced meaning—such as could not be expressed without a mastery of language. This was most evident in public office[5] but was judged essential also in the world of finance and trade; everywhere the literary man, who could express his thought concisely and well, reached high positions.

This is evident from the tax rolls. Giovanni de'Medici, the first of the family to play fully the role of leader, was a banking genius. He devised a system of taxation called "il catasto". It was the first form of progressive income tax, a system that no modern State has yet been able to improve. Each citizen was called upon to pay a part of his income and—in times of grave emergency—even of his capital to the State. Severe with himself, Giovanni de'Medici, invariably had his name at the top of the list. He was the one who paid most.[6] As decade followed decade and governments changed—the Florentines who constantly appeared high on the tax roll because their earnings were high, were practically all men of learning and humanists.

The Rinuccini—men dedicated to the classics—were eighth on the list. They were followed closely by the humanist Leonardo Bruni, who had come to Florence from his native Arezzo and had risen to be Chancellor of the Republic, because his "Epistulae", his letters, provided some of the clearest and best written Latin prose of the Renaissance.

An exception to this general trend was Leon Battista Alberti, but the reason is simple. His family had been exiled a long time before. He himself had been born in exile and previous governments had deprived the Alberti of all their Florentine property. His main income was derived from his post of "Writer of Briefs" at the papal court in Rome, an office he held until he was sixty. This was not a Florentine income and he was not a resident of Florence. His name appeared low on the rolls because he paid only on properties and moneys he owned in the Florentine State.

The great humanist Coluccio Salutati was among the 2 per cent who paid the highest taxes in the whole of Florence, despite the fact that his considerable salary as Chancellor of the Republic was exempt from "il catasto".

Another great humanist Chancellor, Poggio Bracciolini, the son of a debt-ridden apothecary, attained such wealth that he too paid considerable taxes, though—like Coluccio Salutati and Leonardo Bruni—he was not required to pay it on his salary but only on his private property.

It is amusing to note that Bracciolini provides an exception to the general willingness with which literary men paid their 'Catasto.' He—with a good deal of effrontery—claimed exemption from payment on a large sum he had borrowed from the Medici bank years previously. It amounted to 715 Florins. The Medici not only did not insist on repayment of the debt which Bracciolini could easily have afforded, but shouldered the tax on the amount because it figured as one of their 'Claims and assets.' This is a remarkable indication of the tolerant help always extended by the Medici to men of learning. It is all the more commendable in that Bracciolini—while not dreaming of repaying the money he owed—made a great show of his opulence and bought, over the years, a large palazzo, two farms and four lots of land while, at the time, investing considerable sums in government stock, the interest on which was borne by the taxpayer, among whom the Medici, to whom he owed money, were prominent.

But Bracciolini—it must be stressed—was an exception. Literary men under the Medici became wealthy through their merit. Though with Tuscan thriftiness they husbanded their assets—they willingly paid their dues to the Republic, which held them in such great esteem, provided them with the most prestigious posts, and made them the object of continuous admiration and applause. It was to them that the Florentines looked for their supremacy in culture, which was the city's lustre and pride and made every Florentine hold up his head as he travelled through Europe on his banking or trading business. It was not arrogance such as the pride of the Venetians, the empty pomposity of the Romans or the hauteur of the Milanese tended to be, but intelligent realisation that—through her literary men and artists—Florence was giving to the world something the world had not had since the days of Periclean Athens.

CHAPTER TWO

Enlightened Leadership

T was with Lorenzo de'Medici
that the Renaissance reached its peak and this 'Golden Age' may well be
said to have been a renascence in itself.[1] It was during the Laurentian
Era that the use of Latin was largely abandoned by scholars and the
vernacular rose to the full dignity of the writer's language.

This great step towards the popularization of culture was due in very
large measure to Lorenzo himself.[2] His was a complex personality in
which an unquenchable love of poetry—sacred and bawdy—sentimental
and sporting—philosophic and rustic, blended with hard political realism and a banker's ability.

Lorenzo, called *Il Magnifico*, the Magnificent, personified the great
quality which was fundamental to the spirit of the Renaissance: the joy
of living. He was filled and he filled his contemporaries with an irrepressible delight in the world and in the era in which they had been born
and lived. He saw and led others to see in each challenge that arose, a

welcome test of ingenuity, of powers of judgement, of foresight and understanding and—in extreme cases, such as when he was suddenly threatened by an assassin in Florence cathedral—of the swiftness of his steel. He loved to excel in physical prowess but delighted even more in seeking perfection in writing—poetry as well as prose—and his writings at times attained to unprecedented depths of neopaganism, at others reached unknown heights of christian piety and at other moments were profligate and libertine. But, even when he sings of unrequited love, of sighs and tears and heartache, Lorenzo's delight in living surges through the lines and bursts forth in the most varied ways. At one moment, he would discuss philosophy—Aristotelian or Platonic—and rise to the serene heights of the Infinite. The next minute, he might be keeping ribald company and describing it with an acuteness of observation and a choice of words and style that make him a fine writer. Like Leonardo da Vinci after him, he also made himself thoroughly acquainted with and imitated with much success the songs of Domenico Burchiello, who, from his barber's shop, in the heart of Florence, with trivialities and riddles had won fame as the scourge of Florentine customs and politics.[3] But Lorenzo could with equal ease—as he demonstrated with his Nencia da Barberino, a jocular poem of peasant life and loves—enter into the spirit of the people of the countryside. It was this ability, so developed that it amounted to genius, of being able to adapt himself to the moods of the common people and become one of them, that gave Lorenzo his authority by popular consent. He could rely on this acceptance of his power even when—as at times he did—he strained the Florentine Constitution.[4]

At any moment, he knew—perhaps better than any of his informers or advisers—what the Florentines were thinking. He found it out through constant contact with them, on their own level. His devices were an ease of manner and an expert scale of variations in the use of the language, from common speech to learned dissertation, from prose to poetry, from conversation to song. To this skill he added the adroitness of listening patiently and making the right remarks at the right moment to humble and exalted alike. These were his instruments of government far more than the manipulation of the laws.[5] With such awareness of what was going on, he could often afford to be lenient even to his opponents and so enhance his popularity. On other occasions, when he knew the people would approve, as after the Congiura de' Pazzi, he could safely deal out the harshest punishment.

It will never be known whether he delighted more in power or in knowledge. What is certain is that, rather than a great author himself, he was an unswerving enthusiast of literary and artistic perfection for its own sake and one feels he often wrote more to arouse others to surpass him than to win personal renown. This enthusiasm explains why he was so steadfast in his support of writers and philosophers.[6] His help reached them unwaveringly through wars and pestilence even, at times, though they showed themselves in rebellious mood. Few people have surpassed him in generosity, but his assistance to men of letters stands out because it did not depend on whim or chance—was not patronage—nor paternalistic or benevolent concession by a man in power. Lorenzo's were favours to equals, tendered as from friend to friend, when they were not—as often happened—tokens of reverence from an admiring Magnifico to an admired writer.

If we stop for a moment to consider our own day and the influence of Florence on our civilisation, Il Magnifico's conviction stands out as no imaginative fancy. Our times would be different—they might be better or they might be worse—had not Florence pointed out the truth that art and literature, by their nature, must be free.

In our own day we hear and read of brave, often heroic, men who for the sake of freedom of expression in the arts and sciences imperil themselves, their families, their future and their lives. With this afterknowledge Lorenzo's treatment of writers, sculptors, painters, philosophers, astronomers, of anyone in short involved in any branch of learning, shines as a prophetic intuition most highly civilised.

It was freedom that provided Florence with her cultural leadership. Some leadership was her due, Lorenzo sensed, because of the intelligence, creativeness and taste of the Florentines. It could not be military leadership, hemmed in as the Republic was by grasping neighbours. It could only be leadership in culture and in trade and Florence secured both. In commerce and banking, every Florentine was out for himself, but in the arts and poetry all grew under the Laurentian laurel. In Il Magnifico's Florence, writers came to enjoy prosperity, respect, admiration, prestige and a secure, serene way of life, such as existed nowhere else and, in very many countries, does not exist even today.

Perhaps one of the most telling examples of how literary men were treated under Il Magnifico is that of Poliziano, the poet who first combined the polish of the classics with the tuneful vigour of a language in everyday use. Lorenzo knew that Poliziano's verses were far better than his own and that Poliziano could turn into memorable poetry even subjects that seemed mean and, for these reasons, he loved him and felt happy in his company. And Poliziano felt at ease when talking to

Lorenzo, so much at ease, that he did not hesitate to upbraid him on many occasions.

On one occasion, when Florence was stricken by plague, Lorenzo, who remained in the city to share the fears and hardships of the poorest Florentines, entrusted Poliziano, who was a doctor as well as poet, with the care of his family. He was to accompany Lorenzo's wife and children to the country, near Pistoia and act as guardian to the children. Poliziano accepted with what can only be termed bad grace. He wrote numberless letters to Lorenzo—who was extremely busy with the affairs of the State and fighting the results of the epidemic—and, in each letter, he complained of the boredom of being secluded in the country especially in what he hinted was to him the very dull company of Lorenzo's wife, Madonna Clarice. Things failed to improve when the family moved to Cafaggiolo the original country mansion of the Medici. Writing from there to Florence,[7] Poliziano complained of having to spend his days by the fire in sleeping attire and slippers, while the children entrusted to his care, kept indoors by the continuous, pelting rain, played ball games in the room to keep fit. He was delighted with the children but complained bitterly of having no one worth talking to, an evident shaft against Madonna Clarice. Things came to a head on the 6 May 1479. There is no doubt Clarice's literary merits were nil. There is even less doubt that she was a religious bigot and a fanatic. On the other hand it is positively certain that Poliziano's temper was never of the best. The medieval ideas of Clarice—the first of three generations of Medici wives not to compose a single verse—collided head on with Poliziano's convictions and taste. He could not stand what he called the interference of this retrograde and obscurantist woman in the education of Lorenzo's children. Refusing to admit that they were also Clarice's children, he deplored the influence she had on her eldest son Piero, once so promising and now, as Poliziano complained, giving signs of growing bigoted and with a mind closed like his mother's to the classics, just like his mother.[8] He concentrated all his teaching on the second born, Giovanni, who was later to become Pope Leo X and link the glory of the House of Medici with the building of St Peter's as it stands today.

Clarice, sensing perhaps with a mother's instinct that three year old Giovanni, the way he was lapping up secular knowledge, might lose interest in religious subjects[9] one morning, when she caught Poliziano teaching him the ancient pagan classics, demanded haughtily that he stop at once and instruct the boy in the Psalms instead. Poliziano, in a fury, with equal disdain, insisted in a loud voice that Clarice expound all she knew and understood about the similarity of the symbolism of the

Laws of Moses and the sayings of Socrates. As Poliziano had expected, Clarice knew nothing whatever concerning the wisdom of the ancient Jews and even less about that of the Greeks.[10] Moses she may have heard of in church. As for Socrates, she had just heard mention of his name by Lorenzo and his friends. That was all.

Poliziano, literally in a paroxysm of rage, told her, with the greatest possible rudeness, that a woman of her despicable ignorance should have no place in a household of the highest intellect such as the Medici household undoubtedly was, that her influence over her children was most obnoxious[11] and that he would write to Lorenzo at once and have him forbid her to have anything to do with their instruction.

So two messengers with two fiercely contrasting missives to Lorenzo set out for Florence a few hours later.

Clarice, in her letter, wished her Lord well and expressed the hope that he would continue to escape the epidemic to which he was exposing himself so valiantly in his struggle to stop it from spreading or at least to limit somehow its terrible effects upon the city. She assured him she prayed for him constantly and expressed her fears for him and his health. Then she told him of the incident with Poliziano. She said it was the last of many and begged Lorenzo to remove the poet from the household. She ended by saying that she would abide by his decision whatever it might be, but that she felt cruelly insulted by Poliziano's leering presence.

Poliziano's letter contained no good wishes for Lorenzo's health. It went straight to the point and voiced the poet's resentment at the effrontery of ever having been asked to live under the same roof with a woman of no intellectual quality, who should have no business with him but be confined to her section of the house and gardens, if not, more appropriately ... to the kitchen.

It is at this moment that Il Magnifico, in plague-stricken Florence, despite the danger fulfilling the duties of his office and rank, shone forth as the patient friend of poets and poetry and learning. In answer to Poliziano, he wrote that he understood his friend's difficulties and invited him to go at once to a villa[12] he would be honoured to provide him with at Fiesole, sure that he would find it more congenial and cozy; many other poets and Marsilio Ficino, the neo-platonist, lived there. Poliziano would be able to converse and pass the time with them in discourse at the highest level. Lorenzo begged him to go straight to Fiesole—not to pass through Florence on the way—lest his precious health be endangered. Though he did not say it, one cannot help feeling he may have been a little tired of his argumentative friend, and wanted to avoid seeing him just then.

Poliziano was delighted in the new magnificent villa and the prospect of cultured friends but was only partially appeased. In a letter to Lorenzo, he complained of having found insufficient wine in the house. Patiently, Lorenzo took him the wine himself and spent an afternoon with him discussing neo-platonism and Socrates and—what pleased Poliziano most—listening enraptured to Poliziano's verse. He returned to Florence (leaving the poet in the safety of the hills of Fiesole) and himself feeling fitter to fight the plague. At least there was one less problem to cope with.

In any other of the Courts of Italy and the rest of Europe, Poliziano would have fared very differently in similar circumstances. But to *Il Magnifico* even deeply felt family affection could not rank above literature. One was transient; the other still lights the world. He surrounded himself with poets, philosophers and artists. With a collector's eagerness, he sought out artisans, decorators, medallion makers. He relished contact with intelligence and talent and perhaps that is why he understood Poliziano's predicament at Cafaggiolo.

Another cantankerous poet, friend of *Il Magnifico*, was Luigi Pulci, the author of *Il Morgante*, who many think was to inspire Ariosto. In 1466, from the franciscan monastery of La Verna, high up in the Casentino mountains, Luigi Pulci wrote to Lorenzo who had been sent by his father Piero de'Medici on a mission to Rome: "Do you really think of leaving me stuck in these woods amid this snow, alone and comfortless while you go to Rome?" He complains in his letter "I shall get well only when I know you love me" and upbraids Lorenzo for not having provided him with a horse with which to reach Rome, "where I would have been no weight to you at all as you fear, because I am clever at making friends and would have found someone to support me". That Pulci wasn't quite so clever at making friends as he claimed but had to rely on his real good friend Lorenzo instead is shown in a letter he wrote in 1468: "I have been short of money for some while and have made use of your name. Wherever I let myself be seen, people whisper to each other: 'This is Lorenzo's great friend' ". So Pulci managed to live from day to day. And when his brother Luca went bankrupt he wrote to Lorenzo: "I came into the world as one whose destiny is to be the hunter's prey. My luck was to love you and to be, for a while at least, in your company." What Lorenzo's love meant to Luigi Pulci is clear from a letter the poet wrote to *Il Magnifico* on 14 May 1479 asking him to use his good offices with the Medici Bank so they would prolong the term of his repayment of a debt of one hundred Florins he owed them.

Another literary man with whom Lorenzo was ultimately to have some difficulty was Alamanno Rinuccini, who, rather than a great writer himself, was the emulator of great authors. He belonged to an ancient noble family with a castle at San Donato on the way to Arezzo, and to this he ultimately retired when he had run foul of Lorenzo. Under *Il Magnifico*, he had reached high positions in local government and had held the delicate post of overseer of the High Schools of Florence and Pisa. But to him, Lorenzo was not a real protector of the arts in that *Il Magnifico*, in Alamanno's view, failed to encourage architecture, and did not see the connection between what Rinuccini termed eloquence and the other arts. He said so in writing on two occasions, both in 1473. Once in the dedication of his own translation of Philostratos to Federigo of Urbino, the other in a letter[13]. In both, it is clear that he considers Federigo the real patron to whom 'modern' writers and artists should turn.[14]

He was also a non active opponent of Lorenzo's emergency measures[15] particularly after the Pazzi conspiracy, when he retired to San Donato there to entertain his own circle of literary friends.

Quite a different sort of problem, created by a totally different sort of person, arose in Lorenzo's household through the beautiful and witty Alessandra della Scala. She was the daughter of Bartolommeo della Scala, an extremely lucky man who, in the course of his life, occupied most of the most exalted posts in the Florentine Government. He was a great latinist and a good Chancellor and, even after the fall of the Medici in 1494 remained in the government. His ability in the Latin language and in the marshalling of facts secured for Florence the sympathy of most European governments, even when the Republic was attacked by such powerful adversaries as the Pope and the King of Naples simultaneously.

Bartolommeo della Scala was one of the few humanists of Lorenzo's circle who never caused him any worry but his intellectual and charming daughter Alessandra more than made up for it. It was not her fault. God had made her beautiful; her manners were captivating; her brains of the first order. From her earliest youth she had studied Greek[16] under some of the eminent erudite Greeks who had fled Constantinople (when it had fallen to Sultan Mehmet II) and had found a generous welcome, warm appreciation and sincere reverence in the home of Lorenzo de'Medici. Alessandra was a diligent and enthusiastic pupil. She was soon composing Greek verse. If to some her rhymes were charming, to Poliziano they soon became enchanting. When she exchanged messages in Greek verse with him, he became quite enraptured. But if she accepted the flowers he

89059

College of St. Francis Library
Joliet, Illinois

showered on her, the presents he sent her, she was very far from recip-
rocating his adoration. She told him so and she married a Greek poet
Marullo.[17] Poliziano unleashed all the jealousy he felt in hundreds of
verses in which Marullo is spared no insult to which Marullo replied with
equally vicious invectives. No one, not even Lorenzo, could stop the two
from hurling epithets at each other. At last, Alessandra, a widow by
then, retired to a cloister.

Two shining stars of Lorenzo's circle were: Leon Battista Alberti,
perhaps the most versatile and gifted of all the geniuses of the Renaissance, who wrote prose and poetry on the most varied subjects from
architecture (he drew up the plans of the facade of Santa Maria Novella
in Florence—for the courtyard of the Lateran in Rome and many other
monuments and wrote the treatise *De Re Aedificatoria*) to philosophy, to
the duties of fathers, husbands, sons and all the family.[18] He was for
many years at the Papal Court but always was in close relationship with
Lorenzo de'Medici who often visited Rome. The second star was
Michelangelo whose greatness in sculpture (he studied it in *Il Magnifico's*
Academy in the Garden of St. Mark) has often obscured the fact he was
also a poet. He developed his poetical talent through his contact with
Poliziano, whom he met in the Medici Palace.

But "the finest expression of the ideals of Lorenzo's Florence" as he
has been described, was Pico della Mirandola. He certainly embodied *Il
Magnifico*'s versatility and love of God through the world's beauty
instead of through asceticism and sourness.

It is no wonder that even Niccolo' Macchiavelli—no benevolent
critic—should describe Lorenzo as "the greatest patron of literature
and the arts than any other prince has ever been". Lorenzo often
repeated that he was ready to ruin himself if necessary to acquire
ancient manuscripts for the poets his friends and with whom he spent his
happiest hours. Amid the cares of State,—the watchfulness necessary to
keep the turbulent Florentines from leaping at each other's throats, the
attention to trade and banking that made the City of Florence one of the
richest in Europe, the delicate diplomacy to keep the Republic's enemies
from growing too powerful and, at times, the wars—through it all,
Lorenzo never missed an occasion to listen to poetry or to write it,
constantly encouraging others to compose verse and search through the
classics for ways to improve their rhymes. He had a large network of
messengers, dispersed through every part of the world then known, all
of them engaged in collecting books and documents on every branch of
knowledge and particularly ancient classical manuscripts. This involved
great expense as well as careful thought and Lorenzo spent his money

gladly—not with a collector's covetousness but to advance knowledge and spread it in the world.

To Mattias Corvinus, King of Hungary, who had written him concerning an ancient document he knew Lorenzo had acquired, and who ended his letter saying: "How jealously you must guard so precious a piece of writing and its contents" Lorenzo replied by sending a copy of the precious manuscript as a gift.

CHAPTER THREE

The Poetry and Prose of Love

S if he had known from youth that his lifespan would be short,—only forty-three years from 1449 to 1492—Lorenzo early dedicated himself to developing his talents.

The most youthful of his poems to have come down to us is "La Altercazione"—"The Altercation" which is an exposition in verse of neo-platonism, a system of philosophy taught him by his preceptor and later close friend, Marsilio Ficino, head of the Neoplatonic Academy, founded by Lorenzo's grandfather Cosimo and which Lorenzo was to support generously and frequently throughout his life. In the "Altercation"[1] Lorenzo describes himself as setting forth from Florence, leaving "Il bel cerchio delle patrie mura" "The graceful ramparts that surround my native city" in search of peace and quiet and the pleasures of the countryside. While he sits in the pleasant shade of a laurel tree, with a babbling stream running amid the grasses and flowers by the side of it, he imagines himself enjoying "tanti vari e dolci odori" "various shades of fragrance" (Lorenzo had a strange deficiency: a total lack of the sense of smell). A shepherd arrives and taunts him for celebrating the pleasures of the countryside, which to him are sheer drudgery; cold in winter, heat in summer, hard work in every season.

While Lorenzo praises country life—the shepherd speaks vehemently of his longing for the comforts of the town. But then Marsilio Ficino arrives and explains to both that happiness lies not in the environment. Bliss arises from contentment not from outside circumstances. Lorenzo is persuaded; the shepherd remains doubtful and announces that the hour is come to lead the sheep back to the fold and that he "must back to his customary struggle" and "tu dove il desio tuo ti conduce" "and you to where your fancy leads you."

"The Altercation" is certainly not a classic but it shows us a very young Lorenzo, already deeply interested in every avenue of wisdom and in every problem of life: from the shepherd's to those of the highest philosophy.

But very soon Lorenzo, then nearly twenty, was attracted by lyricism and his poetry became less solemn. One day in Florence, he saw a crowd and he always loved a crowd. But this time when he mingled with it, he found that it was not a joyous gathering. The people were following an open bier, in which lay, dead, a young bride of exceptional beauty. Lorenzo does not tell us who she was, but, from other sources she appears to have been the lovely, goldenhaired Simonetta Cattaneo. Her married name was Simonetta Vespucci and her likeness, painted by Botticelli hangs in the picture gallery of the Prussian State Museum in West Berlin[2]. Such was her charm that the whole of Florence felt bereaved and sorrowful. Lorenzo dedicated to her the first four sonnets he ever composed. He wrote the first the evening of her burial. For the first time too in his poetry he left lofty philosophy aside and—looking romantically at a star that shone that evening unusually bright,[3] he imagined poetically that it was the girl's ethos, her spirit, her ideal essence arrived in heaven that lent the star its radiance:

> "O chiara stella che co'raggi tuoi
> Togli all'altre vicine stelle il lume,
> Perche' splendi assai piu' che di costume?
> Perche' con Febo ancor contender vuoi?"

> "Bright star whose radiance
> Robs the neighbouring stars of all their light
> Why are you more than usually resplendent?
> Why do you contend with the sun's rays?"

He then continues: "Haply those beauteous eyes, of which cruel death robbed us, lend you their light."

The lyricism grows in the same mood.

Despite the melancholy one cannot help feeling that Lorenzo was really delighted to have discovered he had a poetic vein in him. When at times it inevitably eluded him, he tried to recapture it, but, unable to do so in rhyme, he wrote a commentary to these first four sonnets.[4] In it he tells the details of the circumstances in which he composed his verses as if he were anxious to re-evoke his feelings of that hour—how it was April when the young lady died—how later the same day the whole of Florence had followed her to her last resting place, he had been sitting in a garden, enjoying the first warm evening of spring with a friend and suddenly he had noticed what he calls "a new star" in the heavens and had been led to imagine it was the embodiment of the departed Simonetta, whose name however he mysteriously still insists in not revealing, calling her simply "quella gentilissima" "that most gentle being". But, after recalling his romantic sentiments that day, he has to admit that, with the passing of time, his sorrow has waned and he cannot re-live that moment, nor does he feel inspired to write more poetry.

Ever practical, he decided he must find some way of reviving his feelings of bereavement so inspiration would come back to him. The composing of verse had become for him an end in itself. Confirming the truth of William Roscoe's judgement of him, 400 years later:—"In the usual order of things, it is love that creates the poet, but—with Lorenzo—poetry seems to have been the occasion of his love."— Lorenzo goes on to make it even clearer: "Better to understand and feel the sentiments of those who have lost a dear one, I searched for another girl in Florence—a living girl—on whom I might bestow my affections and in whose absence I might feel the pangs of love."

The search did not prove easy until one day: "A festival was held in our city and almost every beautiful young lady in Florence was there. I had gone to the celebration without really wanting to, but destiny, in the shape of some friends of mine who, after much insistence, had persuaded me to go, willed otherwise. And there I saw her. She was suddenly before me in a group of other ladies, matchless in her beauty." Lorenzo was particularly attracted by the splendour of her eyes and her expression, by which he judged her to be intelligent and delicate in her feelings.

Because of Lorenzo's passion for keeping the objects of his admiration incognito, we have to turn to other sources to learn that the girl's name was Lucrezia Donati.[5]

And he immediately broke forth in a poem of 141 stanzas—Selve d'Amore—Woodland of Love—in which platonic love is described at all stages—the first vision, the tremulous hope, the servitude, the sense of loss at the departure of the loved one—all of it crowned by the vision of the loved one transfigured herself by love.

But love of Lucrezia Donati could not be confined to writing poetry. Lorenzo was also determined to show her his manly qualities. No sexual intercourse is described or even mentioned, but he did want to show her that he excelled in feats of prowess. It came easily to him. A complete "Man of the Renaissance", avid for knowledge and direct personal experience in every field of activity, he had, from his earliest youth, tried every branch of sport. It has been written that his horses would not take food except from his own hand. This is most unlikely not only because of the nature of horses but because it is unthinkable that a man of State and a poet would find time to visit his stables every day. But the legend, however deplorably wrong, indicates in some measure his passion for sport. His poems on falconry and hunting point the same way and certainly show him to have been a very knowledgeable sportsman, who evidently practised a variety of sports. He was an athlete and the twist in his nose[6] may well have been due to an early love of boxing. It was not the sort of boxing that we know today with its umpires and its rules. Ducking was allowed but that was about all. The contestants stood each with one foot firmly planted on one of the opponent's feet to make retreat out of the question. Often the noses of the fighters would be almost touching, not unlike the beaks of two fighting cocks. This was for protection of the eyes and—partially—of the face also. For the rest, they pummelled each other to a finish with their bare fists.

This form of boxing was not only allowed but formed an essential part of every football game, most aptly called "Il calcio" "The kick". Any member of the two twenty-seven-man teams could resort to kicking not only to punish a foul but as a normal expedient to keep at least one of the opponents away from the ball.

Horse racing was equally rough. It took place along the cobbled streets of the city and often proved deadly to both horse and rider.

There is no definite proof that Lorenzo took part in these sports when he was a teenager but his later insistence on his own physical strength and the determination (that never left him) to excel in every physical contest, seems to show that he was at least very interested in them from early youth.

What we do know for certain is that on 7 February 1468, when he was twenty, he was a winner in a tournament and that, although he was to be married to Clarice Orsini the following June, he wore the colours of Lucrezia Donati. According to some, this was his farewell to Lucrezia. But there is no doubt that he corresponded with her throughout his life and many of his poems that make allusion to unnamed ladies and love, appear to have been dedicated to and inspired by her. On the day of the tournament in 1468 he wore her colours openly for the last time and Verrocchio had painted on his standard the image of a girl that very closely resembled Lucrezia[7].

The joust took place in the piazza in front of the church of Santa Croce. It cost 10,000 Florins.[8] The procession of the competitors— eighteen in all—was opened by nine trumpeters followed by mounted noblemen and finally came Lorenzo in magnificent array. His coat had puffed red and white silk on the shoulders and his black velvet attire was studded with pearls and rubies and diamonds. He rode a horse that had been sent to him in recognition of his rank by King Ferrante of Naples.

When it came to the actual fighting, he and all the other contestants exchanged their magnificent headwear for a helmet. Lorenzo also changed horses—the one Ferrante had given him for another also sent to him as a gift by Borso of Modena, who, three years later, was to become Duke of Ferrara.

However Lorenzo was not only a sportman but also a poet. Unable, because he was in it, to sing the joust in verse, he commissioned his friend, Luca Pulci to write about it. Though the resulting poem is of no great poetic value, it provides minute, detailed information of the tour- nament: the appearance and names of the competitors, who were the umpires and so on. It tells us that Lorenzo's first encounter was with Carlo Borromeo (Carlo ended up with second prize the first going to Lorenzo.) Then Il Magnifico was himself attacked by Braccio de'Medici, who rode at him with such fury that "if the stroke had gone home, the great paladin hero, Roland himself"—or so Luca Pulci assures us in perhaps his only flight into poetic imagination—"could have withstood the shock."[9]

Lorenzo counter-attacked with great speed and this was perhaps the reason why his spear flew into hundreds of pieces and failed to unhorse his opponent. But he did succeed in pushing his antagonist out of the saddle so that he was left clinging to his horse as best he could, while Lorenzo—swiftly drawing his sword—turned on another knight; Carlo de Forme, and split his helmet with a mighty blow.

After this, Lorenzo changed horses again and immediately set on Benedetto Salutati. Luca Pulci writes (in Roscoe's spirited translation):

"Hast thou not seen the falcon in his flight
When high in the air on balanced wing he hung
On some lone straggler of a covey alight?
On Benedetto thus Lorenzo sprang."

"Achille's rage their clashing strokes inspires
Their armour's sparks rival Etna's fires."

Lorenzo evidently thought that Luca Pulci had let himself be carried away by his poetic vein because—after the joust—he wrote: "Although I was not very brawny, I was awarded first prize." This seems to indicate that he had no illusions about his true worth and that he liked sport for its own sake, like poetry.[10]

After the tournament, which one might define as his bachelor's farewell though it was by no means a final goodbye to Lucrezia, he felt the need of seclusion with highminded friends. Cristoforo Landino,[11] one of the most distinguished humanists of his time and Chancellor of the Signoria of Florence (he was born at Volterra in 1424 and died in Florence in 1498 six years after *Il Magnifico*) tells us in the beautiful Latin of his "Disputationes Camaldolenses" the day after the tournament, Lorenzo and his friends rode the forty-five miles to the monastery at Camaldoli, high on the hills of the Casentino not from Arezzo.

The group from Florence arrived late in the evening and had the delight of finding Marsilio Ficino and Leon Battista Alberti already there.

Landino writes: "The following day, after the performance of religious duties, the whole company agreed to go up through the woods towards the top of the hill. They reached a solitary spot where the extended branches of a large beech overhung a clear spring of water."

There, at Alberti's suggestion, a conversation took place, Alberti saying that the happiest people are those who—having improved their minds through study—know how to withdraw at intervals from public engagements and private anxiety, indulging in some agreeable retreat, in a wide-roaming discussion on matters of the natural world and aspects of moral existence. Alberti then turned to Lorenzo and to Giuliano, Lorenzo's brother and addressed them saying: "If this be a habit advisable to all men of learning, it is particularly required in your case, since it is on you that the direction of State affairs is soon likely to devolve because of the growing infirmities of your father."

Then to Lorenzo personally he said: "Both you and the Republic, which you are shortly to lead and which, in practice is already to a great extent in your care, derive great advantage from the hours of leisure that you may spend either in solitary meditation or in friendly discussion for it is impossible for any person, however great, to conduct public affairs wisely, unless he has trained his mind to discern clearly what is due to others and what is due to himself."

In any case, solitary meditation or discussion with a small, selected and enlightened group, was to Alberti the prerequisite of real happiness.

It is remarkable that Lorenzo, then only twenty, should contend that "no essential distinction can be made between active and contemplative life. Each should assist and improve the other—the contemplative preventing physical exertion and practical activity from leading to uncouthness and excessive preoccupation with material things. Physical exercise and the practice of material arts and everyday human business saving contemplation and study from slipping into pedantry."

It is clear that Lorenzo was well on the way to being thoroughly fit to rule and conduct affairs of State, as he was already doing, surrounded by men of learning who were called upon to underwrite his own unspoken decisions, give him the comfort of their reassurance.

A few months after the joust in honour of Lucrezia Donati followed by the Camaldoli meeting, Lorenzo was married to Clarice Orsini. He laconically recorded the spectacular event in his Memoirs: "Today, fourth of June 1468, I took to wife the daughter of Prince Jacopo (Orsini) or rather she was given me." Strangely he was to grow very affectionate towards her almost immediately and remain so all his life, though this did not prevent him from having amorous adventures and loving Lucrezia with all the strength of his poetic imagination.

The Orsini are a great princely family in Rome, who once ruled over practically the whole of the Balkans, from Albania to Rumania, and vie with the Colonna for the first place in the ranks of the Roman aristocracy. At the time of the betrothal of their daughter Clarice to Lorenzo, they had already had one Pope in their family, Niccolo' III in 1277—80. Proudly, they let the Medici know that they considered they were conferring a signal honour on them and on the Florentines in giving a daughter of the Orsini in marriage to one of them. To have said so openly would have been an insult. They did it by a simple device: they assigned Clarice a dowry of only 6000 scudi (less than half the sum young Lorenzo had spent on the tournament for Lucrezia Donati).

The Medici—who knew the extent of the Orsini's liquid funds from their agent in Rome, Luigi Tornabuoni, brother of Lorenzo's mother—may well have been aware that the puny offer stemmed as much from lack of ready money as from a deliberate intention to snub them. Anyway money and dowries were not the aims they were pursuing. The main consideration that had prompted Piero to ask the hand of Clarice in marriage for his son was that the Orsini had promised to provide mercenaries for the defence of Florence and her interests, should ever the occasion arise. The Medici knew very well that their fellow-citizens relied on mercenaries in times of war—not through cowardice but because they judged it more profitable to attend to their trade.[12] But mercenaries cost money and the dilemma the Florentines had to solve every time war threatened, was whether it would be more profitable to hire mercenaries or to plunge into the struggle themselves. And here were the Orsini offering mercenaries free or—if not completely free—in exchange for a marriage bond with the Medici[13]. So long as the Medici remained in power, mercenaries would be cheap, a good claim to popularity in times of war.

The second motive that convinced the Medici of the desirability of a marriage with one of the Orsini was perhaps more important than the first.[14] Had they requested the same honour from any one of the leading Florentine families with daughters of marriageable age, all the others would have felt insulted and this might have proved highly dangerous.

Therefore when—in the spring of 1467—the Orsini approached him with suggestions of a marriage between Clarice and Lorenzo, Piero lost no time and asked his wife, Lucrezia Tornabuoni, to go to Rome, visit the Orsini and look into the matter. She wrote frequently to her husband as the negotiations proceeded and from her letters we gather she did not think much of Clarice's looks, manners or brains. Neither did the Orsini appear anxious to show off her looks, for in her first letter Lucrezia wrote: "She is fifteen or sixteen years of age; when I first met her she was dressed in the Roman style with a handkerchief over her head. She was veiled so I could not see her very well."

At their second meeting, the girl's veil had been removed, but Lucrezia's appraisal remained guarded. She wrote home: "The girl is certainly of above average height." It seems impossible she should not have noticed this at their first encounter and one cannot help feeling, that she was desperately trying to find some good qualities in the bride chosen for her son. As if to confirm this, the letter continues "Her complexion is fair; her manners have become more pleasant. Though she is definitely less beautiful than our daughters, she is very modest so it will be easy to teach her some graciousness. She is not a blonde—no one is fairheaded in Rome—but her thick hair has a reddish tinge. As for her face, it is round but, all things considered, not displeasing. She does not hold her head confidently as our girls do, but it hangs forward down on her breast. This I ascribe to shyness which seems to be her predominant characteristic." One may wonder how it could have been otherwise under such severe scrutiny, but at last Lucrezia concludes: "On the whole the girl seems to be above the ordinary, though of course not to be compared to Maria, Lucrezia, Bianca nor any other young lady in Florence."

The marriage was first celebrated by proxy in Rome and the Archbishop of Pisa represented the absent bridegroom. Then there seems to have been no hurry whatsoever to consummate the happy union. Not until a year later and four months after Lorenzo had, with his tournament, outwardly bidden adieu to Lucrezia Donati, was the wedding solemnised with all splendour in Florence.

The festivities lasted three days, during which five banquets were given; 150 calves were eaten up by the more than 800 guests. Whatever the feelings among the families whose hopeful daughters had been passed over, there was no prominent citizen of Florence who did not do his utmost to be invited.

The bride's table was set in a garden. Thirty-six married women sat round Clarice while fifty dancing girls pivoted round as the guests ate and conversed with each other. The men—as the custom then was— were strictly separated from the women and sat under porticoes surrounding the garden. At Lorenzo's table sat the seventy most distinguished guests.

Poetry and the arts were represented and Lorenzo composed ballads and sonnets for the occasion. Strangely enough, not one of them seems to have been dedicated to Clarice herself but there is no report of her having been surprised at this. She was already and always would be a dutiful and respectful wife.

We do not of course know Lorenzo's thoughts and hopes during those three days. As he sat there feasting, he could not foresee that the elder son to be born of the marriage, named Piero after his grandfather, would bring ruin and shame to Florence by disgracefully handing over, without a fight, the key fortresses of Sarzana, Seravezza and Lucca to the invading armies of Charles VIII of France. Nor, on the other hand, carousing on that fourth of June 1468, amid the dancing and the songs for which he improvised verse could he bask in the thought that his second son, Giovanni, would one day become Pope Leo X and dedicate all his efforts to embellishing Rome in the Renaissance style though he could not succeed to bring the Renaissance spirit, with its thirst for free inquiry, to the Eternal City.

Out of his love for art and artists, this first Medici Pope was to devise a scheme for selling indulgences to provide the funds needed for the renovation of the Basilica of Saint Peter's. No use appealing to the Romans, always ready to receive but never to give. So Pope Leo was to turn the whole of his pressure for collecting money on to Northern Europe and Germany in particular. A certain friar, Tetzel, unknown for anything else, travelled through the country, chanting the slogan "Wenn das Geld in der Kasse klingt, die Seele aus dem Fegefeuer springt" which means "As soon as the coin tinkles in the almsbox, a soul is delivered from Purgatory." Many simple souls, not wanting to be a party to the sufferings of those who had preceded them in this life, rushed to the friar with their savings. But when it became known that part of the money went to the Fugger Bank, which had advanced the sums for the rebuilding of Saint Peter's, popular annoyance grew into resentment. To give utterance to the increasing anger became the courageous task of an Augustinian monk: Martin Luther. Pope Leo, lover of the arts, completely failed to realize the importance of what was happening. While hunting in the Roman Campagna or blissfully listening to the beautiful Latin verse of his State Secretary, Bembo, he never understood why Luther raised theological problems as to whether sins could be pardoned against payment of money when, to him, the real question was that the money was needed to raise works of art and subsidise poets so they could dedicate themselves wholly to verse. The result was schism and, what vexed Leo far more, no more money to go on building Saint Peter's with.[15]

In his momentary despondency, he sent Cardinal Caetano to offer Luther not only pardon but promotion, if only he would not oppose his theological views to the Pope's quest for money. Caetano's instructions were to appease Luther not condemn him, possibly make him see how much contribution to the raising of monuments added to the glory of God. The cardinal acquitted himself very badly and merely asked Luther, in no polite fashion, for a full recantation, and the schism which might have even then been averted, became a reality and is, in some ways, a wound to Christianity that must be laid at the door of a Medici Pope.

Lorenzo could not know all this as he sat at his wedding feast. But we may sense some disquiet in his feelings when we come to know that of those three festive days he left no enthusiastic description. Unlike in the case of the joust in honour of Lucrezia Donati, he did not ask any other poet to sing of his wedding with Clarice.

A few weeks later, at the beginning of July, he was off to Milan on a political mission for his father. With the seriousness he brought to all he did, he had already assumed the role of a dutiful husband. Perhaps too, the first hints of an affection that was to grow throughout the years had already begun to show themselves. On 22 July he wrote to Clarice: "I arrived here safely and am in good health. I believe this will please thee better than anything except my return; at least, so I judge from my desire to be once more with thee ... I shall make all possible speed to come back for it seems a thousand years till I see thee again."

These are affectionate words, words a young husband owes his bride. But—alas—no poetry. How different his first sonnet to a girl to whom he had never spoken.

> "O chiara stella che co'raggi tuoi
> Affievolisci all'altre stelle il lume
>
> Bright star that, with your rays,
> Dost cause all other stars to appear faded.

CHAPTER FOUR

Barbo the Barbarous

NLY six months after Lorenzo and Clarice were married, Piero de'Medici died on the 3 December 1468. We have Lorenzo's own account of what followed: "On the second day after my father's death, although I, Lorenzo, was very young, only in my twenty-first year, leading men of the City and the State came to our house to condole with me and with my brother, Giuliano, on our loss and to persuade me to take on myself the care of the City and the State, as my father and grandfather had done."

So Lorenzo became First Citizen of Florence,[1] at an age when most young men are taking only their first, bold but often inexperienced, steps into the world. He was not unprepared for his new condition. During his father's long illness, he had often had to help him and take his place in matters of diplomacy and government. He had often been called on to fulfil important tasks and had acquitted himself well.

Even though the way he rose to be First Citizen was not strictly constitutional, Lorenzo certainly did not usurp his new rank. The Florentines, judging with shrewd realism the situation in which they found themselves, realized that this was no time for constitutional niceties and possible discord. The danger that confronted them was that of finding themselves again under the sway of the old aristocratic factions which ultimately would bring ruin to the Republic and perhaps even cause it to fall victim of a foreign Power. Florence that might have repulsed Lorenzo with the greatest ease, called on him instead to seize the reins of government. And his first nine years of rule proved to be years of joy and laughter, a time when the bright side of life dispelled all shadows and each day seemed happier than the last, despite poetic sighs and tears. The State waxed stronger and more prosperous, music was encouraged, art protected, poets were supported and inspired.

Conditions were very different elsewhere, even just on the borders of Tuscany—in the Papal States. Here the reigning Pope was the Venetian Pietro Barbo, who had been elected in September 1464. Roscoe describes him as "a cruel and unrelenting persecutor of men of science and letters, who exhibited, in inflicting them suffering, a constancy and resolution which might have raised them to the rank of martyrs."[2]

But Roscoe was a Protestant and—though he is a most precise and honest writer—it is interesting to note what a Catholic apologist, Dr Ludwig Pastor, an ecclesiastic—a professor at Innsbruck University in Catholic Austria—author of one of the most accurate *History of the Popes* finds himself compelled to write in the desperate attempt to defend Pope Barbo.

The learned Austrian Professor begins by admitting that this Pontiff is generally represented as "a barbarous enemy of classical studies and of all intellectual activity, in fact a hater of learning". When he had been elected Pope, the cardinals had had the utmost difficulty in persuading him not to adopt the name he had chosen: Formosus—the Beautiful, the Shapely one. Understandingly, Pastor, Catholic apologist glides over this and merely tells us he was given the name of Paul II.

Pastor, devout and sincere as he was, wrote at a time when the line of demarcation between those papal pronouncements which are infallible in catholic eyes and those which are not or should not be, was not as clear as it is today.[3] It was even less clear in Paul II's time and many seconded the villainous treatment he meted out to men of learning because they believed the Head of the Church could do no wrong. Among those who, blinded by an unswerving conviction of Papal infallability at all levels, acquiesced in his iniquitous oppression of the learned, there were even lovers of the classics and scientists.

Today, theologians have progressed far in their studies of the dogma of infallability.[4] It is now recognized that, to make a statement that Catholics will be bound to accept as infallible, the Head of the Catholic Church must precede it with a definite, clear, unequivocal announcement that what he is about to say is divinely inspired by the Holy Ghost and it is usual though not essential for such pronouncements to have the assent of at least a large number of bishops and of the faithful. If a Pope does not make such a declaration beforehand, his Letters Apostolic, his Encyclicals, his exhortations, however authoritative, however correct, however praiseworthy, may be well-based interpretation of Church teaching, but are most definitely NOT infallible articles of Faith.

Infallible pronouncements are and have always been very few and announced at long intervals. They have been sustained by Councils and consultations of Bishops, prior to being made publicly known. In our twentieth century only one infallible pronouncement has been made; that of Pius XII on the Assumption of Our Lady, with the assent of a majority of bishops and all cardinals but one. Of course members of the Roman Church are bound to accept the Pope's guidance (not imposition) as their leader. It is like asking a fireman how to quell a fire. His experience makes him authoritative but he may not necessarily be right.[5]

Pastor however did not know all this and neither did the men of the early Renaissance,—at least not in Rome where the Pope's powers of coercion were greatest. And it was coercion the Roman Curia believed in, not persuasion, not the powers of inducement such as had been shown by Pope Barbo's immediate predecessor, Pius II, and were to be the endearing characteristic of John XXIII's reign.

Pius II—himself a great writer—had included among the functionaries of his Court, several men of learning, who, like Pius himself, studied the texts of antiquity and became conversant with the symbolism of heathen gods. To Paul II they were anathema and he saw in their enthusiasm for the classics a return to paganism and he summarily dismissed these men who had grouped themselves in what they called "The Roman Academy."[6] Pastor derisively suggests they had been admitted to the Curia only because they had paid for their posts. His disparaging remark on what was, at the time, the intelligentsia in Rome, is followed by expressions of great indignation at the decision of these humanists to appeal to "the kings and princes of the World" (we would say: 'to public opinion') to set up a Council to judge whether this dismissal had been fair.[7]

The Pope's answer was to throw into the papal dungeon the classical scholar who had compiled the letter of protest. He was Bartolomeo Sacchi known by the name of Platina from his native village Piadena. He was kept in the dank fearful bowels of Castel Sant'Angelo for four full months and many feared he would be beheaded when they heard the way Pope Paul spoke about him. But this first imprisonment of Platina was interrupted through the efforts of a worthy Prince of the Church, Cardinal Gonzaga, himself a humanist and a former pupil of Platina's, who interceded with the Pope in the scholar's favour.[8] Platina was indeed in a pitiful condition. When he had the pluck to meet again with his friends of the Roman Academy to learn how they in their turn had fared during his incarceration, he still could hardly stand. As was customary at their meetings, the members of the Academy addressed each other with names derived from antiquity and read poems by Latin authors. Pastor indignantly tells us: "They displayed an infatuated admiration for the ancient Roman republic." Present at the gathering was the leader of the Academy, Pomponius Laetus, who lived in what Pastor calls "haughty poverty" a condition which evidently irked wealthy clerics and, in particular, Pope Paul who loved gaudy apparel and rich palaces.

When the Pope heard that Platina had met with his friends again, he imagined it was to plot against him and had Platina and as many of the classicists he could catch thrown into gaol. Here, Pastor piously tells us "they were examined by torture". Rumours were put about in Rome that the Academicians had intended to solicit the calling of a General Council, not merely to seek redress for themselves, but to depose Pope Paul. However, the Pope seems to have at least suspected that this was a trumped up charge. When the Milanese Ambassador asked him about it, the Pontiff's reply was that the Academicians "despised the Church— ate meat on fast days—said that priests had invented fasting and for their own ends forbade men to have more than one wife". The Pope stressed what to him was the enormity of their habit "of being ashamed of their christian names and giving preference to heathen appellations". He said they circulated predictions that "Pope Paul would soon die." It seems unbelievable but Paul II went as far as to assert that "some of them" contemplated an alliance with the Turks. (The Academicians were less than a hundred!) Somewhat inconsequentially he also stated that he believed they were in league with the King of Bohemia. All these garbled accusations, some of them conflicting, are faithfully enumerated in four letters (now in the State Archives of Milan) sent to Galeazzo Maria Sforza, Duke of Milan, sent him by his two separate representatives at the Papal Court: John Blanchus and Augustine de Rubeis. In his concluding letter, written on 4 March 1468, de Rubeis says "as for the attempts on the person of the Pope, of which I wrote in my previous letters, a diligent inquiry has established only "parole paze e vane", "mad and empty words".

It was on the basis of these hollow rumours, that the classicist Literati continued to be kept in prison. In his zealous attempt to white-wash Paul II, Pastor tells that there is no evidence they were tortured. But it is difficult not to surmise that they were, when Pastor ungener-ously adds that Platina—who had hitherto shown himself an intrepid man—"abjectly" vowed he would abandon all classical studies and even promised he would celebrate in verse and prose what he now called "the Golden Age, the most blissful of all Pontificates" that of Paul II. And Pomponius Laetus, whom the Venetians had ungraciously handed over to the Pope, after he had sought refuge in their territory, "soon followed the example of his friend Platina and sought by obsequious flattery to win the favour of his jailer and the Pope". (The original text of one of his letters is preserved in Cod.161, in the Library of Corpus Christi College, Cambridge.)

But it was all of no avail. Platina, after his agonized grovelling promise, made the fatal mistake of saying that "Poets confer immortal-ity on Princes, just as Homer made Achilles known throughout the centuries". At this mention of a heathen poet and a pagan warrior, the torturer went to work again and, when he had finished with Platina, threw him back into solitary confinement. Through the agony of the martyred limbs and the despondency of his dignity crushed and des-troyed, Platina sent a desolate appeal to the Prefect of the Fortress, Bishop Rodrigo Sanchez de Arevalo, begging him, for mercy's sake, to allow him to break his intolerable solitude by writing to him, and to let him nourish the hope of an answer.

The "kind Prefect" did grant Platina's request. He even replied to his prisoner, but his missives to the tormented victim, took the form more of religious exhortation than of a comforting exchange. Pastor comments and we don't know whether his comment is wry or based on conviction: "It is curious to see how difficult Platina found it to respond to the Bishop's thoughts. In spite of some convulsive snatches at Christ-ian reminiscences, the antique element predominates in his letters." It is not clear whether Pastor, like Pope Paul, thought that sufficient reason for keeping him in prison.

As for Pomponius Laetus, we learn that, when he begged for some books to read and expressed his preference for Lactantius and other classical writers, Rodrigo de Arevalo sent him a treatise on the errors of the Council of Basle, which had questioned the authority of the Pope. Laetus was incensed and thanked the Bishop with a letter, which the recipient considered offensive. It is not recorded whether he was subjected to torture for this, but it is more than possible since, a short few days later, Pomponius wrote his "Defensio Pomponii Laeti in carceribus et confessio" ("Defence and Confession of Pomponius Laeti in prison") in which he suddenly admitted to being an homosexual and confessed that he had spoken against the clergy and broken the laws of fasting. After a weak defence, which only confirmed his gaolers in the fundamental perniciousness of classical study, (Laetus claimed that in his homosexual practices he had only followed the example of the great Socrates!), the unfortunate scholar concluded with the cry: "For the sake of the risen Saviour, let mercy prevail over justice."

Pastor tells us this pitiful document saved Pomponius. The Holy Father (Paul II) came to the conclusion that the writer of such a letter was incapable of originating a conspiracy. And Pastor—like the Milanese envoy centuries before him, reached the conclusion: "The obscurity in which this conspiracy is shrouded will never be cleared away." Inquiries were finally abandoned for want of evidence, yet the prosecution of what was described as the "heresy" of the Academicians (their classical studies and their contempt of riches) was carried on. From many sources we learn that Paul II contemplated further extremely severe measures against "the heathen philosophical extravagances" of professors and literati. He is known to have said: "I shall do two things if God preserves my life. In the first place I will forbid the studies of histories and poems. They are full of heresies and blasphemies. Children, when hardly ten years old, even without going to school, know a thousand villainies. What then must become of them when, later on, they read Juvenal, Terence, Plautus and Ovid? Then, perhaps thinking of the supposed prediction of his death which had been laid at the Literati's door, he said he would forbid the study of astrology and the spreading of false rumours and assured everyone "I shall do these things if God gives me life".

God didn't. Paul died within two years, one 26 July, 1471.

From the long list of sovereigns and statesmen who, dutifully, sent in their condolences, one name was missing. That of the First Citizen of Florence: Lorenzo de'Medici.

CHAPTER FIVE

Driving a Bargain

ORENZO de'Medici's silent reproof of Paul II and of the dead Pope's persecution of men of learning was meant to show everyone, not least the new Pope and the Curia, that, unlike others, *Il Magnifico* knew how to discriminate between what was Church doctrine and error or infamy. Keenly aware that a sharp distinction must, at all times, be clear in free men's minds between religious authority and its distortion for worldly or personal or base ends or even through well-meaning mistakes, he never for a moment doubted that the infamous Paul's excesses were the evil fruit of an individual aberration, aided by an hierarchical structure that provided no check and allowed no criticism. Theological schools, based on literal, narrow-minded, legalistic and scriptural interpretation without recourse to open-hearted charity, did the rest. The fact that some of Rome's inquisitors might have acted in good faith appeared to Lorenzo all the more tragic in that it proved that good faith might, at times, exclude good sense. In other words, Lorenzo saw clearly that the Church of his day acted on a set of rules and based many of its actions neither on the heart nor on the intellect. In fact many churchmen, foremost among them Paul II, were determined to crush the intellect. But the sense of proportion that springs from the mind at its highest level, might yet be instilled into the Papacy by the Renaissance—that flowering of men's free reasoning of which he felt himself the apostle together with the literary men with whom he surrounded himself and those of their number with whom he corresponded.

Lorenzo de'Medici arrived in Rome immediately on the accession of the new Pope: Sixtus IV. The new Pontiff—Francesco Della Rovere—a Franciscan monk—had a reputation for scholarship. As Lorenzo saw it, it was not unreasonable to suppose he might have vision. He had. Unfortunately, it did not develop as Lorenzo hoped and led to Sixtus's murderous hate for all the Medici and the freedom they stood for.

However—in that summer of 1471—both the new Pontiff and the Ruler of Florence were full of good will towards one another. Not only had the sombre clouds of Paul II's reign been lifted, but Sixtus was downrightly anxious to have a friendly power to the north of the Papal States and Lorenzo on his side wanted fervently to enjoy the benevolence of his southern neighbour. There were other considerations—some of them extremely practical—on both sides. Paul II was known to have amassed a vast collection of jewels. As much a coxcomb as a pervert, he had had a tiara[1], the last of many—fashioned for himself and it had cost as much as a palace. Shrewd Lorenzo realized that, after so much squandering, the Holy See needed cash and must turn Paul's valuables into money and he wanted to be the first to come up with an offer.

Officially he had come to Rome at the head of a deputation of the most prominent citizens of the Florentine Republic to congratulate Sixtus IV on his elevation to the highest rank in the Church. Unofficially he went immediately into consultation with his maternal uncle, Giovanni Tornabuoni, Head of the Roman branch of the Medici Bank. He wanted to secure first hand knowledge of the more recent reports on the Pope's finances and to know how much money he himself might lay hands on at a moment's notice should he be making an offer to the Pope in competition with another purchaser ready to pay immediately.

Actually, the developments of the next few days were rosier than his hopes. He found himself formally entrusted with the office of Treasurer Extraordinary of the Holy See, Guardian of all the valuables, Administrator of all the Finances. He could not simultaneously hold these positions in Rome and be in Florence to head the Republic. So, he appointed his uncle to act as his proxy during his absences from the Papal Court but, before he left Rome, he and Tornabuoni had succeeded in buying from Sixtus most of the priceless jewels left by Paul II. The new Pope had been in no condition to insist on too high a price as Lorenzo had correctly surmised: to the normal difficulties that beset the beginning of any pontificate were added several claims that first one cardinal, then another advanced demanding settlement of sums said to have been lent to the dead Pope and not repaid. The amounts of money found in the Vatican coffers at Paul's death were negligible. With them were several written statements, signed by the dead Pope, purporting to indicate the hiding places where large sums were supposed to have been concealed to meet these debts and provide for the Holy See. These statements—all of them—proved to be either untrue or mistaken unless of course someone had read them and profited by them before an inspection could be carried out. The hard truth was that each and every hiding hole was empty. Debts were therefore pressing and Lorenzo de'Medici and his proxy Tornabuoni were on the spot, full of money, plenty of it. It is not surprising that they were able to buy all they wanted and buy it cheaply. The large collection of jewels that Paul II had frantically amassed to the dismay of those who believed the Pope should spend on charity and good works, all ended up in the Medici bank. Roscoe tells us "Tornabuoni sold them to much advantage to different Princes of Europe."[2]

Lorenzo also made valuable additions to the many works of ancient culture that he already owned. The Pope himself—how different to Paul II!—wishing to add to the collection Il Magnifico was known to possess in Florence[3] presented him with two busts, one of the Emperor Augustus and one of Agrippa. In their discussions on antiquity both the Pope and Lorenzo lamented that Paul had had no regard for classical monuments and had even destroyed part of Flavian's theatre to build his palace. This palace, since Paul had been a Venetian, became, in the end, the property of the Venetian Republic and is, to this day, known as the Palazzo Venezia. In the twentieth century, it was assigned to Mussolini as his office and from its balcony "Il Duce" declared war on Britain, America, France and the other Allies.

But it was not of war that Lorenzo and Sixtus IV talked in those halcyon days of 1471. Neither could know that less than seven years were to go by before Sixtus would connive in a conspiracy to oust and kill Lorenzo and murder his brother within the sacred precincts of a church, so that Macchiavelli was to write of him: "Sixtus was the first Pontiff to show how far a Pope might reach and how actions, which had always been regarded as sinful, lost their iniquity when committed by the Head of the Church."

The nineteenth century historian Leopold von Ranke, whose pride
and art it was to relate events without comment but with teutonic precision, as they were told in Archives and documents, has this to say of
Sixtus: He "never hesitated to make use of his spiritual power for purely
worldly projects. He lowered the prestige of his heavenly mission by the
intrigues he wove for purely material ends."

Gregorovius, for his part, in his monumental "History of Rome"
says: "It is in Sixtus IV that the facets of the Prince prevailed over those
of Supreme Pontiff, Shepherd of Souls. From him began a succession of
Popes who seemed in effect to be only tyrants to whom chance had given
a tiara—instead of a ducal crown."

But all this was unknown to Lorenzo and, perhaps, even to Sixtus, as
they conversed of classical matters as well as business in 1471. Though it
is not recorded that Lorenzo had anything to do with it, before the year
was out, the members of the Roman Academy whom Paul II had persecuted, were re-instated. Pomponius Laetus was restored to Rome University. Platina was assigned to compiling a "History of the Popes." A
broken man, he failed to accomplish this or perhaps prudence kept him
from a subject that, if truly told in all details, might lead him straight
back into gaol. His salary continued to be paid to him however and in
1475, Sixtus appointed him to the important post of "Librarian" of the
new Vatican Library of which Sixtus must be acknowledged the founder.
It is to him too that we owe the Sistine Chapel, the Sistine Choir, a fine
bridge, a fountain, the Via Sistina and many other embellishments of the
Eternal City. All this must be recognised to his exceptional merit, but
the unbridled and temporal power which the Popes then exercised led
him to adopt expedients that brought shame to the Papacy. Not only did
he indulge in financial speculation, the sale of favours, the granting of
office, even of spiritual office, to the highest bidder—but he resorted to
political subterfuge, was unscrupulous to the point of murder, and
instituted what came to be called through the centuries by the name of
'nepotism': the assignment of exalted and lucrative offices to members of
the Pope's own family. It was he who started the practice whereby the
"nephews", (often the illegitimate sons of the reigning Pope) exploited
their family connection, going about Vatican circles with what can only
be termed insolence when it was not raffish arrogance. It was he who,
not content that his nephews should impose their will on Rome and in
the Papal States, made plans and carried through designs for them to
attack or purchase free cities and turn them into fiefs that would entitle
them to a nobleman's crown before the Pope would die and a whole new
generation of "nephews", of another Pontiff and with another name,

should displace the relatives of the Pope who had passed on.

With his nepotism and the extremes he went to to assert it, Sixtus IV more than counter-balanced all the good he did to the arts and learning, to him only means of self glorification or of the advancement of church power. His was the deathblow to the freedom of expression of the writers of the Renaissance. After him, we are confronted with the paradox that while many rulers, first of all Il Magnifico, surrounded themselves with and sought the advice of men of learning to whom they were happy to entrust the highest offices, the spiritual heads of the Church of Rome placed their confidence instead in their nephews and illegitimate sons to help them widen their temporal power. The nephews became in practice the instruments whereby the living Pope governed. They became ministers—admirals—generals—cardinals whatever their natural abilities made them best fit for, or the Pope's choice. All this stemmed from Sixtus IV. Even that dutiful defender of the Papacy, Ludwig Pastor, is compelled by his conscience, the moral sense of a truthful historian, to admit that "The admirable energy with which Sixtus devoted himself to the defence of Christendom is clouded by the extravagance with which, from the moment of his accession, he heaped favours on his numerous and—in many cases—unworthy relatives."

The new Pope had lost no time. Barely three weeks after his coronation, his nephews were already well established in the Roman Court. A short three months more and Sixtus elevated to the Sacred College of Cardinals two of them: Giuliano della Rovere, who was only twenty-eight, and Pietro Riario, son of his sister Bianca, who was even younger: a mere twenty-five. Another son of Bianca, also inducted into the Papal Court was to play the leading part in the attempt to do away with *Il Magnifico* and in the murder of his brother, Giuliano.

But all this was in the shrouded future during the honeymoon of 1471 between the new head of the Catholic Church and the youthful first citizen of the Florentine Republic. Relations were genial and business was brisk on both sides. The Medici leased from the Pope some alum mines that had just been discovered in a locality called La Tolfa, to the northwest of Rome not far from the border with Tuscany. Lorenzo found himself compelled to agree to what—by all standards— was an excessive annual rent. This transaction might seem unimportant but it was to play a vital part in the history of Florence and of the Writers of the Renaissance there and in the rest of Italy.

At the time, Lorenzo's hands were tied. Florentine trade and consequently Florentine banking rested, to a great extent, on the excellence of the wool fabrics made in Florence. They were sought after, not only for their texture and durability, but for the beauty of their colours. Now, at that time, alum was essential to fix colour on wool—to make the colours 'fast'. Without alum, the whole trade of Tuscany would have been jeopardized. It had previously come from the East, but, with the fall of Constantinople, that source had dried up. Just as in the twentieth century industries all over the world are thirsty for oil, so in Lorenzo's time, textile manufacturers and particularly the Woolmasters of Florence, were frantic for alum. The Pope knew all this and pressed his advantage home and Lorenzo had to comply.

The excessive annual payment to the Pope for the alum mines at La Tolfa was certainly a heavy burden on Tuscan trade but far more dire consequences arose, a few months later, early in 1472, as the result of a rebellion, which broke out owing to the scarcity of alum, in the territory of the Florentine republic itself.

Here is what happened: the ancient fortress-like Etruscan hilltown of Volterra was an important bulwark between Tuscany and the States of the Church. There were some disused alum mines nearby. The scarcity of the mineral prompted a group of people—Florentines, Sienese and Volterrans—to try to reopen the mines, which had proved unprofitable when alum had been plentiful but might not be so now. Not unlike the Pope, the Volterrans asked the Company formed to revive the mines—a very sizeable annual payment. In the hopeful expectation that inadequate supplies would push the price of alum up to any level, the Company agreed too readily and the Volterrans became suspicious that the rent they had asked might be too low. They increased their claim until it became excessive and the Company, eager to get its hand on the desperately needed alum, cut negotiations short and took the matter to Florence, the State capital, for mediation. The answer of the people of Volterra was to prevent anyone from going near the mines. The unrest grew into open rebellion against the whole Tuscan State, when Florence came out in support of the Company, declaring that the alum mines were not the exclusive property of the people of Volterra but were a vital prop to the industry of the country; the Volterrans might lawfully negotiate what rent they wanted but, on no account, must they stop work at the mines and jeopardize the search for desperately needed alum. The Florentine Signoria also pointed out that there were two Volterrans on what we would now call the Company's "Board of Directors" and they would surely look after their city's interests. The reply of the people of Volterra was to seek out their two co-citizens, brand them as traitors and hunt them down. Their fury grew when they discovered one of them, Paolo Inghirami, had taken refuge in the palace of the Florentine

Governor. They broke into the palace, found Inghirami in a hiding hole and smoked him out with burning sulphur. He was already dead when they hurled him from the top of the palace tower, la Torre del Topo, the Rat's Tower. They turned on his brother Giovanni who managed to flee the target of arrows shot from the crowd in the square below. The Florentine Governor was also threatened and this was open rebellion.

The Signoria in Florence took the matter seriously. It was not only a question of the alum mines, important as they were, but Volterra was on the border with the Papal States and might call in Papal aid and other towns along the border might follow Volterra's example. The whole State in fact was in very real danger.

Despite the urgency of the situation, the Florentines were divided. The woolmerchants, fearing that an expedition against Volterra would endanger their slender surplus of alum, were for appeasement; others were for the use of force. It was at this moment that Lorenzo came to the decision, the consequences of which would be with him for life, would lead to his being wounded by a Volterran in a Pope-inspired conspiracy, would destroy the serenity of the cultured Court he had created, would set the freedom of Renaissance thought back for years, would cause Renaissance writers to slide from their places of men of authority down to the role of courtiers. The decision was: raise an army and march on Volterra.

Five thousand five hundred mercenaries were hired and placed under the command of a renowned Condottiere: Federigo da Urbino.

The expedition against Volterra was not yet a major war. It seemed on the face of it easier than it turned out to be. The prospects became yet more favourable when news came that Federigo da Urbino's army was to be swelled by another 600 soldiers, sent by Galeazzo Sforza from Milan. This was not a large force but it meant that if the Volterrans were to turn to the Pope or to the Kingdom of Naples for support, they would have the Milanese as well as the Florentines against them. In other words, they would be faced by a large-scale war. This was what it seemed at the moment but actually the presence of the Milanese was to lead to dire consequences that were to stain forever the name of Lorenzo de'Medici, despite all his merits.

This is what happened: the Volterrans sensing perhaps they were no match for Federigo da Urbino and Galeazzo Sforza's professional soldiery or else—like the Florentines—wanting to attend to their daily business instead of fighting—made a fatal mistake. They too hired mercenaries, mostly Venetians, always ready to fight against their rival: Milan.

Now the hiring of mercenaries can be very profitable in two sorts of war: when victory is likely to be easy in which case the mercenaries will try to win it quickly so as to collect their dues and move on to someone else's service or when the war is likely to drag on with only desultory fighting. This means they need only fight sporadically meanwhile living off the land in the combat area and as likely as not, plundering.

In this case, the hiring of mercenaries was favourable to the Florentines: either they would subdue Volterra in a matter of weeks or their troops would lay waste Volterra's surroundings. The situation of the Volterrans was very different. The Venetians could not conquer Florence. Volterra was an impregnable fortress and it looked as if it could only be vanquished through a long siege. The proud Volterrans were certainly ready to undergo the consequent hardship, but why should the Venetians? Perhaps they also judged that Volterra's money would run out long before that of Florence and that, after suffering months of hunger and thirst inside Volterra's walls, they might get no final pay at all. It seems besides, according to some accounts, that some of them had fought as mercenaries in the service of Milan,—not against Venice to be sure, but against other northern Italian cities. What is certain is that many of the Venetians had friends and acquaintances among the Milanese troops opposing them. Perhaps all these reasons concurred to what happened: Venezio, commander of the mercenaries in the service of Volterra, in the dark of night, let the Milanese into the Volterran fortress through a breach in the walls. As might have been expected, the Milanese were followed by Urbino's troops. The result was massacre. The soldiery went wild and began to sack the town. Drunk with victory and eager to secure as much profit as they could from their shortlived war, (if war it could be called) they respected no one. In all fairness, it must be admitted Federigo da Urbino tried to stop the plunder. But about half of the pillagers were not under his command but under that of Venezio and the Milanese captain who had started the raid. Federigo frantically searched for Venezio and, as soon as he could lay hands on him, had him executed, intimating that the same would happen to anyone found pillaging. But, in the tortuous alleyways of the fortress town, even his own troops proved uncontrollable.

The result was that Volterra suffered one of the most fearful devastations in her history.

Lorenzo de'Medici's admirers say he had no part in the outrage, while his detractors maintain that he was responsible for the Volterran slaughter because it had been he who had persuaded the Florentines to go to war against Volterra. Many feel however that Lorenzo could not

really be called to account for the guilt of troops that were not under his
control (some of them, as we have seen, were actually in the pay of the
Volterrans). Besides, he was far off in Florence when the outrage occurred.

That he felt some pangs of conscience for having started hostilities,
however, appears certain. When news of the sack of the rebellious town
reached him, he rushed posthaste to Volterra and, finding that order
had already been restored by Federigo da Urbino, he distributed large
sums to alleviate the distress of those who had suffered most. Many
critics suggest this might have been an attempt to pacify the Volterrans
after their defeat. If this was his intention, he was signally unsuccessful.
To this day, let no one call Lorenzo by the appellation of "Il Magnifico"
in Volterra or the Volterran countryside. He is still looked on as "the
evil force that destroyed our ancient Etruscan city."

The saddest part of the story is that the alum mines, after all, did not
prove profitable. The Volterrans would never have made much out of
them anyway. Too late did they discover that the value of the site was
not what they had thought, or, it might be more apposite to say had
"hoped."

Florence, on the other hand, secured many very evident advantages:
First she had forcibly discouraged armed interference in the territories
of her satellites by foreign Powers. To put it bluntly, this meant the
Pope, already scheming to find new fiefs for his host of 'nephews' and to
enlarge the dominions of the Church. Secondly, the Florentine State had
shown its dependants and allies that rebellion against Florence could
prove very costly.

And if Florence had reaped undoubted gains, Lorenzo personally
saw his position as ruler, as the guide to follow in an emergency, firmly
established in Florence, the whole of Tuscany subjected to Florence.
Even in distant lands, his authority came to be acknowledged and
respected not only, as was natural, by Federigo da Urbino, but by the
Gonzagas of Mantua, the Estes of Ferrara, the Duke of Milan and even
by the Kings of England, Aragon and France, by Edward IV and Louis
XI.

Sixtus IV too was compelled to recognise it, however grumpily, and
malevolently, and it may have been just then that he decided that one
day he would do away with Lorenzo or at least oust him from government. It may have been only a vague fancy, but it is certain that, from
that moment, the idea of warring and plotting against the Medici began
to take shape in his mind.

Lorenzo—this is known and he said so himself on his deathbed when dying men don't lie—bitterly regretted the Volterran incident. At the time, his emotions were divided between vexation and distress at what had happened and gratification at the fact that the glory of being undisputed First Citizen of Florence. This seesaw of emotions seems to have worried him since he chose that moment to take refuge in the solace he most delighted in: letters and learning and the spreading of culture.

To show the satellite and allied towns that, if he could be forceful against rebellion, he also had at heart, and the Florentine republic had at heart, first and foremost the civil well-being and happiness of all those who owed allegiance to Florence, he undertook to bring back to the ancient university of Pisa to its former splendour.

There is no doubt that Lorenzo loved power but the delights of poetical emotion and this enthusiasm for learning, in all its forms, prevailed and gave him greater satisfaction and happiness than the will to command. He seldom sacrificed his thrill at discovering some novel aspect of erudition to his ardour to lead men and the State. In the case of Pisa University, the two quests converged. By a single action, he could both enhance his power and spread culture.

Wasting no time, he moved his residence from Florence to Pisa and, to the 600 florins provided by the State for what was to become known as the "Pisan Academy", he added large sums of his own. At no period had professors of literature, or law, men of medicine and science, been offered such high rewards as Lorenzo proffered, if only they would come and teach in Pisa. Francesco Accolti from Arezzo, who taught Civil and Canon Law, received the highest salary—1,440 Florins—Baldo Bartolini 1,050 Florins; Bartolomeo Mariano Soccini—a Sienese—700 Florins. For the Faculty of medicine, for which Pisa remained famous for many centuries, Lorenzo found Alessandro Sermoneta, Giovanni d'Aquila and Piero Leoni.

Not all went well however. Men of science and poets are like other men and, inevitably, with them too, there is the chaff among the wheat. In this case, the chaff was the Sienese Soccini. For his 700 Florins salary, he had signed a contract to stay and teach in Pisa for at least three years. His lectures were vivacious, original, controversial and attracted students from many lands. His widespread reputation induced the Venetians to make him a higher offer than Lorenzo's, but he was to come to Venice at once. This meant breaking his contract with Il Magnifico and Soccini broke it. He tried to abscond taking with him several ancient manuscripts that were the property of the University.

He arranged the documents in long narrow boxes, sufficiently narrow to go through the neck of a wineflask. He sealed them well, slipped them through and then—to conceal them—filled the vessels with dark red wine. But the Tuscans were not fooled and Soccini, arrested, was taken to Florence. The judges proved unusually severe. He was found guilty on three counts: of breach of contract which was obvious; of theft, equally evident, and then came the most damaging charge of all: using the advantages of his public office for purposes of collecting information for a Foreign State. They found that the fact that the information was cultural made the crime all the more heinous in a man of learning, especially as he must have known that Florence made no monopoly of the contents of her documents, but certainly did not want to lose the originals to a country that, in all probability, would have kept their purport out of reach of anyone not Venetian. They condemned Soccino to die.

But this time too, Lorenzo asserted his authority. He stayed the execution and—with impassioned oratory—persuaded the judges that, however despicable Soccini's crime "so accomplished a scholar could not be made to suffer an ignominious death". He pressed the point that the loss to culture, were he prevented by death from continuing to teach, might be as great as or greater than the loss of the manuscripts.

Roscoe, in his *Life of Lorenzo de'Medici*, expressed disapproval of Lorenzo's gesture. He argues that Soccini was all the more guilty because of his learning and must have been fully aware of the loss he was inflicting on a foremost seat of learning and on a friend who had trusted him. Lorenzo held a different opinion and in his reverence for learning, he reinstated Soccini in his office within three years and—to prevent temptation getting the better of him again—raised his salary to 1000 Florins. Soccini ill repaid his benefactor. He broke his contract once again; but this time he took care to flee taking nothing with him, not even his belongings. As if this were not enough, later, after Lorenzo's death he led a Pisan rebellion against the Medici. Lorenzo however had secured his services for at least a while and his enlightened teaching had created a discriminating generation of Pisan students. And this had been Lorenzo's aim.

Mrs Oliphant in her *The Makers of Florence* expresses strong disapproval of Lorenzo's indulgence toward Soccini. She also remonstrates against aspects of *Il Magnifico* that the puritanical nineteenth century of Victoria, Louis Philippe, and Franz Josef, in which Mrs Oliphant lived, did not approve at all. She writes: (Lorenzo's time) "was the very height of the classic revival, so famous in the later history of the world, but Florence was as near a pagan city as it was possible for its rulers to make it". She continues in shocked tones: "Lorenzo—a man of superb health'' (actually Il Magnifico died of intestinal trouble that was his bane throughout his life) ''and a man of superb physical power—who can give himself up to debauch all night without its interfering with his power to work next day and all the day—whose mind is so versatile that he can sack a town one morning and discourse upon the beauties of Plato the next, and weave joyous ballads through both occupations, gives flatterers reason to applaud him, but never had Society been more dissolute, selfish, hopeless morally, believing in nothing but Greek manuscripts''.

Mrs Oliphant's scathing remarks, which fashion has caused many later researchers to re-echo, seem to be a grudging praise of *Il Magnifico*, though they are not exact in all details. Still we feel that if Lorenzo were to appear at Mrs Oliphant's door, she most decidedly would not ask him in to tea. But she might winsomely regret it afterwards.

CHAPTER SIX

Poliziano

HE Literati, whom Lorenzo had left behind in Florence when he had moved to Pisa to set to rights the ancient University there, missed his presence sorely. Poliziano particularly—who was only nineteen—felt he needed his friend's guidance and help. The young poet was desolate but tempered his sense of loss by writing affectionate verse in honour of his benefactor and there was also an intense exchange of letters between the two. To this circumstance, posterity is indebted for several notable epistles that tell us—with the freshness of contemporary language—how men of letters lived in Florence at that time; what their thoughts were, their problems, their hopes and preoccupations and—above all—their delights.

The pervading sentiment, besides affection, is one of complete frankness and Poliziano's letters are only one of many examples of the freedom of expression writers enjoyed in Medicean Florence[1]. In this, Florence under the Medici, was ahead of most Italian Principalities and of most of Europe.

This was the real achievement of that season of rebirth. Because of it, literary production, even in its highest form, was no pompous rhetoric as it was later to become, but a clear and concise endeavour to exchange ideas. An attempt to generate convictions freely reached, an instrument of persuasion not an imposition by force or authority or worse still, fashion. It was more highly civilised not only than in most contemporary States, but also than in many nations in later centuries, such as the seventeenth, when under absolute monarchs and the Inquisition, "the maximum care" was recommended "at city gates and along travelling routes" to stem the flow of books, particularly those printed at Basle or Frankfurt, considered "vehicles of pernicious ideas". (2) Nor can letters, free, frank and sincere be exchanged within many countries today.

Poliziano's epistles, on the other hand, showed he had not the least inkling of fear when he wrote, no apprehension, nor prudence because none was needed. He was no courtier, nor even a subordinate but wrote to Lorenzo as from one equal to another. He seems to have had no doubts that, because he was and intended to grow into an ever greater man of culture, he was destined to become *Il Magnifico*'s collaborator; in his work and in his leisure; when State problems were pressing and in the gentle hours devoted to learning and meditation in the company of Marsilio Ficino, and, in time, Pico della Mirandola and others. And again he would be by Lorenzo's side in the hours given over to merriment with the Pulci brothers and Matteo Franco. He was also destined to be close to Lorenzo when death threatened and to be the means whereby Lorenzo survived. Though Poliziano was the closest to Lorenzo, the same bond existed between *Il Magnifico* and most other men of culture in Florence at that time. Their influence on the State, on the way of life, in short on the society of their time was so great that it is difficult at first for us to appreciate its full extent, accustomed as we are to the far more oblique sway on modern thought of our contemporary writers, even the most eminent and weighty.

"Lorenzo represents in Italy the peak of the civilisation of the Renaissance, after whom begins the period of decline" writes the left-wing author Lucio Lombardo Radice[2]. The retrogression was slow, almost unnoticed at first, but by the sixteenth century, even the great Leonardo, who knew how to build bridges and self-dredging harbours as well as to create unequalled works of art, was compelled to look for a master to serve: first Ludovico il Moro, then Cristina of Mantua and then the King of France. Finally in the seventeenth century, writers and artists were reduced to the rank of mere courtiers to Popes and Princes or forced to be sour moralists to avoid the censure and extreme rigours of the Inquisition and the Counter-reformation.

But in Lorenzo's time this was not so and writers could write freely. The fruits of Lorenzo's and Poliziano's collaboration began to make themselves apparent when both were still extremely young. *Il Magnifico* entrusted the young poet with the sorting of the valuable books and documents of antiquity that numerous, hardpressed agents collected for him at almost any price in every part of the world. They are still gathered as Poliziano screened them in the Laurentian Library in Florence and are, to this day, among the most precious assets of Western civilisation.

Lorenzo did not mind the great expense they entailed because as he said: "I think they cast a brilliant light on our city." From 1434 to 1471, his family had spent no less than 663,755 Florins on embellishing Florence and contributing to its finances[3] and he was determined to continue at this pace, even though it would mean large inroads into his private fortune.

He would spend as much as he dare afford not only on books but also on writers too. He was determined he would create a generation of writers if he could and he began with Poliziano. He must have done it very gently as between friends with a deep affection for one another and it gave rise to a period of such happiness for both that as Adeline Nesca Robb writes "The emotion that stirs the two poets (Lorenzo and Poliziano) is the regret that their joys cannot endure." Their gladness and their verse were of a different nature surely, but it did not seem to matter.

Poliziano, in his own words, had been "naked, unlearned, destitute", had seen the hand not of a benefactor but a friend stretched out to help him and could now delight in fulfilling his aspiration to describe the beauties of nature as he saw it—the charm of the pursuits of country folk—the art, the learning and the graces of a brilliant society of which he became a dazzling part and whose admiration warmed and encouraged him.

Lorenzo—on the other hand—could write with zest of the crudities and vulgarity of his times but, at other moments, his poetical emotion was intertwined with a mystical rapture and depth of philosophical expression, bound with the religious sense he had learnt as a child by his mother's side, for Lucrezia Tornabuoni had been a poetess whose musical rhyming had expressed in each verse an adoring faith.

Poliziano, on the contrary, was no mystic and no philosopher. He invariably went to sleep during the lectures of Marsilio Ficino, the fore-

most neoplatonist of the Medicean Era. Lorenzo instead believed in the
uses of philosophy as a guide and balm to practical life. Poliziano saw in
it only a soporific.

Il Magnifico was pained at this but it did not diminish his love for his
friend. Realising that his young companion had in him the makings of a
great poet, he set about to develop Poliziano's talents to the full. This
for Poliziano meant long and arduous practice. To express himself as
one day he would do and make nature and the heart quiver with life, he
must first of all become master in the choice of words. The best exercise
for him to develop a perfect appreciation of their value and music would
be for him first to learn to render with exactness the words of another,
written in another language. So Lorenzo set Poliziano to translate
Homer's *Iliad*. Poliziano showed his talent and hard work by sending
Lorenzo at Pisa as early as 1472, the first three books of his translation.
He was rewarded by becoming a permanent guest in Lorenzo's palace in
Via Larga as soon as *Il Magnifico* returned to Florence in December the
same year.

But Poliziano had a fiercely independent disposition. Despite all
Il Magnifico did not to make him feel the weight of his benevolence,
he applied for an emolument from the young cardinal Raffaele Riario, a
nephew of Sixtus IV, though the Riarios were rivals of the Medici for the
Pope's favours. Faithful to his tenet, that "genius must be humoured",
Lorenzo took no umbrage. On the contrary, not long after, he showed
his complete trust in Poliziano by confiding him his own son Piero, to be
educated. It was Lorenzo's dream that Piero, his first born should, one
day, prolong the Medicean Golden Age, so it is all the more remarkable
that he should have entrusted his upbringing to Poliziano, who was only
twenty-one. Perhaps because of the young teacher's age, certainly
because of his comical looks[4] and prominent nose, little Piero, who was
only three years of age, laughed uproariously when he first set eyes on
the preceptor his father had chosen for him. Somewhat put out,
Poliziano wrote to Lorenzo saying he had found his son "leggeretto e
disubbidientuzzo" "fickle and tending to disobedience" which sounds a
severe appraisal of a three year old mite. But they made friends for—
three years later—in 1478, Poliziano wrote in quite a different vein
describing his young charge in a letter to Lorenzo as "Piero vostro e
mio." "Your and my Peter". With someone as sensitive as Poliziano, we
may safely infer that his sentiments towards the boy were reciprocated.
This is all the more remarkable in that we learn from various sources the
most notable of which is that of Picotti[5] that Poliziano put the little boy
through the most strenuous mental and physical exercises—made him

learn the classics by heart and repeat hourly the sayings of ancient writers. Not content with all this, he also insisted the boy learn Greek, a language which even many adult scholars didn't know at that period. Neither Poliziano nor Lorenzo considered Piero a prodigy when, at six and a half, he could recite most of Virgil by heart, (he had read Livy correctly since he was four) and at seven he translated consistent passages from the Latin into Greek and then back into Latin. When he was eight—on 16 April 1479, the little boy wrote, unaided, a letter to his father from Cafaggiolo, the Medici's country seat. It was couched in such perfect Italian that even Poliziano, rigorous stylist and grammarian that he was, praised it for the appositeness of words and flow of phrase.

But if the pupil had been worked hard, the master most certainly had not spared himself. He had been asked to look after his charge's physical health as well as his intellectual upbringing and he had taken this mission very seriously. He had gone to the length of learning and elaborating something approaching modern medicine in an age when this science was more akin to astrology than to the body of knowledge we have amassed today, thanks in no small measure and surprising as it may seem, to Poliziano. Juliana Hill Cotton in her "Poliziano and Medicine" writes: "The study of medicine was part of Poliziano's activity in the service of the Medici and sprang from his intellectual curiosity."[6] She also points out that the Medici family, the adults perhaps more than the infant Piero, were beset by many ailments and these, particularly in times of pestilence and war when doctors were likely to be more scarce than usual, required the attention of a competent man on the spot. Poliziano, in the intervals of tutoring Piero and writing his own verse, set to and learnt medicine. He mastered it so well—for his times—that, at a later date, he even taught it. Robert Weiss reveals that Thomas Linacre, the Founder of the Royal College of Physicians in London, on his way through to Rome to carry out a mission from Henry VII to the Pope, had decided to stop and stay in Florence for many months "to study under Poliziano."[7] Poliziano's proficiency was due in large measure to his being able to read the ancient Greek medical texts in the original and Linacre—who already knew the rudiments of Greek—developed a high degree of familiarity with it under Poliziano and was able, in his turn, to consult the ancient authors and make their deductions and experiences his own and this played no small part in the progress and the glory of London's College of Physicians. To this glory, it may be said, Poliziano had, in small part at least, contributed. He contributed to the growth of Pisa University as a seat of medical learning.

To realise how far he had progressed beyond his times, it is sufficient to recall he was one of the first diagnosticians. Before him, most doctors hardly examined the patient, analysing as best they could his various symptoms but chiefly looking into books for the movements of the stars above the patient's head. To Poliziano, the perusal of a sick man's urine was more important than the stars of which he sang so melodiously in his poetry.

For despite all his occupations, didactic, social and scientific, he found time to write harmonious verse. Though at times he still felt an irrepressible urge to buck under Lorenzo's guidance, he was evidently deeply grateful to him when at last he wrote:

> "High born Lorenzo—Laurel in whose shade
> Thy Florence rests nor fears the lowering
> storm . . .
>
> Nursed in the shade thy spreading branch
> supplies
> Tuneless before, a tuneful swan I rise."

> (William Roscoe's translation.)

But this did not prevent him from raging at Lorenzo when he thought he ought to. *Il Magnifico* was rudely awakened on the morning of July 3, 1477 by Poliziano hammering on his door. Half dazed with sleep, Lorenzo learnt that the poet, doctor, preceptor of his child, friend or what have you, had just had news of the death during the night of the Prior of a church in Florence, St Paul's to be exact. Shaking off his sleep with difficulty and wondering why this had necessitated his being awakened so roughly, Lorenzo further learnt that the Priory carried an emolument paid by Rome and that Poliziano wanted to become its incumbent. For this it was essential he have a recommendation from Lorenzo to the Pope, and Poliziano informed him he must have it at once. Il Magnifico, raised from slumber, still dazed and wanting to go back to bed, may have had it on the tip of his tongue to assure Poliziano that he would always take care of his needs but the memory of Poliziano's sensitivity on the subject pulled him up short. He sent a messenger posthaste to Rome to do as Poliziano wanted. But the clouds of Sixtus IV's hatred for Lorenzo were already gathering. Less than ten months hence it would break in the open and assassins would try to kill Lorenzo in Florence cathedral with the Pope's concurrence. So

Lorenzo's recommendation wasn't as decisive as Poliziano imagined. There were other candidates. Among them one put forward by Tornabuoni, Lorenzo's uncle. So the reply was delayed. But Poliziano was impatient. He sat down and wrote a furious letter: "What delusion for me, who had been led to believe that Lorenzo's word was his bond. Poor was I born and lived though poor. I shall not die if I become poor again."

It was an unkind way to reward his benefactor. It shows Lorenzo's liberality that he remained unruffled by the insult. As it was, Poliziano was appointed Prior and became a proud taxpayer on an income of 100 Florins a year[8] that made him (if need be) independent. Perhaps he was more grateful to *Il Magnifico* for that than almost anything else.

After that Poliziano was often asked to act as Lorenzo's secretary on matters of State and *Il Magnifico* often praised him for the discretion with which he kept a secret: those of Lorenzo's bedchamber no less than those of the Republic. Certain it is that, voluble on any other aspect of life, Poliziano never wrote a line of verse on either subject. He did write on law—just as he had written twelve volumes on medicine—but only when asked by Lorenzo to clarify the Justinian Code which had been discovered among the treasured documents of Pisa University.[9] According to Poliziano's convictions, the perfect jurist must be able to grasp the intended meaning of a legal document and express it in lucid phrases over which there can be no equivocation. That is what he accomplished with the Justinian Code, which became the charter on which the whole system of jurisprudence rested in the fifteenth century.

Poliziano also tried his hand at philosophy but in this case with no marked success. While Lorenzo often basked in spiritualness, Marsilio Ficino's, Poliziano was happiest and at his best when he could draw Il Magnifico along some country lane and they happened on a group of country girls:

> "When the full rose quits her tender sheath,
> when she is sweetest and most fair to see,
> then is the time to place her in your wreath
> before her beauty and her freshness flee."

(William Roscoe's translation.)

Poliziano was not wrong. Awesome clouds were gathering against the Medici and the Golden Age. The threat came from retrograde Rome and her greed.

CHAPTER SEVEN

La Congiura dei Pazzi (1)

HE *congiura dei Pazzi*—the conspiracy of the Pazzi family to murder Lorenzo which led to the violent death of Il Magnifico's younger brother Giuliano—may, at first sight, seem to have sprung from economic motives chiefly the possession of the town of Imola, which lies astride what was then the most direct route from Florence to Venice, the port for Tuscany's trade with the East at that time.

Dread of seeing this line to the sea—so vital to Florentine economy—under the control of Milan's great power or that of the Papal States, who already controlled the routes southward, induced Lorenzo to make an attempt to buy the town from the Duke of Milan, under whose domination it was at that moment. He made an extremely handsome bid of 20,000 ducats for it and the Duke of Milan, always short of money for the wars he was waging or intended to fight, accepted. But once Imola had become the property of the Florentine Republic, trouble started.

Pope Sixtus IV, ostensibly bent on making noblemen of his nephews, had long intended that his sister's son, Girolamo Riario, should become Lord of Imola. This he gave as his pretext for wanting possession of the town at all costs and in a heart-rending letter to the Duke of Milan, he adjured Galeazzo Maria "by all that is holy" to rescind the agreement he had concluded with Lorenzo.

Galeazzo Maria believed firmly and devoutly in God, but he was also a businessman and a politician. He sensed that the real reason for the Pope's wanting just Imola (Girolamo Riario could well become Count of anywhere else) was that he intended not only to ennoble his family, but above all to control Florence's lifeline to the sea and, in consequence, all the Tuscan economy. Galeazzo Maria mused that if the Pope stood to gain two advantages from owning Imola, while Florence had aimed at one advantage only, then it was clear the Pontiff must pay twice as much. He replied to Sixtus's adjuration that, as a dutiful son of the Church, he would comply with his request, but the price of Imola, contested by two buyers, was up to 40,000 ducats. He may well have known that there were no 40,000 ducats in the Papal Treasury as Lorenzo, who was still the Vatican's Treasurer, could have told him. He hoped the Pope would have to renounce Imola and all sides would be satisfied. But Sixtus was unswerving in his determination. With considerable brashness, he turned to the Medici bank for a loan of exactly 40,000 ducats. So the Medici would not only fail to secure Imola, but would also risk twice the capital they had spent in acquiring it. Lorenzo was furious not so much for the hazard the loan implied, but for the attempt to use Medici money for the purpose of throttling the Florentine State. Giovanni Tornabuoni, Lorenzo's agent in Rome, refused to advance the money. The Pope turned to the rival Pazzi bank. The Pazzi came up at once with the 40,000 ducats and Imola—lost to Lorenzo—became the Pope's and Sixtus furthermore deprived Il Magnifico of his post of Vatican Treasurer and gave it to Francesco de'Pazzi. All this raised the terrible threat of a stranglehold on the Tuscan economy, and, as a consequence, on Florentine independence.

Lorenzo was too shrewd a politician to meet the Pope head on. He accepted with good grace the Pontiff's decision and vented his anger on the Pazzi instead. The measure he took, morally justifiable since the Pazzi had handed the Pope the means to hurt the Florentines, was legally dubious and perhaps actually high handed. He introduced a retroactive law which deprived the Pazzi of an inheritance—a very large one into which they had just come. It was a gesture that was just short of an abuse of authority and juridically defensible only at times of great national emergency and the extension of the Pope's power to include Imola, though certainly a threat to Florence, did not amount to an emergency yet. As it was, *Il Magnifico*'s decision may well have contributed to bringing the emergency closer. What had till then been the Pazzi's concealed enmity swelled to hatred—mortal hatred. But outwardly they took to heart the admonition that Lorenzo's action against them implied: "Harm the republic and stand against me and you may lose yet more money. With me and with the Republic you would gain in wealth, advantages, prestige."

Towards Girolamo Riario—now Lord of Imola—Lorenzo adopted the policy he was in fact proposing to the Pazzi: that of making friends now the storm was over. This policy is described nowadays with the hackneyed cliché: "If you can't lick them, join them".

Lorenzo offered Riario assistance in any difficulty and made it clear to him that the portals of the Medici banks were wide open to him should he want a loan. This must have been a tempting offer. The Pazzi, after lending 40,000 ducats (pretty well unrecoverable) to the Pope and the loss of their sizeable inheritance, were no longer able to help Riario financially. Riario and the Pazzi knew only too well that lending money was one of the ways the Florentines controlled foreign lands.

Lorenzo accepted Girolamo's refusal with grace and proclaimed himself his friend. But both Riario and the Pazzi continued to see in him the most formidable opponent to their own aggrandizement. So did the Pope.

The result was—as Roscoe puts it: "An event of an atrocious nature—the greatest proof of the practical atheism of the times in which it took place—a transaction in which a Pope, a Cardinal, an Archbishop and several other ecclesiastics associated themselves with a band of ruffians to destroy two men who were an honour to their Age and country. They perpetrated their crime violating hospitality and desecrating a cathedral at the very moment of the Elevation of the Host, in which Catholics revere God Himself and others solemnly commemorate Christ's Last Supper."[1]

Roscoe's impassioned, outraged words are not accurate in every detail but the main purport of what he says is true. It is drawn from the accounts given of the felony by three eminent intellectuals and literary men of the period.

First there is the cold, bureaucratic, juridical document of Matteo Toscano, an historian as well as a magistrate, who based his report strictly on the answers to questioning of one of the principal conspirators, the one who had been chosen to cut Lorenzo's throat.

Then there is the virulent description, full of invectives and passion, written by Poliziano a few days after the crime.[2] Poliziano was at Lorenzo's side when Il Magnifico was attacked. It was Poliziano who slammed the door that prevented the assault from being carried home. It was Poliziano who saw the enemies of the Medici hanged from the windows of the Palace of the Florentine "Signoria" immediately afterwards. He was in fact not only present at but extremely close to each principal event of that horrifying day. With a poet's genius he recreates the atmosphere of each succeeding scene and brings the feelings of the participants to life. But not all his details are accurate because of the stress of the moments when he witnessed what was happening and also because—as he has no false shame in confessing—he was the prey not only of horror but of absolute abject terror during those hours. Most of those present must have shared the feeling and Poliziano is the writer who brings the scene and sentiments to life in their stark reality better than anyone else who has written about them. But—just because those sentiments of consternation and horror were prevalent in him as in others—his account, like theirs, is confused when it comes to detail. Moments of fear can seem far longer than they are and those of intense excitement far shorter than they have been. So, while Poliziano concurs with most, for instance, Landucci[3] and the Mantuan Ambassador[4] in saying that the Medici brothers were stabbed at the moment when the Host was raised for the Elevation, the Milanese Envoy speaks of the attack taking place later, at the moment of the Agnus Dei.[5] Gregorovius,[6] who, though not there, was always very careful of his facts, agrees with Poliziano while F. Strozzi writes the two brothers were set upon at the end of Mass. This is most unlikely since that would have been the moment when the victims could more easily have fled or fought in the confusion of people leaving the church. Besides, witnesses would have actually seen the event since their eyes, instead of being lowered in adoration, would have been turned to the people around as is only natural in the relaxed moments that follow the conclusion of a religious service. Strozzi's account must be put down as an attempt to absolve ecclesiastics from responsibility in the sacrilege that occurred at the culminating moment of the divine Service. Poliziano's on the other hand must be accepted as, in the main, correct.

The third account, which Roscoe draws on, is less emotional than Poliziano's but not as cold as the precise rendering by Matteo Toscano. It quotes Matteo Toscano but is severely limited to telling only the incidents that are absolutely certain and have proved so after lengthy and careful inquiry. It omits no provedly true detail but mentions none on which there could be a shadow of doubt. It is contained in the letter—written in beautiful Latin—by the erudite Chancellor of the Florentine Republic, Bartolomeo della Scala, who took three months to collate all his facts and wrote them with the clearness and style of the great humanist he was.

Roscoe draws also from other chroniclers who have drawn their narratives from sources other than the three that he himself drew from. The most important of these chroniclers are: Michele Bruto in his *History of Florence* written in 1515 and Machiavelli with his *Historiae Fiorentine*. Although Machiavelli may have been in the cathedral when the Medici brothers were set upon, he can have only been a very small child. It is no wonder that his narrative seems based on earlier authors and not on his own appraisal of the events at the time they occurred. Michele Bruto also bases his account on earlier authors.

The fact is that literary men were deeply, personally, involved in the actual aspects of the crime and in establishing responsibilities afterwards. Nicolai Rubinstein[7] who has sought for proofs of a possibly justified opposition to the Medici, believes that "The contemporary Florentine evidence on the conspiracy is almost exclusively pro-Medicean" and that "The only contemporary Florentine source which decidedly takes the side of the Pazzi is Rinuccini's *De libertate*, composed early in 1479." He adds that it is as biased against the Medici, as Poliziano's account is biased in their favour. But Alamanno Rinuccini was not the only man of culture on the conspirators' side. One actually took part in instigating and carrying out the crime. But he—like Rinuccini—seems to have failed to have an impact on the society of his day.[8] He was Jacopo Bracciolini son of Poggio Bracciolini. Poggio had been one of the Florentine Chancellors, whose elegant classical style had delighted the Courts of Europe some years earlier, and young Bracciolini was anxious to keep his father's fame alive. It is due to the son if Poggio's works are known to this day. This is so at least in very large part because Jacopo translated Poggio's *History of Florence* and also, as we know thanks to a recent discovery by Nicolai Rubinstein, young Jacopo was indefatigable in defending his father, when his works and the value of his collection of ancient documents were attributed to another. We know from Rubinstein that what riled Jacopo particularly was that the tracing down of some documents of antiquity his father had found in Germany were later attributed to Petrarch.[10]

The *Congiura dei Pazzi* was so complicated that it is essential to examine the main sources in turn.

The first is the full confession—made after his arrest and before his execution—by Giovan Battista Montesecco, a mercenary captain in the service of Girolamo Riario, the Pope's nephew. It was he who should have killed Lorenzo but refused when told that as a last minute change the murder was to be perpetrated inside a church on holy ground. The confession was taken down by Matteo Toscano, with the rigour of a magistrate who was also an historian. It is countersigned by him as *Podestá* (magistrate) of "this magnificent sovereign city of Florence" and several ecclesiastics witnessed his and Montesecco's signatures. This last circumstance is most significant, when one considers that the Head of the Church, the Pope himself was involved certainly indirectly and probably directly, in the crime. The independent integrity of judgement of these ecclesiastics, as common in Tuscany as it was uncommon in Rome and other States, was further proved when later Pope Sixtus excommunicated the Florentine Republic and the whole Synod of Florentine Bishops did not hesitate to reject the excommunication. They went so far as to hurl epithets of such violence against the Pope that Roscoe shrank from repeating them because of their downright virulence.

Strangely Pastor dismisses Montesecco's confession as "dealing merely with the preliminaries of the crime", but then is at pains to show that the plot was hatched not inside the Vatican at all, but in the Pazzi palace at Via del Banco di S. Spirito close to Castel Sant'Angelo. (About half a mile from the Vatican!) But Montesecco, about to die, had no reason for whitewashing anybody.

His confession begins: "The first contact concerning this matter was with Archbishop Francesco Salviati and Francesco de'Pazzi in Rome. The meeting took place in the rooms of the aforesaid bishop. (Not at Santo Spirito.) They told me they wanted to reveal to me a secret they had long harboured in their hearts. They made me take an oath that I would keep this secret."

After he had taken this oath, according to Montesecco's sworn confession: "That Archbishop was the first to speak. He gave me to understand that he and Francesco de'Pazzi had ways and means for changing the government in Florence—that they were determined to accomplish this but they needed my help to do it."

These words of Montesecco dispel any possible doubt that, whoever was the first to dream up the conspiracy against Lorenzo, the initial, concrete step to bring about the events that culminated in *Il Magnifico* being wounded and his brother murdered, was taken by an ecclesiastic, who was a member of the Papal Court, and took this step in his own apartment at the Vatican and not in de'Pazzi's quarters. This first essential move was not made by Girolamo Riario, though Montesecco was in his service. What need was there for an archbishop to step in and give Montesecco orders unless it was to calm Montesecco's possible doubts and lead him to believe that whatever he might be asked to do had the seal of ecclesiastical approval, notified him in such a way that the order seemed to carry the assent of the Pope himself? Surely enough, Montesecco's reply was to request for further confirmation of Pope's interest in the undertaking. The captain's words were: "I answered that I would gladly do all I could to please their Lordships, but I was bound by compact to serve the Pope and the Count (Girolamo Riario) so I could not enter the service of others. They exclaimed: 'How could you imagine we would undertake anything without the consent of Girolamo Riario!' "

Although this answer begs the question of whether the Pope was involved or not in the conspiracy at this stage, we must assume that the bishop's words were intended to convey that Sixtus was not mixed up in it at that moment and that the assertion is true. However, Montesecco continued to insist that he was Riario's vassal and would come to no agreement with anybody else.

"Things stood at this point for several days" Montesecco's confession runs "and nothing was said to me but I know very well that the Archbishop (Francesco Salviati) and Francesco (de'Pazzi) and the Count (Girolamo Riario) talked over these matters several times.

"Then, one day, I was called by il Signor Conte to his apartment. The Archbishop was there and we talked of matters in Florence. The Count said to me: 'The Archbishop tells me they have talked to you concerning a certain business we have on our hands. What do you think of it?' I replied: 'Sir, I don't know what to say about it because it has not been explained to me. I don't understand it. I cannot express an opinion until the business has been made clear to me.'

"The Archbishop interrupted testily: 'What is this? What are you saying? Did I not tell you we intend to bring about a change of government in Florence?' I answered: 'You certainly told me that but you did not say how you propose to do it. Not knowing the ways you intend to follow nor the means you think of using, I don't know what to say' ".

So at last the Archbishop and the Count stopped speaking in riddles. They were long in coming to the point. They began by saying that, should the Pope die, Lorenzo de'Medici would vent against the Count the ill will he was known to feel against him. But, if the government of Florence were changed before the Pope's death, the "Signor Conte would be established in his domain and no one would harm him." This was the reason for their plan, they said. Reasonably enough, Montesecco asked what the plan was and how they intended to carry it out. They explained that "There are two noble families in Florence, the Pazzi and the Salviati, who, together can count on the support of half the people." Montesecco asked how they proposed to win the consent of the other half and, at long last, came the damning admission: "This could not be accomplished any other way than by 'cutting to pieces' Lorenzo and Giuliano de'Medici".

Montesecco was taken aback by the enormity of the proposal. He shrank from all its implications and said: "Sirs, you must watch out. Firenze e'una gran cosa! Florence is great and powerful! *Il Magnifico* enjoys great popularity there. I am positive of what I am saying."

The Count broke in severely "Others assert quite the contrary. They say he does not enjoy the support of the people. They tell me he is hated and that, once the two brothers are dead, all Florentines will lift their hands in gratitude to heaven." It became evident who it was who asserted all this when Archbishop Salviati burst in: "Giovanni Montesecco, you have not been to Florence. We know the situation there better than you do. We know the feelings of the people. We know towards whom they are well disposed and towards whom they are rancorous." Finally the Archbishop caught his breath and then exclaimed, "Have no doubts. As certainly as we stand here our plan will succeed." And then added prudently: "Of course we have to work it out properly." Montesecco agreed that this was necessary and asked what it was they all intended to do and the answer was: "What we have to do is to draw into the scheme Jacopo [Jacopo was the head of the Pazzi family and uncle of Francesco.] At present he is colder than ice about the idea and is altogether lacking in enthusiasm about our plans." These words were spoken by the Archbishop clearly indicating that he was taking an active and leading part in organizing the details of the plot. Montesecco inquired: "How will His Holiness the Pope take all this?" and they answered: "Nostro Signore li faremo fare sempre quel che vorrimo noi. (As for His Holiness, we shall always make him do that which we want.) Besides His Holiness hates Lorenzo and wants him out of the government."

"Have you spoken to him about it?" asked Montesecco.

"Certainly and we shall see to it that he speaks to you also and lets you know his mind." Here then we have a clear statement that Sixtus IV already knew of the plot or would soon be drawn into it and Pastor is wrong when he takes to task Luigi Villari for writing of the Pazzi conspiracy that "It was planned in the Vatican by Sixtus IV and many mem-

bers of the most powerful Florentine families took part in it.'' Salviati's
words leave no room for doubt that the final word to Montesecco was to
come from the Pontiff himself.

Meanwhile, Montesecco must make preparations. Archbishop Salviati gave him instructions to go to Florence and do three things: check
the general situation in the city—visit Lorenzo de'Medici so as to get to
know his victim well; and then contrive to be seen in *Il Magnifico*'s
company often so that, on the day of the killing, he could keep close to
him without arousing suspicion. Meantime he was to allay Lorenzo's
misgivings regarding Imola by pretending to ask his advice as to what
Girolamo should do to govern it properly. Finally Montesecco was to get
in touch with Jacopo de'Pazzi and persuade him to join the conspiracy.

Montesecco was a methodical soldier. He seems to have concluded in
his mind that he could not begin asking questions about the Florentine
situation without first establishing contacts with people of political
importance; and who was more important than Il Magnifico himself? So
he decided to see Lorenzo before doing anything else.

Montesecco's confession goes on: "I arrived in Florence in the evening so could not see His Magnificence Lorenzo at once. I saw him the
following day. He was dressed all in black because one of the Orsini a
kinsman of his wife had died. I said to him that the Count my master
wanted him to know that he trusted His Magnificence more than any
other single noble personage in the world. Indeed there had been
divergencies and misunderstandings in the past, but the Count was
determined to lay all animosities aside.''

One is led to wonder whether Lorenzo really believed all this or
merely pretended to, so as to establish a closer contact with Girolamo
and win him over to his side with his unfailing charm and persuasive
ability. Whatever his reasons, he accepted at once Montesecco's over-
tures at their face value. Montesecco was encouraged to go further and
in his confession he tells us he said: "The Count wished His Magnificence
to consider himself as if he were a father to the Count who badly needed
a father's advice. This is what I had been told to say and I said it''. Poor
Montesecco under questioning by the Florentine Magistrate concludes
shamefacedly at such arrant nonsense.

His Magnificence was no fool. Deliberately bent on establishing good
relations with Girolamo and the Pope, he pretended gladly to accept the
proffered fatherhood and Montesecco says: "His Magnificence's answer
literally astounded me; he expressed himself with such feeling that he
might indeed have been the Count's father''. Further to add to the
honest soldier's conclusion that everything appeared the exact opposite

of what he had been told in Rome and Lorenzo had no hatred for the Count, "His Magnificence added very sensible suggestions as what I should do better to further the Count's interests once I got to Imola. Lorenzo may have had his tongue in his cheek when he ended saying: "Yes, go to Imola to see how things stand there. Then come back and let me know what I, for my part, can do for the Count."

All this left Montesecco very confused and doubtful. Wisely he decided "to go to the hostelry of La Campana and have my meal". When he had thought things over while eating he drew the conclusion: "My instructions were to see Jacopo and Francesco de'Pazzi. I sent one of the attendants to advise them that I was in Florence. Word came back that Francesco had gone to Lucca. I sent another message insisting that I had to see Messer Jacopo on a very important matter. I said I was ready to go to his house or wait for him at the hostelry, whichever might be more convenient for him but I must see him." Messer Jacopo came to the hostelry but would not be seen with Montesecco in public. They met in a side room where they would be alone.

Jacopo de'Pazzi's first words were to the effect that if Montesecco had come to talk of matters concerning the government of Florence, he wanted to hear nothing about it. He explained testily that if Salviati, Girolamo Riario and Francesco de'Pazzi intended to become lords of Florence "they will end by breaking their necks". These words by the man who was vital to the conspiracy and knew about the situation in Florence certainly more than Cardinal Salviati should have warned Montesecco to steer clear of the plot. But how would Riario his master take it? And he was in Riario's service. And the Archbishop would egg Riario against him; and above the Archbishop towered the Pope, who, he now revealed, had also spoken to him. In his confession Montesecco told how he had said to Jacopo: "I am speaking to you on the part of His Holiness who received me in audience just before I left Rome. His Holiness said I was to encourage you to expedite this affair ... he said it would be unwise to delay ... he was set on a change of government in Florence and equally determined that no one should die in consequence of it." This to Montesecco seemed an impossible order. Sixtus was evidently thoroughly misinformed about the situation in Florence and the popularity of the Medici. But even his advisers, Salviati and Riario, were of the opinion that their aim could not be achieved without "cutting the Medici brothers to pieces". They had said so openly to Montesecco and repeated it, in Montesecco's presence to Pope Sixtus.

Even Montesecco saw no other way. He told Jacopo "In the presence of the Count and of the Archbishop, I said plainly to the Pope that it will be difficult to overthrow the Medicean government without putting to death Lorenzo, Giuliano and probably other people too. But His Holiness cried out 'I don't want the death of anyone. It is not my office to consent to the death of anybody. But I do want a change of government!' '' It was most confusing for Montesecco and very nebulous to Jacopo de'Pazzi. Someone was playing hide and seek. How could the Pontiff, if he wanted no bloodshed, entrust the whole affair to people who told him it could not be carried through without killing the Medici?

Montesecco in his confession goes on to say that, after the Pope had told him to bring about the fall of the Medici without hurting anyone "The Count then spoke and said: 'All that is possible shall be done to avoid anyone dying, but—should it happen that someone is killed—surely Your Holiness will pardon those who shall have been responsible for it.'

"The Pope answered: 'You are a brute. I am telling you I don't want the death of anyone but only a change of government in Florence. This I definitely want.'

"His Holiness then turned to me: 'Giovan Battista Montesecco, I am telling you that I very much wish the State of Florence to undergo a change—that Lorenzo be taken off our hands—that he is a villain who has no consideration for me. If he were only out of Florence we could do with that Republic what we want ...' ''

Here we have the admission that the *Congiura dei Pazzi* was intended not "to bring liberty" to Florence but to extend the Pope's power over the Republic. The conspirators then repaired to the Count's rooms and came to the conclusion that, if they were not to disobey the Pope and leave the Medici to rule Florence, they could not do other than bring about the death of Lorenzo and Giuliano.

The argument has raged for centuries whether Sixtus della Rovere was or was not guilty of instigating the murder of Giuliano and of Lorenzo. Henry Edward Napier—Fellow of the Royal Society and a member of the Royal Navy, wrote in his *Napier's Florentine History:* "With respect to the Pontiff's guilt in the bloody portion of the conspiracy, two opinions may be entertained. The most direct evidence of it is in Montesecco's confession. There it appears that, after repeated orders to shed no blood, Sixtus is content to give the whole management of the plot into the hands of those who had just declared it could not possibly be carried out without bloodshed."

On the other hand, Giovan Michele Bruto in his *History of Florence* reports Montesecco's words and draws the opposite conclusion. The Pope was convinced, according to Bruto, that the conspirators would obey him when he reiterated that no one must be killed.

The Florentines of the Medici epoch took a more practical view. Toscano the inquiring Magistrate, who took down Montesecco's confession from the Captain-at-arms' own lips, either thought it prudent or deemed it useless to delve into Montesecco's words about the Pope and ask him to make his meaning clear. The Florentines could do nothing against Sixtus and merely to protest would only harm relations between the Papacy and the Republic. Lorenzo did not go into the matter at all. He was sure of the Pope's enmity but knew he could do nothing about it. He was primarily concerned with the threat to Florence and her free way of life and was determined to defend both.

The very detailed confession by Montesecco goes on to tell at length of many hesitations and the final lukewarm agreement of Jacopo de'Pazzi to join the conspiracy, showing that the Pazzi on the spot were far less certain of popular support than Pazzi far off in Rome.

After meeting with Jacopo, Montesecco, as ordered, went off to Imola and, on his way back, went to visit Lorenzo at Cafaggiolo, the Medici's original country seat. From Cafaggiolo, the Captain-at-arms travelled back to Florence in Lorenzo's company and again was surprised at the cordial and almost affectionate terms Il Magnifico used when speaking of the Count.

At the end of his confession, Montesecco wrote in his own hand: "I, Giovan Battista Montesecco, confess and swear and vouch that all the above things, written on a foolscap sheet and on another half sheet, are true and written under oath."

Then follows the statement of the Magistrate: "I—Matteo Toscano—Knight and honoured at present with the rank of Magistrate of the Magnificent Republic and City of Florence, was present—together with the Reverend Fathers whose names appear below—when Giovan Battista Montesecco wrote down all that appears on this foolscap sheet and on the accompanying half sheet and when he stated on oath that all this corresponds to the truth and that he himself wrote this fact down in his own hand. Dated 4th May 1478."

A representative of the Archbishop of Florence, numerous heads of monasteries, ordinary monks and friars and many notaries also affixed their signatures to Montesecco's confession all testifying that he had written with his own hand and stated on oath that what he wrote was true.

CHAPTER EIGHT

La Congiura dei Pazzi (2)

MONTESECCO'S confession is an official document. Its contents have never been denied and must be accepted as an accurate account of the preparations that led to the murder of Giuliano de'Medici, the wounding of Lorenzo and the attempt to overthrow the government of Florence and seize power over the Republic by calling the people to rebellion.

Whether Florence was to have become incorporated in the Papal States or whether the Pope would have held it under his sway through leaders who would in effect have been his vassals, is debatable. But there can be no question that, either way, this would have meant an end to free thought and research and a dark cloud would have spread over the City of Flowers, heralding the end of its Golden Age.

The people sensed this and—in the half hour when Florence was practically without a ruler—when Giuliano lay dead and Lorenzo was believed killed—they rose for the Medicean party and against the Pazzi and the Pope. The few opponents acted in self interest or judged according to a distorted view of the situation.[1]

But the conspiracy also failed because of the muddleheaded preparation for it particularly in the last stages. Last minute changes were made several times for the most absurd reasons.

A fundamental deviation from the original plan occurred when Montesecco flatly refused to kill Lorenzo within the precincts of the cathedral, during a religious service. His place was taken by two priests: Antonio da Volterra and Stefano di Bagnone, a preceptor of the Pazzi children. Because of this change the conspiracy lost a cool, military mind and was left to courtiers, incompetent ecclesiastics and common ruffians, all, except these last, persons discontented but utterly unpractised in the use of arms.

The conspirators moreover committed a huge organisational mistake. They planned an attack against the two Medici brothers in one place and another assault, concomitant with the first, on the Palazzo della Signoria, seat of the Florentine government, which was a good half mile away. No system of communication had been set up between the two groups carrying out the two separate actions, except for the peal of the cathedral bells, which would signify the moment to act had arrived but provided no certain news to either attacking party that the other had been successful. And if either the massacre in the cathedral or that in Palazzo della Signoria failed, the whole conspiracy was doomed.[2]

But the basic reason for the failure of the plot was that, as Montesecco had shrewdly judged from the start, Francesco de' Pazzi and Archbishop Salviati had very much overrated their own popularity. They relied on the support from half the population, but it turned out to be that of a few hotheads only. Here is the sequence of events that led up to one of the most infamous crimes in history, a grievous attempt against men and modes of life to whom our civilisation and our present times are much in debt.

The Medici had no suspicion that a plot against them was in the making, nevertheless, for added safety, the conspirators planned to act so as to dispel any possible misgiving Lorenzo and Giuliano might have. They went a roundabout way about it. There was, at that time, a young nephew of the Pope, Raffaele Riario, seventeen years old but already a cardinal, who was studying at the University of Pisa and had never seen Florence. What better excuse for effecting a contact with the Medici than that Riario should visit them.

All unawares, the young cardinal took up his residence at the Pazzi villa near Fiesole across the Mugnone valley. It was only natural that a feast should be given to celebrate the arrival of the Pope's nephew, himself a prince of the Church and that the highest authorities in Florence, the Medici brothers, should be the guests of honour at the reception. Outwardly the party was to appear as the seal of reconciliation between the Medici and the Pazzi, Salviati, Riario and of course the Pope. In reality, the conspirators had planned that Lorenzo and Giuliano should both be killed before the celebrations were over.

But things did not go according to plan. Giuliano excused himself on a plea of ill health and Lorenzo arrived alone. This seems to have thrown the plotters into complete turmoil. What should they do? Kill Lorenzo there and then and hope that Giuliano would not be able to rouse sufficient support to hold on to the government and get them arrested? Suddenly the confidence in their own popularity which had seemed so bright and encouraging in Rome, appears to have deserted most of them. In rapid, covert consultation they quickly agreed that even a single Medici and ill at that, was too much for them. The massacre must be put off. It was agreed that the brothers must be killed simultaneously to prevent the one who happened to survive proving an obstacle to rallying the people of Florence to the Pazzi faction.

With hindsight, it may appear surprising that all the whispers and machinations at the feast should have escaped the notice of Lorenzo de' Medici and his followers, but they may have thought that the consultations had something to do with the entertainment in progress. Besides the principal plotters were only eight in number and in a large unsuspecting crowd it was possible for them to whisper to each other without attracting undue attention.

Poliziano provides a full list of conspirators[3]. They were: Jacopo de' Pazzi whom he describes as "a man who spent his nights and days with dice continually in his hands and, when he lost the game, blasphemed God, man and mankind. At times, blind with rage at his losses, he would throw the dicebox straight into the face of anyone who happened to be near him. A bad administrator of his wealth, he had torn down to the foundations the palace his father had left him and begun to rebuild it with many hired hands whose wages he never paid in full." Hinting that full payment would only take place on completion of the work, Poliziano adds "In this way he forced them (his workers) to live miserably though he made them work all day." This vivid description of Jacopo de'Pazzi would make anyone doubt, in any age and under any circumstances, that he would be able to win popular support, unless it were that of the rabblerouser. But the Florentines were no rabble. Their frame of mind and habits of judgement were such that they would have shared

Poliziano's contempt for Jacopo de'Pazzi. Lauro Martinez in his remarkable work "The social world of the Florentine Humanists"[4] tells us that to be considered a man of the ruling class an individual must be the owner of honourably acquired wealth and be a good administrator and show at the same time a willingness to spend for the good of the city. Jacopo de'Pazzi may have inherited honourably acquired wealth but he neither administered it well nor spent it for the good of the Florentines. He exploited his workmen, and looked for an increase of his possessions neither to work nor to trading but to the throw of the dice. Poliziano concludes his appraisal of him with sarcasm "He contrived the miracle of being, at the same time, a miser and a squanderer".

As for Archbishop Salviati he too had never done anything to make the Florentines regret the old oligarchy with its arrogance, bullying and perpetual gambling and fighting. He too was much addicted to dice. Even if Poliziano was exaggerating when he described him as a gambler there can be no doubt that he judged him well when he wrote of him in beautiful Latin: "Omnis divini atque humanae juris ignarus et contemptor"—"one who held in contempt and wilfully ignored every divine and human law" and neglected no felony nor ribaldry however infamous. Nevertheless the Florentines (and probably Poliziano) could not have been expected to know all this until after the conspiracy had been discovered and his being in Florence and at the Pazzi reconciliation party aroused no suspicion. Though he was one of the prime movers in the plot to kill Lorenzo, his coming to the feast appeared mainly as a wish on his part to bury the differences he had had with Il Magnifico over his own appointment with the archdiocese of Pisa, which Lorenzo had strenuously opposed knowing Salviati to be one of his enemies.

Francesco de'Pazzi—the next on the list of conspirators—was the man who had supplanted Lorenzo as Vatican Treasurer after supplying the funds for the Pope to acquire Imola and so deprive Florence of the town. One might have thought Lorenzo would grow suspicious at his presence, but he seems to have taken it as a part of the reconciliation for was not this the occasion for forgetting grievances, starting afresh in concord for the good of the Republic.

Poliziano's indictment of the next plotter on his list appears less objective and it is difficult to resist the conclusion that there was not something very personal about it. It is directed at Jacopo Bracciolini, third son of the great Florentine humanist, Poggio and the invectives hurled at Jacopo seem more venomous than those aimed at the other plotters. Poliziano begins by saying that Jacopo "was of the sort that is always ready for any kind of sedition because of the economic straits he was in, burdened by debts." Though, with these words, Poliziano shows himself a true representative of the general opinion of the Florentines of his day that honour is due to wealth acquired honourably and not to the squanderer, his fury against someone in debt is unexplainable considering he often incurred debts himself; but then it was always with the Medici and he considered them merely advance payments for services he was determined to render, as writer, doctor or legal adviser. His was not a case of running up debts with no idea of where the money to pay them would come from. Perhaps one of the few mistakes made by Lorenzo de'Medici was that he had not subsidized Jacopo Bracciolini's translation from Latin of his father Poggio's *Florentine History*. Had he not heard of it?[5] There is nothing to show that the lack of help for Jacopo Bracciolini was in any way due to Poliziano and we must hope it was not. It would be a tragic reflection on the Literati of the time if one writer's jealousy towards another proved to be the cause that led two eminent Humanists to be on opposite sides in the *Congiura dei Pazzi*. As the conspiracy developed, Jacopo was entrusted with the all important, the culminating, dastardly final act of physically seizing the Chief Magistrate of Florence, the Gonfaloniere, and killing him after the two Medici brothers had been murdered. He was to do this under the personal direction of Archbishop Salviati, who would appear to place the seal of Pontifical approval on the crime.

Poliziano's treatment of the remaining three conspirators is different. No venom wasted here. Bernardo Bandini, the hooligan who murdered Giuliano and came very close to killing Lorenzo is merely termed "a common criminal". The others were minor characters and treated as such. Among them is the only one who was driven by honourable motives. He was a priest, Antonio da Volterra, who meant, by killing Lorenzo, to avenge the destruction of Volterra under the Medici. He had been picked after Captain Montesecco had refused to carry out the deed himself on the holy ground of a cathedral in front of the high altar during divine service.

Poliziano does not tell us how the conspirators were to have taken control of Florence and how troops were to be moved up from Siena and down from Imola, once the Medici brothers, Lorenzo's son Piero and Poliziano himself had been murdered. It was left to Montesecco to reveal all this in his confession. The extent of this military project shows that Salviati and the Pazzi were not sure of their vaunted popular support.

Nevertheless there must have been others, besides the "seven citizens" at the heart of the plot, who knew about it and, though taking no immediate part in it, were expected to go into action once the murders had been committed. Meanwhile they were vowed to silence or kept in total ignorance of what was going on.

For the next step in the active unfolding of the plot, the conspirators once again used the unsuspecting young cardinal Raffaello Riario as a decoy; Poliziano tells us that the plotters made it known to the Medici that the cardinal longed to see their palace in Florence and, particularly, the famous collections that were in it: the tapestries—the jewels—the works of art and many other precious objects. He further tells us "The excellent young men (the Medici brothers) harbour no suspicion. They put all ornaments in display for the cardinal's visit—arrange the statues—the basreliefs and the jewels."

According to some authors, the murders were to have been carried out in the palace, but this seems very unlikely as the assassins would have been completely surrounded by the Medici's retinue and followers. What is certain and what did in fact happen shows that the place chosen for the outrage was Florence cathedral and the day fixed for the murders was the Sunday preceding Ascension Day. This Sunday in the year 1478 fell on 26 April. It was for this day that the cardinal's visit to the Medici palace in Via Larga was arranged. They would all meet there. They would then go to church in the cathedral and afterwards return to the palace where a banquet would be held followed by a protracted visit to the Medici collections and galleries.

The cardinal arrived early on horseback and was ushered upstairs where he changed into his more sumptuous ecclesiastical vestments—then the cortège proceeded to the Duomo, the cathedral, for divine service.

Once again Giuliano, unwittingly, almost foiled the plot when, at the last minute, he suddenly decided he would not go to church. The cortège arrived at the cathedral without him. The murderers were already inside, each waiting close to his own station. Matteo da Volterra with the other priest, Stefano, preceptor of the Pazzi daughters were close to the high altar on the gospel side where Montesecco should have been had he not refused. Strangely, where a soldier had flatly declined to spill blood in church, the two priests saw no harm in it. Was it because Archbishop Salviati, a high Vatican prelate, was one of the leaders of the conspiracy and, the two priests thought, the Pope must have approved of it? Matteo da Volterra, we know, saw in the deed the just revenge for hundreds of Volterrans killed, but Stefano? It is hard to believe that one in holy orders would commit a sacrilege merely out of devotion to the Pazzi. Did he not think rather that the plot had the Pope's blessing? There is no other apparent reason to explain his part in the conspiracy. He was not a murderer nor even a violent man by nature.

The two men who waited for Giuliano on the other side of the high altar were of a very different stamp. They were killers. Francesco de'Pazzi, driven by an almost insane hate for the Medici. Bernardo Bandini ready to murder anyone for what he considered his advantage. Unlike the two priests across the altar from them, neither worried about who might or might not have originated or supported the plot. They wanted to kill.

The procession reached the high altar. The cardinal, in full pomp, was ushered to his throne, his priests all around him. Lorenzo took his place in his pew on the gospel side of the altar and, finding Matteo and Stefano close to it, became automatically separated from his immediate followers: Poliziano and some members of the Platonic Academy.

Across the choir, Bandini and Francesco de'Pazzi looked in vain for Giuliano. Dismayed at his absence, they exchanged glances and stole from their pews and out of the church. As fast as they could, they ran to the Medici palace in Via Larga. They found Giuliano in a state of undress, about to prepare for the party that was to take place after the church function. The minutes were flitting by—the service in the cathedral was about to begin—the moment of the Elevation would arrive—Lorenzo would be murdered and Giuliano would remain alive in the palace—they could not possibly kill him in the palace with all the Medici servants around. They pleaded with Giuliano. They stressed it would be a slight to the cardinal not to attend Mass. They told him ribald jokes to put him in good humour and, at last, he was dressed and they were all on their way to the cathedral. The service had started but they managed to reach their pews. The scene for the outrage was set at last. A matter of minutes now. They sighed with relief.

And the moment came—bent over the altar, the priest spoke the words of Consecration and lifted the Host—the people in the church bowed in adoration, praying, their eyes covered, in the presence of God.

Not so the assassins. On one side of the altar, Bernardo Bandini drove his dagger straight into Giuliano. Across, on the other side, Matteo da Volterra aimed his knife at Lorenzo's throat. Far above, in the church tower, the big bell echoed the tinkle of the silver ones on the altar steps. Its boom through the crystal air told the Florentines that the service within the cathedral had reached its most solemn moment. It also told Archbishop Salviati and Jacopo Bracciolini—half a mile away in the Piazza della Signoria—that the moment had come for them to attack the Government palace and do away with the liberties of Florence.

Inside the cathedral, all was confusion. On being struck Giuliano had cried out in a loud voice and taken a few steps, then Francesco de'Pazzi was on him, plunging his knife viciously into his prostrate body, again and again and yet again. In his fury, he even wounded himself badly in his own thigh.

Opposite, across the front of the altar, Matteo da Volterra had blundered. In the instant when—steadying himself with his left hand on Lorenzo's shoulder, he had aimed his steel straight at his victim's throat—*Il Magnifico* had bowed his head low in reverent worship of the uplifted Host. Matteo's blow miscarried, struck not the windpipe, missed the jugular, made a gash in the neck below the right ear. It was a bad wound but it left the intended victim all his physical powers.

The old habits of Lorenzo's football days now proved their full value. He drove his nose straight into Matteo's face against the sinus and began pummelling Matteo's sides with his right and left, trying at the same time to place his feet over the Volterran's to prevent him running away. Matteo—blinded and winded by the blow on his face and the hammering on his lungs—managed to slip away and was gone. Stefano had already disappeared.

With one mighty leap, Lorenzo was over the choirscreen. And there, just rounding the back of the altar, Bernardo Bandini was rushing towards him, his long dagger red with blood: Giuliano's. One of Lorenzo's retinue, Francesco Nori, tried to bar Bernardo's way and was felled with one stroke. Bernardo was running again towards Lorenzo, his steel now dripping with the blood of two men.

Il Magnifico was unarmed except for a small stiletto he carried as an ornament as was then the fashion, something like a penknife against a foe with a dagger. With the swiftness that was so marked a characteristic of all his decisions, Lorenzo planned and acted. He whirled his cloak off his back and threw it over his left arm, holding it high as if to shield himself—from under it peeped the point of the stiletto clenched firmly in his right. He held it at arm's length trying, desperately trying to make it appear that what he held was a sword. It fooled Bernardo for a fleeting moment; a precious moment, just long enough for Lorenzo to reach the sacristy behind him. He was across the threshold; Bernardo was running at him again. Someone slammed the door shut, right in Bernardo's face.

The hand that slammed the door just in time was Poliziano's who can therefore rightly be considered a major participant in the day's events. In his account of them, he had no false shame in admitting that he had already fled to the sacristy before Lorenzo got there. He writes frankly: "One could see the people in tumult. The women, the priests and the children ran hither and thither, fleeing not where safety was but any-where their feet would carry them. When Lorenzo repaired to the sac-risty, I had already got there. With the help of others, I pushed and closed the door, which was of bronze. So we shed our fright." He didn't shed his altogether however for he adds: "We kept our eyes on the door. Would it hold? Some of us were dithering with terror."

He was so much the prey of panic that he even neglected the friend he had just saved: Lorenzo de' Medici. He shamelessly writes that while he was still paralysed with fright "Others felt great sorrow for Lorenzo's wound. Antonio Ridolfi—a young boy—dried the wound and cleaned it." This alone, the fact that Poliziano—who knew about medicine—left the care of Lorenzo to another, tells us more than anything else of the utter dithering fear that possessed him in those moments. And if further confirmation were needed, we have it in his silence, in his failing to notice what other authors tell us: that Ridolfi, fearing that the dagger that had cut Lorenzo's neck might have been poisoned, bravely began to suck the wound so that he would draw the poison into himself and save Lorenzo. Poliziano's terror will simply not leave him and he shakes uncontrollably again when someone from the outside raps on the closed door and he hears shouts addressed to Lorenzo: "Come out, come out, Lorenzo, show yourself before our opponents gather strength. We are a group of friends of yours." Poliziano says: "We inside trembled. We wondered whether they were really friends. We asked 'Is Giuliano safe?' They gave no answer and our uncertainty grew. Then Sigismondo della Stufa—a very courageous young man—climbed up the stairs to the small gallery reserved for the musicians, who played and sang up there with-out being seen from below in the cathedral." Della Stufa's first news was yet more disquieting. He reported he could see Giuliano's dead body lying on the floor. Then at last, he gave the reassuring tidings "The group round the sacristy door are really our friends. We can open the door."

What is remarkable about Poliziano's account of the massacre is that—in those obviously awful moments—he could not sever himself from literary expression. In his terror, details, even essential details go unnoticed, but his rendering of the emotions of those present is master-ful as always. No one can deny to Poliziano's story the praise due to perfection. Some, exaggerating, have compared it to Cicero but cer-tainly he reaches the heights of Sallust. What is indisputable is that Poliziano—then only 24—described the agonising and recurrent terror within and around him with a musicality and choice of words that not only bring the scene to-life again but re-arouse horror and consternation.

We may be moved to pity for the young poet who, until then had sung of a world governed by love, was suddenly brought to realise, with the hollow bitterness of disenchantment, that the liberal, free life of Renaissance Florence, with its dances, carousels, severe search for truth in philosophy, the arts, the sciences, was not the only kind of life and that there was another world where terror made the blood freeze, the heart race and the knees, the hands, the head, the lips shake uncontrollably.

He was quaking with fear, when Lorenzo's friends, realising that any opponents, wherever they might be were not in the cathedral, nor in the adjoining streets, decided to carry him to his palace in Via Larga where his wound could be better attended to.

CHAPTER NINE

La Conguira dei Pazzi (3)

HE ringing of the bell in Giotto's tower at the moment of the Elevation in the cathedral down below, re-echoed in the spring air and those in Piazza della Signoria heard it.

Archbishop Salviati, Jacopo Bracciolini and their followers knew it was the signal to go into action. The Archbishop was the first to enter the Palazzo della Signoria with a large retinue and Jacopo followed. Their attendants[1] did not go up with them to the Gonfaloniere's floor but dispersed in various waiting rooms the better to escape notice. On reaching the first floor of the palace, Salviati asked to see the Gonfaloniere, the Chief Magistrate of Florence, Ceasare Petrucci, whose duty it was to attend to the practical enforcement of law and order. Petrucci had dealt with conspiracies before. Some years previously, while he was Governor of the town of Prato, he had actually been taken prisoner by rebels who wanted to capture the town. They had been about to hang him, but his determined manner and the forcefulness of his powers of persuasion had saved him and, in the end, he had arrested and hanged the leaders of the sedition.

Interrupted now in his dinner, he was not impressed by the Archbishop's opening remarks. The prelate stammered, appeared highly nervous and his arguments were confused. With some unctuousness, he said he had come from the Pope because Sixtus wanted to confer some sort of honour—it wasn't quite clear what—on Petrucci's son. The Gonfaloniere thought of his meal getting cold and judged that the message might well have been delivered, if not after the siesta, at least after he had finished eating. Snappily, he asked the Archbishop for the Papal document. At this point, Salviati, who had felt so confident when originating the conspiracy in the safety of the Vatican and asking Pope Sixtus for complete authority "to steer this bark", now that the moment was come, completely lost his head. He stuttered uncertainly that he had no letter from the Pontiff (Sixtus would never have been such a fool as to entrust him with a written document proving his own participation in the conspiracy—Salviati's trumped up tale was idiotic from the start). As if this were not sufficient blunder, he paled and made for the door. Petrucci, only too glad to see the last of him, opened it to let him out and found himself confronted by Jacopo Bracciolini. If the Bishop had seemed unsure of himself, there was no doubting Bracciolini's intention, but, though unprepared, Petrucci was quicker. Before the son of the famous Florentine Chancellor could make use of the knife in his hand, the Gonfaloniere had him by the hair, knocked him to the ground and kicked the steel out of his grasp.[2] Behind Petrucci, the Archbishop clamoured, calling loudly to his retinue that the moment had come for the general attack. Like most of Salviati's plans, this too went awry in the most absurd manner. All the men-at-arms of the Archbishop's retinue had distributed themselves, in several rooms. They had been careful to close the doors so as not to be seen. This proved fatal to them for they had not reckoned with the wily Gonfaloniere. Upon taking office, Petrucci had had every lock of every door of the Palace changed taking care that the ones he had had fitted should open only from the outside. In their effort to escape notice, Salviati's would-be assailants had automatically locked themselves in and become prisoners.

Petrucci was a man of quick decisions. He hanged Bracciolini there and then flinging him out of the Palace window on a rope that kept his body dangling only just above the heads of the crowd that was gathering in the square; a sad end for a brilliant literary man. His influence on Society was now reduced to a mere warning, silent but eloquent.[3]

Up in the Palace, Petrucci told the Archbishop he would be next but he yielded to Salviati's entreaties that he be allowed to go to confession and receive communion first.

If the Archbishop thought this might be a way to gain time and ultimately escape the rope, he was quickly disillusioned; from the square below came the cries of the people: "Palle, Palle" the insignia of the Medici crest, threateningly signifying that the people stood by Lorenzo, dead or alive.[4] Then came the news that Lorenzo had reached his own palace—he was wounded but safe in his home.

Petrucci's fury mounted as the minutes went by. And then Francesco de' Pazzi, who had tried to hide and nurse the wound he had inflicted on himself when he had raged over Giuliano's dead body, was caught and brought naked and bleeding to the Signoria. A rope was thrown about his neck and his body hurled from the window. The Archbishop went over next. Poliziano, who, by this time, had rallied on seeing the Medici victorious, had reached the square in front of the Palace. He writes that the Archbishop "was hanged close to the dead body of Francesco and, as the rope round his neck choked the breath out of him, his eyes grew red as embers and he bit into Francesco's body either out of rage or trying to get a grip of something in his despair."[5]

But what struck Poliziano most and provides the tangible proof that the Pazzi had no following worthy of the name in Florence, was that, as he says in his Commentarium: "Even from the countryside in the neighbourhood of Florence a multitude was pouring into the square and similar scenes occurred round the Medici Palace in Via Larga, where Lorenzo, weakened by the loss of blood, had been put to bed." Poliziano tells us vividly: "Townsfolk and peasants offered their sons, their servants, themselves, to do anything they could to help—countrymen brought meats and bread and all that is necessary to life."

As for the young cardinal Raffaele Riario, who had been by the altar at the moment of the crimes in the cathedral, he barely escaped alive because the people—wrongly but not unnaturally—thought him a party to the conspiracy. Some of the priests, who shielded him, were killed, but Petrucci, however much infuriated, had not lost his judgment. He despatched, at the double, a body of armed men of the Signoria to escort the cardinal to the Palace. The unhappy prince of the Church was led with some difficulty through the angry crowd that hurled insults at him as, paler than death (it is said he never recovered his earlier rosy complexion) he was at last carried into the Palace. Here, Petrucci set him down at a table, gave him pen and ink, enjoining him to write immediately, while everything was fresh in his mind, to his great-uncle, Pope Sixtus IV, stating the exact details of all that had happened. He also told him the report would be taken to Rome at once. The Pontiff must learn of the day's events from one of his kinsmen one in whom he would have complete trust.

In those moments, with Lorenzo disabled, Petrucci was in fact the supreme power in Florence and he adapted well to this situation. All his acts confirm he was a man of extreme determination. He hanged the guilty—set in motion the report to the Pope—called the Florentine Chancellor, Bartolomeo Della Scala, to draw up a full account of the day's happenings to be sent to the sovereigns of Europe. There was one thing he did not succeed in doing. He couldn't. For all the evident popular support and love for the Medici, there might still be ill-intentioned individuals or groups lurking somewhere and he just did not have sufficient men-at-arms to guard the Signoria, protect the Medici Palace, arrest the suspects (all of which he did) and, at the same time, prevent the people from venting their anger against any of the Pazzi faction they happened to apprehend.

Jacopo, the head of the family, who had joined the conspiracy so unwillingly, had fled Florence together with Bernardo Bandini, Giuliano's assassin. Bandini got away but a shepherd recognised Jacopo and, when offered a large sum in gold if only he would let him free, answered by beating him severely over the head with his crook and leading him back to Florence to be hanged—a clear indication that the people of the hills and the countryside shared the feelings of townspeople and fully supported Lorenzo.[6]

All of these events together constitute the greatest possible disclaimer of the conspirator's assertion that the people of Florence were crushed by Medici rule and wanted its overthrow, a thesis even some erudite persons have sought to find evidence for. When it came to the point, in the moments when Florence was practically without a government and a free for all reigned in the streets, the people of Florence and the countryside identified the Medici with themselves and their way of life and stood firm against change. The few signs of not dishonest opposition confirm this. The solitary lament of Alamanno Rinuccini,[7] the one most worthy of notice, stands as the cry of a man whom personal choice had set apart from the life of the state so that he could no longer understand it and its working in periods of emergency. It is the sigh of a contemplative not the yell of a man of action. No one listened to it and probably nobody heard it. It was prudently spoken almost a year later.

What the Pazzi conspiracy showed was the remarkable efficiency of the Florentine government under the Medici. When its leaders had been struck down and all was disarray and the religious conscience of the people might be divided by the Pope's part in the affair, the Magistrates of Florence—Petrucci in particular—showed they knew how to deal with a situation that appeared desperate. But even the Gonfaloniere could not have done what he did, if the people had not rallied to him.

The effectiveness of the Florentine government was given full recognition far and wide. Within forty-eight hours an envoy brought the condolences from Venice to the Florentine Signoria. A missive expressing horror arrived on 12 May from Louis XI of France. Messages followed from England—from Mattia Corvino in Hungary and, despite the Pope's involvement, also from Catholic Spain.

The Turkish Sultan sent his own kind of message: Bernardo Bandini in chains. Bandini had been apprehended trying to hide under a false name in the territory of the Ottoman Empire and had been arrested only six hours after his arrival on Turkish soil. The Florentines beheaded him.

As for the Pope, his reaction was strange for the Head of a Church. He turned his rage not against the perpetrators of the crime but against its victims. He offered only perfunctory expressions of condolence for Giuliano's death and Lorenzo's wounding, but was particularly incensed by the fact that the Archbishop had been hanged in his robes to the indignity of his ecclesiastical garb and rank. (He made no mention of the Archbishop's neck). He had a second reason for his fury and perhaps this was more understandable. He appears to have been frankly worried about the possible fate of his nephew, cardinal Raffaello Riario and protested violently against his detention in Florence, even though he was surrounded with all the honours due to his rank. As a reprisal, Girolamo Riario proceeded with 300 halbadiers to arrest the Florentine Ambassador in Rome, Donato Acciaiuoli, who protested violently against this affront to an accredited representative of the Florentine Republic. In order that Sixtus should not again evade his responsibilities, he demanded to see the Pope personally. The Pontiff's first intention was to commit Acciaiuoli to Castel Sant'Angelo. Only the very firm protests of the Venetian and Milanese ambassadors, who declared they would follow their colleague into imprisonment, brought the infuriated Pope to reason.

Acciaiuoli however had succeeded in highlighting the fact that Riario, one of the prime movers in the Pazzi conspiracy went unreprimanded while the Pope's indignation was aimed against the Florentine Republic because its people had stood by Lorenzo.

In the circumstances, the Florentine Signoria thought it wise to order its citizens domiciled in Rome to return at once to Florence. Sixtus

commanded they should all be thrown into gaol. This was an overt act of
hostility to the Florentine Republic and its people. The Florentine residents in Rome were guilty of no crime. They could not possibly have
taken part in the killing of Pazzi followers in Florence, following the
murder of Giuliano and the wounding of Lorenzo; they could not have
been among those who had threatened Cardinal Riario and killed some
of his priests. They were plainly innocent and the Pope's high-handed
action gave the Florentines a taste of what might have happened in their
own homeland had the Pazzi conspiracy been successful and the free
Republic of Florence become a tributary of the Pope or, worse still, if it
had been incorporated in the Church's oppressed dominions. Nor was
there any ground for the argument the Pope adduced that the arrest of
innocent Florentines in Rome was a justifiable retaliation for the holding
of Cardinal Raffaele Riario in Florence. The cardinal, unlike the Florentine residents in Rome, appeared very much implicated in the Pazzi
conspiracy. He had twice been used as decoy by the murderers and the
suspicion of evil intent on his part was more than amply justified.
Because it was only a suspicion and not a certainty, the cardinal was not
detained in a prison but in a palatial apartment, surrounded with all
honours, until his situation might be cleared.

The Pope, for his part, had committed an act against Florentine
citizens that was unwarranted and changed the relations between the
Papal States and the Tuscan Republic and might well precipitate a war.
But the Florentine Signoria kept its head. It was chiefly Petrucci's head
and he, unlike Sixtus, knew how to use it. While the Pope raged disap-
pointed at seeing all his plans gone awry and Lorenzo's ascendancy more
indisputably established than ever, the Signoria, respectfully but most
firmly, sent word that Cardinal Riario would not depart from Florence
until every Florentine in Rome—except those who could be proved
guilty of crimes—were set free. The Pope was compelled to give way and
put an end to his grievous breach of international usage.

However, where the appeal to his vaunted temporal power had
failed, Sixtus called on his spiritual authority to help him out. Theologi-
cally he had no grounds to act as he did, but the limits to his spiritual
powers were not so well known then as now (see Chapter 4 above) and on
1 June 1478 Sixtus IV unwarrantably issued a Bull of excommunication
against Lorenzo and placed Florence and her dependent territories of
Fiesole and Pistoia under Interdict. The three bishops of these dioceses
and their clergy with one voice rejected the anathema which they rightly
judged to be an abuse of Pontifical power and they said so in such
vituperative terms and invectives of such virulence that Roscoe writes

"It is not in the power of any language to convey a more copious torrent of abuse than was poured on this occasion on the Head of the Roman Church" and the historian Fabroni begs to be excused from publishing "such contumelious expressions."[8]

Lorenzo was more prudent. On 5 June, when it had been ascertained that cardinal Riario had been the innocent *gobemouche* of Salviati and the other conspirators, he had him accompanied to the border of the Republic with the Papal States, by a guard that was both of honour and protection, seeing the feelings of many Tuscans toward him.

The Pope did not lift the Interdict but reiterated it on 21 July. It had no spiritual effects in Tuscany, where the clergy persisted in rejecting it, but it exposed Florentine trade to confiscation in the Catholic nations. So we have a Pope, abusing his spiritual power to rouse the greed that usually Mammon inspires. Anything to avoid the bitter humiliation of having to bow to the truth of Lorenzo's popularity. He demanded the expulsion of *Il Magnifico* from Florence. The Chancellor of Florence, the great humanist Bartolomeo della Scala sent a missive to Sixtus, telling him he had become "the foe of the City's most precious liberty: that of choosing its own leaders". The Pontiff had claimed in his Interdict that Lorenzo was a tyrant, but the Signoria countered: "On the contrary, we and our people with a single voice proclaim him the defender of our freedom. We are prepared to sacrifice all for his safety, which is the undoubted guarantee for the safety and liberty of our State."

This was della Scala's missive to the Pope, but as we have said, della Scala also had the task to compose and despatch to all the Sovereigns of Europe an *Excusatio: Reply to accusations against the Florentine People*. It was ready by 4 August.

It is the best account we have of the Pazzi conspiracy gracefully told in unemotional terms and in elegant Latin. The Chancellor, who was a scholar of renown, and, within the severe limits of precision and conciseness, which Poliziano, the poet did not have to set himself, we feel della Scala's passion and conviction. He writes: "Rem sumus narraturi inauditam et novam adeo alienam ab omni natura humana et consuetudine vivendi ..." "We are about to relate events unimaginable, so much are they contrary to human nature and to common usage and we have no doubt that all who hear of them will marvel at so much atrocity". It goes on to say that after the outrage, Sixtus turned his wrath not against the perpetrators of the crime but against its victims. Della Scala then goes on to quote the whole of Montesecco's confession and adds the names of the witnesses who testified to Montesecco's having made it.

The list is remarkable in that, although the Pope was involved and there could be no doubt that archbishop Salviati had been one of the prime movers of the outrage, several ecclesiastics were ready to testify to Montesecco's Confession. The first was Frate Battista d'Antonio—the dominican Prior—of Saint Mark's church who certified he was "present at the said confession and vouch that the Montesecco wrote everything with his own hand and what he wrote contains the truth." But St Mark's is a stone's throw from via Larga and the Medici palace and this might have influenced Fra'Battista. But the next on the list is "Benedetto, monk and prior unworthy of the Badia of Florence" which is outside Florence on the slopes of Fiesole. And if it is argued that Lorenzo had a villa at Careggi near Fiesole, the name that follows that of many other priests and monks and several notary publics, among them Piero Betti of Pistoia, outside Florence, is that of the Vicar of the Archbishop of Florence, who hailed from Gualdo in the Appennines, a town within the Papal States.

All sovereigns and princes of Europe, with the exception of the king of Naples, accepted the veracity of Montesecco's confession. Even the Pope did not question it and Pastor quotes it as proof that Sixtus IV had not ordered the killing of the Medici brothers but merely their overthrow.

CHAPTER TEN

Bold Measures

HEN Lorenzo was told that Pope Sixtus IV had tried to imprison, in Castel Sant'Angelo, the Florentine ambassador to Rome, Donato Acciauoli, he thought at first that the angry gesture might just be the outcome of the Pope's raging disappointment that the Medici government in Florence had not toppled despite the Pazzi conspiracy.

When the Pontiff took measures to imprison the Florentines resident in Rome, Lorenzo realized that the fight was not over and that Sixtus intended to follow every path open to him to undermine the Medici's popularity.

When the Pope asked that *Il Magnifico* be expelled and the Florentines with one voice refused and confirmed him as their ruler, defender of their freedom, Lorenzo understood that henceforth it was the Republic of Florence and not him alone that the Pope would want to humble and possibly destroy.

When it became certain that in January 1478, four months before
the conspiracy—Sixtus had contracted a secret alliance with the powerful King of Naples, Ferrante of Aragon, and that Neapolitan troops
under the command of Ferrante's son Alfonsino, Duke of Calabria, were
already in the neighbouring territory of the Sienese Republic, only some
forty miles to the south of Florence, he knew that war would come.[1]

Finally when it was reported to him that troops of Count Girolamo
Riario were being assembled at Imola, some sixty miles northeast of
Florence, he realised the fact that the war would be a hard war.

Immediately, he went before the city magistrates and suggested he
give himself up to the Pope in a last effort to avoid the conflict. Sixtus
had always said that it was with him and not with the Florentines that he
had a quarrel. Let them call the Pope's bluff and put him in a position
that—if he were to live up to his assertions—he could not attack the
Republic. But the Signoria of Florence realised only too well that, if the
Pope's rage was aimed at Lorenzo, his covetousness, his ambition and
his greed were set on a takeover of the Florentine Republic. Unanim-
ously, they rejected Lorenzo's offer. They told him' bluntly he was the
chief authority with a mandate and that he must fulfil his mandate. It
was in him the People placed their trust and they wanted no other leader
in the circumstances. By throwing himself on the Pope's mercy, he
would be betraying that trust.

It was another vote of confidence in Lorenzo and, when Sixtus heard
of it, once again he raged. As a planner of conspiracies he had failed.
Militarily he was weak but he had a strong ally in Ferrante, King of
Naples. Ferrante wanted Siena and possibly other portions of Tuscany
as well. The blessing of the supreme head of the Church might be a help
to getting them and Ferrante attacked.

He, like the Pope, made a pretence that his quarrel was with
Lorenzo de'Medici and not the Florentines, but, what his quarrel could
be, he never explained. Good relations had existed until then between
Florence and Naples. The sudden war was in open contrast with the
cultural and cordial links that had lasted between the two States for over
thirty years: first under Ferrante's father and then during the reign of
Ferrante himself. Florentine bankers had brought prosperity to the
Neapolitan kingdom in good times and been a sheet–anchor in times of
trouble.[2]

When Ferrante opened hostilities, Lorenzo acted wisely. Fully aware
of the disparity between his own troops and those of the Neopolitan King,
he sought allies. He was already bound by treaty to the Venetians and the
Milanese, suspicious of Neopolitan dreams of aggrandizement, so he cal-

led on them. He did not take the field himself as commander. The Pope and Ferrante claimed it was him they would fight against and not the Florentines. They would find they were fighting Milanese, Venetians and Tuscans, not him. He would have no part in the operations and their pretence would be exposed.

The command of the allied armies was entrusted to a seasoned military leader who was not a Florentine, Ercole d'Este, Duke of Ferrara, but the war really turned out to be a conflict between Sixtus wallowing in search of self glory in his own times and posterity, and the poet Lorenzo who did not need to conquer territories, build bridges, open roads, create works of art even, for he was *Il Magnifico*, who did not need to build monuments unto himself because he put Leonardo, Michelangelo, Poliziano and others on the road to the full development of their genius which bore fruit after Lorenzo had gone. (Ludovico il Moro commissioned the Milanese Last Supper but it was Lorenzo who gave Leonardo's talent the opportunity to grow.) If Sixtus built the Sistine Chapel its foremost ornament is Michelangelo, whom Lorenzo first put on his way to greatness.

In one thing only were Sixtus and Lorenzo alike. They both loved books. Sixtus in effect created the Vatican Library by rescuing the forgotten collection of ancient documents of an earlier Pope, Nicholas V. He added to it, till, by 1475, it contained 2527 volumes of which 770 were Greek.[3] But perhaps his greatest innovation was that his library was open to the public. Lorenzo for his part created the Laurentiana Library and was always only too willing to share the contents of its documents with anyone who asked them.

But in all else, the two opponents, both absent from the field of battle, were as different as they could be. Eager to aggrandize his family and widen the domain of the Church, channelling knowledge and art to his own or the Church's glory, Sixtus. Lorenzo with his family at the peak of its splendour or near it, he himself well wedded, was determined to limit the Papacy's temporal power as if uncannily sensing the harm it would lead to right up to the Risorgimento and beyond. As for the encouragement and spread of poetry, art and knowledge, he intended them to lend lustre to Florence not by making of her, as Sixtus wanted Rome to be, the centre to which pilgrims would come to drink at the fountain of the Renaissance, but that she should be the source from which the Renaissance would spread outward to all Italy, to Europe and beyond. An ecclesiastical determination to win power, Sixtus's, Lorenzo's was a poet's dream, and it was the poet's dream that was destined to be fulfilled.

For the moment however luck was on Sixtus's side and the war went badly for the Florentines. Perhaps Lorenzo had not been wise in choosing Ercole d' Este as leader of the allied armies. Ercole had been made Duke of Ferrara by Sixtus, when his claim to the title had been in doubt. On the other hand, he had been guilty of plotting (unsuccessfully) against Ferrante, but then he had turned and married Ferrante's daughter so he was fighting against his father in law and a Pope to whom he was indebted. However there is no definite evidence that this was the reason why the war went on in the most desultory fashion. The opposed armies, instead of engaging with the enemy facing them spent their time plundering the surrounding countryside. This hurt the Tuscans who were plundering their own country and benefited the Neapolitans, who lived off land that lay outside their own territory. Sooner or later, the Tuscans were bound to succumb unless they forced the enemy into action. When they finally succeeded in doing so, the results were disastrous for them. The Neapolitans, stronger in numbers and better led, conquered Castellina in Chianti, pressed on and took Poggibonsi. To avoid any possible danger of attack on their flanks, they laid siege to Colle Val d'Elsa, held by a strong Florentine garrison. For seven terrible months, Colle was pounded for twelve hours a day. Then, with the heat of summer, the water supply failed and the garrison was forced to capitulate. The way to Florence lay open.

Lorenzo de' Medici took a momentous decision—perhaps the supreme resolution of his life. The Pope and the Neapolitans had always claimed that their fight was against him and not against the people of Florence. He had wanted to give himself up before the war had started. The Florentines had prevented him. He would go now without their consent. With his uncanny sixth sense for popular feeling, Lorenzo was aware that the Florentines had begun to weary of a war that seemed to bring few results, and those disastrous. For the present, they were certainly ready to fight on in defence of *Il Magnifico* and their freedom. They even viewed with equanimity a possible siege, but Lorenzo's astounding perception told him that, in the end, not the fear of what might happen to them physically, but the disruption of their trade would tell. Already the Pope's excommunication had laid Florentine merchants and bankers at the mercy of the countries they traded with. He had known Ferrante in the past. He had corresponded with him and, between the lines of the outwardly gracious missives the King had written to him, he had sensed the utter ferocity of the Aragon character. He knew that only a short time before, Ferrante had enticed with a soft spoken invitation, a man with whom he had never quarrelled and after receiving him with all honours, had had him thrown into a dungeon, deep underground and after having him tortured, had had him killed. To hand himself over to such a King was a terrifying prospect but it might help Florence. Lorenzo had heard that Ferrante's alliance with the Pope was not as firm as it had once been. The King of Naples too feared Sixtus's and Riario's ambition and their power, should they extend their domain over Florence.

So Lorenzo made up his mind. "At the beginning of December 1479," writes Horsburg[5] "Lorenzo left Florence without communicating his intentions to his fellow citizens." Once clear of the city, from San Miniato, he wrote to the magistrates of the Republic. "It appears to me that peace has become indispensable to us. As all other means have proved ineffectual, I intend, with your permission, to proceed to Naples, judging that, as I am the chief target of our enemies, I may, by delivering myself into their hands, perhaps be the means of restoring peace to my fellow citizens. I am glad to take this risk upon myself, as it is possible that the aim of our opponents be only the destruction of my person. As I have had more honour and consideration amongst you than my merits claimed and perhaps more than have been bestowed on any single citizen in our time, I see myself more particularly bound than any other to promote our country's interest at any cost, even at the cost of my life .... All I wish for is that my life or my death, my prosperity or my misfortune may contribute to the good of Florence.

"If our adversaries aim, as they say they do, only at my destruction, they will have me in their power. If their intention instead is to bring harm to Florence, this intention shall become manifest to each and every citizen, who will no longer have cause to feel he is struggling to defend a single man and all will unite to defend their liberties to the last."

With this letter, Lorenzo shows his deep perceptiveness of his countrymen's moods, even those of a minority of them. He also gave evidence of his determination to abide by their mood, whatever it might be at any time and whatever it might cost him. And the Florentines paid tribute to this quality in the way they responded.

When Il Magnifico, continuing his journey, reached Pisa, he found two missives waiting for him. Both were written in perfect Latin by Bartolomeo Della Scala, the Florentine Chancellor. Unable by now to stop Lorenzo from going, the magistrates of Florence had devised a plan that would give him some sort of immunity. They invested him with the office of Ambassador Extraordinary to the King of Naples with full powers to negotiate a peace. It was not customary to kill Ambassadors and—though the King of Naples was no respecter of civilized usage—the scheme might work.

The second letter Lorenzo found was a personal message from Bartolomeo who expressed his admiration for Lorenzo's imaginative contempt of danger and voiced his apprehension for Il Magnifico's fate ... "I cannot but admire your fortitude and perseverance, but I feel wan with fear ...".

Lorenzo embarked for Naples. From the moment he put to sea, good weather favoured the journey. Strangely elated by the adventurous nature of his mission, Florentine Lorenzo suddenly found himself sharing that most preposterous and pervasive of all Neapolitan moods: hope. Hope however disastrous the circumstances and black the outlook. Hope that somehow, some day, through someone or because of something, a ray of light will penetrate the darkest gloom. Hope in the morning to earn something for a meal. Hope against hope at the end of a hungry day with nothing gained and twelve mouths to feed. Hope in the throw of dice even when it isn't loaded! With every waft of the breeze, as Naples drew nearer, Lorenzo felt coursing in his veins the thrill of tempting chance as the Neapolitans are compelled to tempt it every day and he already felt attuned with them.

He became conscious of increasing optimism. Had not Alfonso of Aragon, Ferrante's predecessor, thrown himself on the mercy of the Milanese Visconti and found mercy? Had not hundreds of such cases occurred again and again? Yet *Il Magnifico* was extremely shrewd and realistic and must also have at moments felt chastened at the thought of Ferrante's famous cruelty and treachery. He knew he was in mortal danger. But the people of Naples, hopeful themselves, inspired hope. Why not respond to the feeling? He need not prostrate himself before Ferrante. In Naples, as in Florence he would go to the people. He knew they loved drama for drama's sake and he would give it to them with a flourish. Drama so spectacular as to satisfy the most exacting. And there they were! They had flocked by the thousand to the quay to watch the arrival of the man who, by his surrender, had already captured their imagination. They were so many that it would have been impossible for Ferrante's guards to arrest him without creating a tumult. Ferrante—possibly sensing popular feeling—actually received him with the honours due to his new position of ambassador. A palace had been assigned to him for his residence.

Nevertheless, *Il Magnifico* had a hard and perilous task before him. He had won the first round and Ferrante would at least have to pretend to listen to what he had to say, but he was certain the Neapolitan King's mind was far from made up. *Il Magnifico* did in fact hang between death and life at the King's whim for several weeks but, even in the worst moments, his proposals were bold: nothing less than an alliance between Naples, Florence and Milan.

His arguments with the King can only be surmised though the historian Fabroni presents an elaborate speech in which Lorenzo details his arguments to Ferrante. The speech appears too clear and straightforward for it to have been uttered while the hard bargaining, with Lorenzo's head in danger all the time, was in progress. Far more subtly than by enumerating all points, Lorenzo appealed once again to the people of Naples. To endear himself to them he successfully made use of his unrivalled charm but, beside that, he made full and efficacious use of the Medici ability to place themselves in the frame of mind of whomsoever they were speaking to, divining their thoughts and attempting to think as they did. We don't know how he exercised this art on Ferrante, but, as for the people, he identified himself with the Neapolitans as he had identified himself with the Florentines.

One of their great worries was how to provide dowries for their daughters. Without a dowry, a girl not only remained a spinster, but often ended up a prostitute. The lack of money to endow a daughter with, was a real tragedy for the girls, the parents, the brothers and sisters, all her relations in fact. And then Lorenzo—the erstwhile enemy—appeared and distributed dowries to five thousand indigent maidens. Naples went wild with delight. Il Magnifico had surpassed even himself (let alone Ferrante) in their opinion.

But not all Neapolitans had daughters in search of a husband. It is fairly safe to say on the other hand, that almost each one of them had a relation, a father, a brother, an uncle or cousin, or, failing that, a friend in gaol. Lorenzo ransomed prisoners and galley slaves with his generous purse and, as the freed men wandered through the streets and alleys, in a desperate attempt to find work and readjust to normal life, he distributed among them fresh clothes to replace their bedraggled rags and give them a chance of regaining their self respect. The new suits were green—for hope—(and possibly also for easier recognition in case they should fall back into evil ways). The mercurial Neapolitans went frantic with joy and acclaimed Lorenzo more than they had ever acclaimed their own King.

Ferrante himself was of two minds. Twinges of jealousy contended in his breast with fears of a Neapolitan rising should he harm Lorenzo. Lorenzo had gambled on popular pressure and he was winning.

By the end of February 1480, the rough draft of a treaty of alliance between Naples and Florence was ready. *Il Magnifico*—his mission accomplished—embarked for Leghorn and thence on to Florence to receive a hero's triumph. Machiavelli, who, though he wrote in a later age, correctly interpreted the Laurentian era, says: "All men praised him extravagantly, declaring that—by his wisdom—he had recovered in peace all that adverse fortune had taken from the Florentines in war."

This is not quite true. The Florentines had not recovered all they had lost. But they had acquired a powerful ally. With only the Pope against them, they could feel safe—their trade would flow again and their poets sing once more.

A splendid painting representing this great victorious crisis in Lorenzo's life remains to us in Botticelli's picture of Pallas Athena and the Centaur: the goddess of learning subduing with a simple touch the forces of sedition and violence.

Part II

AENEAS

SILVIUS

PICCOLOMINI

(PIUS II)

PROHEMIVM PLATYNAE IN VITAS PONTIFICVM

AD SIX1 CVM PRIVILEGIO ꝺNT.MAXIM.

PLATYNAE hystoria de Vitis pontificum periu
cunda:diligenter recognita:& nunc
tantum integre impressa.

PLATINA, *Vitae Pontificum, frontispiece*

CHAPTER ELEVEN

Peasant, Scholar, Diplomat

NE almost sympathises with Sixtus IV when we learn that he flew into another of his usual impotent rages. The great castles of cards he was always so eagerly intent on building seemed to crash down whenever his dreams of victory appeared on the verge of coming true. His great archenemy—Lorenzo de' Medici— outwitted him every time. In vain did the Pope try to attain his worldly aims by appeals to the spiritual authority of the Church. All his attempts to mix the profane with the sacred failed. Now the purpose for which he had gone to war, the overthrow of Lorenzo, was further from his reach than ever. He had lost his ally, King Ferrante, without whom he could not hope to win and one of the conditions of the peace was that the excommunication of Lorenzo and the Florentines must be lifted so that Tuscan trade could flow again. Melancholically Sixtus had to admit that *Il Magnifico* was more firmly in power. The Pope had no choice but to renounce all further attempts against Florence. It was after this tardy but wise decision that his reign grew glorious. Besides the Sistine Chapel and the Vatican Library we have mentioned earlier, he restored many of Rome's churches—among them Santa Maria del Popolo, fallen into decay during the Middle Ages when the "Eternal City" had been reduced to a village of a few thousand souls. He opened to the public, with an unheard of gesture in that era, the halls of the Capitol with their Art Collections. He modernized the hospital of Santo Spirito, originally built by the English who had resided in that quarter.[1] Had he dedicated himself to these tasks instead of thinking of family and temporal aggrandizement, he might have been a great Pope.

His failure and that of Paul II are all the more surprising in that their immediate predecessor, Pius II of the Sienese House of Piccolomini, had been the most human, compassionate, warm-hearted and to many the most lovable of the Popes of the Renaissance and perhaps of all times. He is certainly the most cultured Pope of any epoch, the one who has left us the most beautiful poetry and lucid writing. Pius II was the typical Renaissance author, different from many writers of today in that writing was not his sole occupation but a corollary to many other accomplishments: in diplomacy, government, theology and travel.

He had been born of an impoverished family of noblemen in the small town of Corsignano, in the territory of the Sienese Republic on 18 October 1405. A few fields were all that remained of the Piccolomini's former wealth and the young boy—Aeneas Silvius, as the future Pope was christened, helped with the farmwork when a boy. It was the first experience of what was destined to be throughout a hard life, but he faced it with untiring good humour.

When he was eight years old he was tossed by a bull. Once it was over, he sat down and wrote in detail what his feelings had been, the way the bull had charged, the nearing horn and the hot breath, and the thunderous thump of the hooves as the bull mercifully passed on, having thrown him. His father, reading what he had written, was most impressed. So was his teacher, a humble priest of Corsignano. They decided to send him to higher school, when the time came. So, when he was eighteen, they despatched Aeneas to Siena, the nearest city. The Sienese were commercially-minded and extremely parsimonious in the endowment of their seat of learning. They had no Greek teachers so at first Aeneas Silvius learned no Greek and, because books were very expensive, he developed his intellect through conversation rather than through poring over manuscripts. This also developed his ability to judge what his contemporaries were thinking and of how to get them to tell him what he wanted to know. Nevertheless, whenever he could, he borrowed books and manuscripts and stayed up whole nights laboriously copying them out and pondering over them.

He chose his companions carefully. His most intimate friend was Mariano Sozzini, a jurist only a few years older than himself but so learned he could have taught law anywhere had not a wife and family obligations kept him in Siena—though he was not by any means a family man. An all-round athlete, an accomplished and graceful dancer, women knew him as a refined libertine. His renown for learning was such that scholars came from as far as across the Alps to be taught by him. He excelled in law but was also a master of mathematics and astrology. He developed through his own efforts a knowledge of Greek and it was as if Siena had hired a professor from Greece.

Another friend, whose influence was also to remain with Aeneas Silvius throughout his life, was Beccadelli Panormita whom William Boulting describes as "a magnificent humanist and the most corrupt of scholars. He wrote obscenities with voluptuous grace.[2]" They could not fail to attract the young Piccolomini and the future saintly Pius II spent whole nights over Beccadelli's libertine book *The Hermaphrodite.*"

Throughout his early years, Aeneas Silvius was victim to the pangs of love. But it was not solitary love. He adored feminine company. He revelled in the voluptuousness of the milk-white flesh of the women of Siena. Throughout his life, until old age caught up with him and he became Pope, he always had a preference for buxom, fairskinned, fairhaired women. He was destined to have two sons: one born in Scotland, the other of an English woman he met on the Continent.

He might and probably would have pursued his lover's course in any case, but, without Sozzini and Panormita, he might not have traced as he did, with the delicacy and grace in which he excelled, every moment of his loves, each patter of the heart and every second of physical delight in affectionate heartfelt sex relations. He did not like bawdiness. He just loved wholly, body and soul, time after time,—so long as the skin was white and the hair golden.

Nevertheless Aeneas, right back from those early days in Siena, always had a strangely dual nature. On the one hand he was under the spell of Sozzini and of Panormita, on the other, he was struck deep in his soul by the preaching of a monk, Bernardino da Siena. At that time, Bernardino was 45. His scholarship was exceptional and this must have been one of the reasons he appealed so strongly to Aeneas. Another no doubt, was Bernardino's overwhelming eloquence which enthralled huge crowds as soon as he began to speak. Some said he performed miracles but Aeneas was always distrustful of miracles even when he reached the Papal throne.

Keenly interested in the world, which held so much beauty for him without the need of miracles, he was lukewarm where the contemplative life was concerned. He was already Pope when he visited the famous monastery of Mount Oliveto near Siena. Though its cloister was not yet adorned by Signorelli's paintings, Pius II wrote that the monastery was very beautiful but "how very fortunate are those who have a chance of seeing Mount Oliveto and are not compelled to remain there."

But when, in his youth in Siena, Aeneas heard Bernardino speak, he was overwhelmed with a spirit of mysticism and decided to devote his life to the service of God and become a priest. Boulting says: "His friends tried to restrain him for they knew him better than he knew himself." So did Bernardino who strongly dissuaded the young man from carrying out his intention. And so instead of growing into a bad priest, Aeneas became destined to be the Pope of his time, who, having had worldly experience not only in diplomacy and travel but in the bedroom too, was the most tolerant and understanding of human frailty. Other Popes contravened their priestly vows. Aeneas Piccolomini did not need to feel a hypocrite when, years later, he wrote to Sigismund of Austria who had asked him for advice on how to win the love of a young lady: "You ask me with some bashfulness to write you such words of love as might persuade a young girl you are courting to yield to you. Another man might deny your request fearing to corrupt you. But I know life. If a man does not fall in love during youth he is doomed to prove himself a fool in his old age". Aeneas then points out to Sigismund all the virtues of love: "One man will put forth his prowess in arms—another his competence in letters. Since reputation attaches to merit, the lad in love will try and develop all the powers he possesses to be worthy of his mistress."[3] Such is the power of love to improve the lover that it is worth being in love even if as he wrote "It may be,—I would even say, it is very likely—that you will find your prize much less valuable than you think but it could be the means whereby you may attain to some excellence. Youth must not be held on a tight rein." The excellence Aeneas would have chosen would have been that of the intellect, in the neatness of an epigram not in the sharpness of the sword.

The passion for the glowing phrase was to remain with Aeneas forever. Years later, when he wrote his history of the Council of Basle, the Assembly in which he played so great a part, he wrote: "I really ought to be putting money by for my old age and not use my powers to write history. My friends ask me 'What are you about, Aeneas? Are you not ashamed to be a pauper at your time of life?' . . . Time after time I have turned my back on poetry and history yet—like a poor moth—I flutter back to the flame. Such is my nature. . . . If it is wretched to discover oneself indigent in old age, it is still worse to be old without the solace of letters.''

It was this conviction that made Aeneas Silvius, if not always a happy, at least a serene personality even in the most miserable circumstances. He had an inner contentment that nothing could dispel and he was genuinely desirous to communicate it to others. Even those who at first despised him ended by liking him.

But during his youth in Siena, everyone held him in high esteem. When Cardinal Capranica passed through the city on his way to the Council of Basle to voice his dissatisfaction with the reigning Pope Eugene IV, he found in Aeneas what he had looked for in vain in Rome: a young man of talent, willing to act as his secretary in his dispute with the Pontiff. "One who was well read in the classics—could give a turn to a clever speech—bestow a sparkle on a letter—had some knowledge of law" and over and above all this, was looking for employment. So Aeneas, the future Head of the Roman Church, began his career on the side of the clergy who believed in Councils more than in authoritarian rule.

Because of the political situation, Capranica and Aeneas could not travel all the way from Siena to Basle by land. They met with almost equal difficulties when they took to the sea and reached their destination only after many painful vicissitudes. At one moment they were driven towards Africa where a slave's lot awaited them. They almost gave up hope. But—when they got to Basle—they found gathered there in Council the flower both of Western Europe and of the Universal Church. Skilful diplomatists mingled with the most profound scholars and humanists. To Aeneas it was a marvellous experience that developed still further his capacity to deal with men and judge them.

But his term of service with Capranica was short. His next post as secretary to Nicodemus, Bishop of Freising, was even shorter and he passed into the service of Bartolomeo Visconti, Bishop of Novara. This nearly ruined him for life. It taught Aeneas a signal lesson in prudence and ever after he took great care in whom he placed his trust.

This is what had happened: one day the Bishop of Novara handed Aeneas a letter of which he did not reveal the contents, merely telling him to deliver it to a famous *condottiere*. It contained nothing less than a detailed plan to capture Pope Eugene and hold him prisoner. It amounted to high treason. The conspiracy was discovered.

Aeneas Silvius realising no one would believe him were he to deny having had any knowledge of the plot, ran away, went into hiding and then sought a new master. He found him in Cardinal Albergati, a carthusian who wore a hairshirt all day and all night—awoke several times to pray earnestly and long in the dark and never finished a whole meal and yet was a man of delicate manners, gracious, cultured, a humanist and a skilful diplomat. Moreover and perhaps this was what drew Aeneas to him at that moment he was reputed to be upright in all his dealings.

It proved a lucky combination at last. He not only won at once the admiration of Albergati himself but made an acquaintance that very soon ripened into friendship, warm and intimate, with a personage who was to play a most important part in his life: Tommaso Parentucelli, the future Pope Nicholas V, an enthusiastic humanist and a Tuscan, who was to make Aeneas bishop first of Triest and then of Siena and so place him on the runway to the Papacy. But in that year of 1433, the Pontificate was still far off for both of them. Parentucelli was Cardinal Albergati's housemaster and Aeneas the Cardinal's youngest secretary. He was at once enthralled by Parentucelli's wide field of knowledge and wrote: "What is unknown to Parentucelli is beyond the sphere of human learning". Parentucelli and Albergati were equally enthusiastic about him and entrusted him almost at once with a very delicate diplomatic mission: nothing less than winning the support of the Scots against the English who were then at war with France. In his lifetime, Aeneas was to be sent on many missions. Not all were successful and this, his first one, was destined to fail. But it taught Aeneas the importance of endearing himself to all men, learning how to deal with them and be worthy of their confidence.

The mission was of course secret—so secret that Aeneas always so careful in noting and setting down all that happened to him and the impressions he formed, does not reveal its main purpose but veils it by setting down a secondary aim : that of restoring a prelate in the Scottish King's good graces, a request to which the Scot King readily acceded.

His journey to Scotland was not an easy one. He had to make two attempts to get there. On the first he crossed the Channel and only got as far as London. On the way his keen Tuscan eyes took in the beauty of Canterbury Cathedral and he marvelled at the[4] "celebrated temple of Saint Paul's" (not the present one) in "the immensely wealthy city of London."

Despite his diplomatic preoccupations, he even found time to observe and note that the tide in the Thames flows out faster than it comes in because of the pressure of the river waters running seaward, a novel experience for someone who until then had only seen the tideless Mediterranean. He had plenty of time to linger and observe the new world around him since he, with good reason, had been considered a suspect in London and cautioned neither to continue his journey nor to return to the Continent. But at last he was allowed to recross the Channel and must have been glad the ebb carried him quickly out of danger. Nothing daunted, he tried again, going this time directly to Scotland across the North Sea. He embarked at Sluys a port near Bruges and, soon after, a storm blew up and grew to almost hurricane force, and kept him in fear of death for fourteen hours. It was almost immediately followed by another which damaged the ship's keel so that it became ungovernable and wandered northward so that (he writes in his commentaries) "the sailors, unable to recognise the position of the stars, lost all hope". Then a freezing but merciful north wind came up and, after eleven desperate days, they were blown toward the Scottish coast. As soon as he got ashore, young Aeneas started off with bare feet for the nearest shrine of the Virgin Mary to offer thanks for having been saved. At the height of the storm he had vowed to do this but was dismayed when he learnt that the nearest shrine was not near at all, but about ten miles away over snowclad hills!

Night overtook him and the southern lad in an unaccustomed land trudged on without shoes through deep drifts of snow so that his feet became frostbitten. He did not complain, and merely noted in his diary that, "The sun in the North shines only a few hours in winter." Finally he arrived! But, after praying at the shrine he was told there was nothing for him to eat and he must go on somewhere else. With the aid of two helpers he dragged himself on, beating his feet on the ground until some heat came back into them, but he was to suffer forever from gout after this experience, a constant reminder of the vow he had taken and kept.

As soon as he could, he rode to Edinburgh to fulfil his mission with the King of Scotland, James I, himself a writer like Pius. The King received him with much kindness but was much more interested in the young man's literary knowledge and news than in the message he carried from his Master. He gave him money, a pearl of great value, and the use of two horses for as long as he stayed in Scotland, but firmly declined to embarrass England in any way.

It is no wonder that the young humanist was in no hurry to leave. He could not understand the language of those around him but he found plenty to write about. Everything enthralled him. To begin with the geography of the place. His mind was already becoming encyclopedic and in Scotland he had the opportunity of observing astronomical phenomena very different to those of the Tuscan and Swiss skies he was used to. Later his geographical writings were judged so valuable that Christopher Columbus obtained them and read them carefully and is said to have taken one of them with him on his voyage of discovery to America. This is not absolutely certain, but we do know without a doubt, that he carried a copy of one of Pius's works about with him before leaving and made notes on its margins and blank pages. No less a personage than Salvador de Madariaga in his *Vida del Muy Magnifico Senor Don Cristobal Colon* tells us that Columbus possessed a copy of *Historia Rerum ubique gestarum*, the work of Aeneas Silvius—printed in Venice in 1477,—and that when the discoverer of the New World urgently needed to reproduce a map that lay hidden and perhaps forgotten under layers of dust somewhere in Portugal, he went to the place where he knew the map to be, carrying with him Aeneas's book, and secretly copied the map on to one of its blank pages. To avoid possible detection, he omitted the more essential calculations from the drawing, but made a separate note of them and then inserted them on the map in his own good time. He showed this map to Queen Isabella of Castile when he sought her financial aid for his voyage to the New World and the drawing, on one of the blank pages of a book by Aeneas Silvius, proved Columbus's scientific credential thanks to which he got the money to sail for what was to be the discovery of America.

There is no doubt that the discoverer of the New World read and studied and thought highly of the astronomical works of Aeneas Silvius Piccolomini, to the point of carrying them about with him continually in his travels.

They were not young Aeneas's only literary output resulting from his visit to Scotland. Besides gazing at and studying the stars on occasional fine nights, he also looked underground and described coal, to him a novelty: "There is a rock in the subsoil here that is of a sulphurous nature. The Scots dig it out and use it as fuel." He has also left us a valuable record of the Scotland of James the First: "The cities are undefended by walls—the houses, for the most part, are put together without mortar—the roofs are of turf—the doors, in the countryside at least, are mere oxhides—the people are poor but there is plenty of meat and fish which they wolf down voraciously—the men are bold—the women are fairskinned, fairhaired and very beautiful." So in Scotland too, Aeneas was victim of his unfailing admiration for fair women. A fair Caledonian bore him a son, destined not to live. She does not appear to have been the only Scot woman in his life because he writes in his

Commentaries: "The opportunity to kiss a woman in Scotland arises as easily as that of shaking hands with Italian women. (The Scots ladies) are marvellously gracious, voluptuous, with skins marvellously white." It is evident that the beauties of the Scot feminine world made a wondrous and deep and lasting impression on him. He went out of his way to find interesting subjects of conversation to attract their attention and win their confidence and he noted that: "There is nothing more pleasing to the Scots than to hear the English abused."

The skipper who had brought him to Scotland and who, Aeneas tells us, "was anxious to get home and marry his young bride" offered to take him back to Flanders in his ship. Quoting from the ancients, Silvius declined gracefully: "The man who has been in peril from the sea, cannot complain of Neptune if, after this warning, he meets with shipwreck". As it happened, Aeneas chanced to be absolutely right. The vessel put to sea without him and, as he watched it from the shore, it keeled over and sank. The skipper went down with it.

More determined than ever not to tempt Neptune again, Aeneas decided to go and embark only at the port of Britain closest to the Continent. He disguised himself as an Italian merchant and crossed the Tweed into English territory. Certain that he would not find them on the way, he carried with him forty litres of wine and some white bread. When the sun was setting, he turned towards a village and sought hospitality for the night in a farmhouse. He dined with his host and the parish priest who had come to see the stranger. Many dishes were brought to the table: chicken, then goose, but of wine and bread not a hint! Aeneas congratulated himself on his foresight and produced the wine and the bread he had brought with him. Then a strange thing happened. Men and the women came crowding in, taking it in turns to gape at him as if he were "an Ethiopian or an Indian". When he spread his wine and bread on the table some took him for Our Lord Himself because he offered it freely to everybody. Those who took most of the bread were the women who happened to be pregnant, of whom there appeared to be many and soon all Aeneas's provisions were gone. But the carousing and feasting continued long after dark had fallen.

At a certain time, the men of the party went off in a hurry saying they were going out to watch in case the Scots took advantage of the low water of the river Tweed to come across and plunder. Aeneas, curious as always and seeking strange experiences as was his custom, would have gone with them, but they refused very firmly and left him with the women, many of whom were girls and young brides of great beauty. There were about a hundred of them and Aeneas spent a happy time with them round the fire till, drowsy with sleep, he was led by two girls to a stable. The two maidens made it quite clear that they were willing to sleep with him. But Aeneas who feared that marauders might arrive at any moment, was in no mood that night for lovemaking and repulsed the protesting girls. They went away grumbling, and Aeneas was left with the cows and goat that kept him awake all night by pulling the straw from under him. As he lay awake, he may have regretted he had sent away the girls, but he tried to make the best of it, endeavouring to convince himself that surely God would protect him from raiders since he had been continent. He was not certain of it however, because when, shortly after midnight, there was a great clamour outside—dogs barked and geese ran hither and thither cackling their loudest—Aeneas felt sure the enemy had arrived and kept well hidden under the straw. But soon the women were back and reassured him through an interpreter that there was no longer any danger of a raid that night. Whether he still felt he must remain continent or whether the girls would by that time have none of him, he does not tell us but says that he felt sure that he had been saved as a reward for his purity. This did not prevent him from being unchaste for many years to come.

Next morning at dawn, somewhat shamefaced at having shown fear in front of the girls, Aeneas went on his way. He reached Newcastle then Durham and went on to York. He wrote of his awe and wonder at York cathedral in his *Commentarii* "York Minster merits to be known in all the world for its magnificence and splendid architecture and for its chapel extraordinarily full of light which rains into it through the walls of glass, supported by astonishingly slender pillars".

He continued his journey south and some preoccupation attended it. He fell in with a party of riders one of whom was a judge returning from assizes. At first Aeneas was happy to speak good Latin once again but soon he became much perturbed when the judge started to inveigh against Cardinal Albergati, Aeneas's master, calling the Cardinal "a wolf in sheep's clothing" and cursing "his intrigues with Scotland against England, carried out through a man who had fortunately since been drowned." Aeneas may have smiled but he was intensely worried. He could not leave the company without arousing suspicion. On the other hand he was in danger of discovery through the slightest slip of the tongue. At last the company reached London and the Judge and Aeneas went each their separate ways.

But even now his relief was of short duration because he was told that no one might leave England without a royal permit and in the case of foreigners this was obtainable only on arrival, never on departure. He pushed on to Dover hoping against hope. There with his Tuscan shrewdness he found some harbour guards open to bribes. This time there was no storm and by April 1436 Aeneas was back in Basle. Albergati was not there but he had left behind Piero de Noceto and to him Aeneas made his report.

CHAPTER TWELVE

The Uses of Latin

HE journey to Britain of Aeneas Silvius had not been a success as far as his diplomatic mission was concerned but to Aeneas the writer and future statesman and Pope it had provided fresh experience of how to deal with men whose thoughts he had been compelled to read, though he could not speak their language and whose ways of thinking and customs were utterly dissimilar to his. And he found he needed all his newly developed faculties the moment he got back to Basle. He was told that the Pope had condemned all those who had opposed him in the Council and that he, in particular, had been singled out as the object of the Pope's animosity. The Pope had not forgotten the part he had played—however unintentionally—in the Bishop of Novara's attempt to take the Pontiff prisoner.

In such circumstances, to go on the side of the Pope even had he wanted to, would have been suicidal. So Aeneas had no choice but to remain in Basle in the service of the Council. He set about to make the best of it and immediately scored several achievements. The first opportunity to show his talent and capture the imagination of the entire Council arose through a strange accident of fortune and Aeneas was quick to seize it. In its anxiety to unite the Church, the Basle Council had invited the Eastern Greek Byzantine Church to send representatives to Basle for discussions. Both the Council and the Greeks were opposed to Eugene IV, so the moment seemed propitious for them to come together. The Greeks agreed but objected to Basle as a meeting place so the question came up as to where to transfer the Council. Four cities were proposed: Florence, Udine, Pavia and Avignon. The first two were the Pope's selection. Eugene hoped that, by holding the new universal Council in a city of his choice, to reabsorb under his authority both his Basle opponents and the Greeks. Avignon was the easy choice of the French Sovereign, who would have dominated the Council. The Duke of Milan for his part offered Pavia.

Formidable, eloquent speeches were delivered in favour of each of the first three cities suggested but, when it came to Pavia, its proponent proved so hopeless and tedious an orator, that he was shouted down by the whole of the assembly. At this moment, Aeneas Silvius was quick to seize his chance: he would defend Pavia and so make it unnecessary for the Council Fathers and their attendants to submit to either Pope or King. Besides winning the Council's gratitude, he would enter the good graces of the powerful Duke of Milan. Moreover, as he says, he was "stirred by the humbling of a noble city" that didn't deserve to become the laughing stock of the Assembly. He sat up throughout the night and composed a speech in defence of Pavia. "Next day" as he writes "I came into the Council Hall and—having obtained permission—spoke for two hours to a most attentive and admiring audience." From that moment, he was more popular in the Council and of course with the Duke of Milan. But he had done more than that. In the course of his speech, which was an oratorical and personal success, he had managed to slip in the suggestion that the Pope's authority be not disregarded until the Council had definitely condemned him. So, without losing the support of the assembly, he had won some favour with the Papal party, and, when he sat down, he was the object of an enthusiastic ovation from all sides. The one exception was, naturally, the unlucky Milanese who had spoken for Pavia. But, as for the Duke of Milan, Aeneas felt he could already count on his favour. Aeneas Silvius had grasped his opportunity masterfully, and stepped out of obscurity forever.

After that he often acted as the Council's secretary and Writer of Briefs, a task that required an elegant diverting use of Latin, such as he had so spectacularly displayed during his speech for Pavia. He also sat on the so-called Committee of Twelve, which carried great weight since admission to the Council and questions to be submitted for discussion were subject to its approval. He was no theologian. It was his literary power that made him wield great influence in the supreme assizes of the Church and, through them, on the whole of Christendom, at a time when he was not yet even an ecclesiastic. He was also sent on several missions for the Council, which felt it could rely on his amiability and discretion no less than on his ability to persuade. They were not always easy missions. One one occasion, on a visit to Milan, he came down with a severe fever and he tells us in his Commentaries that "Duke Filippo Maria Visconti sent him his own physician who administered to him a drug with no effect. The doctor was about to give him another dose when Aeneas's bowels began to work and caused him such discomfort that he became delirious and was brought to the very gates of death so they say. There is no doubt that, had he drunk the second draught, he would have died."

He was still feverish when he made his way back to Basle. Here the plague had broken out. Bravely Aeneas assisted two of his friends who had caught the epidemic and it is no wonder he fell a victim to it himself.

After he had detected the fatal swelling on his body, he tried to find a doctor. He was told there were two celebrated medics in Basle, one from Paris, very learned but whose patients usually died; another known to be ignorant but usually assisted by good fortune. He chose the latter. After all, he reflected, no one really knew what the correct remedy against plague might be. He was right. The treatment he was given was to cut a vein in his left foot to relieve the pressure on the swelling which was on the left groin. He was then kept awake the whole day and most of the following night, and a powder was administered to him, the nature of which the physician would not disclose. Under this treatment and after applications of juicy radish and moist clay to his sores, the fever increased, his headache became unbearable and he was clearly in danger of death. He received the Sacraments just before his mind began to wander, and he could no longer talk to those around him. Then, miraculously, after six days, he began to recover. When finally he offered the doctor a payment of six florins, for—as he says—"the man's kindness and faithfulness had been remarkable and perhaps unprecedented in a physician" the doctor considering himself unworthy of so high a payment exclaimed "If you insist on my taking all this money, I shall attend to six poor men and not charge them anything" and he bound himself by oath to do so. As soon as his health permitted, Aeneas

Silvius plunged back into the Council storm.

On 25 July 1439, the Basle Assembly took a momentous decision. It deposed Pope Eugene IV; Aeneas Silvius, the future Pius II was on the side of those who deposed him. Though a layman, he was included in the special group formed to elect a new Pontiff.[1] They chose him in the person of a hermit, Amedeo, who was in fact the Duke of Savoy and who chose the name of Felice V. One of the first acts of the new Pontiff was to insist that Aeneas Silvius, who was not an ecclesiastic, but whose fundamental honesty and dedication to whatever he undertook were well known to him, should become his secretary. Such was the trust that Felix put in Aeneas Silvius that he despatched him almost at once, to the Emperor of the Holy Roman Empire, Frederick III of the House of Hapsburg, to win his support and that of all his followers against Eugene, whom the Roman Curia still recognised as the true Pope, as indeed he was.

Frederick was a cautious man, never one to make up his mind quickly. Uncertain whether the future would favour Felix or Eugene[2] he meanwhile set about gratifying the messenger Felix had sent him. This was easy. Frederick was no man of culture but the fame of Aeneas as orator, latinist, writer and poet had reached even him and he decided he would give him the highest literary honour it was in his power to bestow. He crowned him "Poet Laureate."[3] There would always be some other honour to confer on an envoy from Eugene should one come.

Such was Aeneas's personality and the sympathy he aroused that Frederick also offered him a post in the Imperial Chancery. Aeneas obtained his release from Felix's service and entered the Emperor's. But a bitter delusion awaited him. Though he could style himself henceforth as 'Aeneas Silvius Poeta' he discovered that the post given him in the Chancery was that of the lowest paid clerk. He was all the more surprised in that the Head of the Imperial Chancery was a noble knight, Kaspar Schlich, who was destined in time to become one of his closest friends and appear in this disguise in Aeneas's writings. But for the moment he found that he had no regular pay and—like all the other clerks,—could not solicit payment from those presenting requests to the Emperor. All he had to content himself with was what a postulant might or might not offer him. It was a painful situation for the poet laureate especially as the other clerks, each vying to secure petitioners who offer them money, resented the competition of a newcomer. One Bavarian in particular hated him. He was Wilhelm Taz and was to appear later, in July 1444, in one of Aeneas's comedies, an erotic piece which realistically describes the ribaldry of some of Frederick's clerks. When we learn how Taz treated Aeneas, we need not wonder that, in the comedy, he appears as the archvillain. What made his persecution more vexing was that Taz was regularly put in charge of the whole Chancery, whenever Kaspar was away. He "outrageously tormented Aeneas at these times but Aeneas made up his mind to conquer evil with goodness. He laid back his ears like a stubborn donkey, vexed by a burden too heavy"[4]. Aeneas was treated as the meanest of all the clerks; not given a place at table nor a bedroom nor even a bed to himself. He had to share with companions who at best snored but more often lay drunk and retched and brought up what they had imbibed. Aeneas took it all calmly and refused to become angry when they taunted him, derided and openly despised him. They dubbed him a heretic and a few for being against Pope Eugene; but with his tolerance, far ahead of that of all who lived in his day, he judged neither of the two intended epithets insulting and did not consider them in any way a diminution of his worth and dignity. It enraged his tormentors, who tried to devise new tricks to vex him. But they never succeeded in shaking his equanimity.

There was one of his fellow secretaries Michael Pfullendorf, who appreciated Aeneas's qualities and engaged in humanistic studies and read poetry with him. He comforted Aeneas, bade him take heart, until Schlich's return when—he promised—things would get much better. They did. Schlich—more intelligent than Taz—quickly came fully to appreciate to the full Aeneas's worth and industriousness. He admired the calm self assurance of the young man and recognised it was based not on fatuity but on the consciousness of a well-developed talent. The result was that the next time Kaspar Schlich went away on a mission, it was Aeneas and not Taz whom he left in charge of the Chancery. He acquitted himself well and so Aeneas came to be considered Schlich's natural substitute. Wilhelm Taz, who had once trampled on Aeneas's dignity, found himself compelled to respect and obey him. Those who had harassed him most now came over on his side and Taz, having no inner resources, and unable to stand his new unpopularity, soon withdrew from the Court. Aeneas on the contrary rose from the level of a clerk to that of an envoy. He was sent to Triest to persuade its citizens to swear allegiance to the Emperor and he succeeded.

Then a task for which he was ideally fitted came his way. Groups were formed to weigh the relative argument of Eugene IV and Felix V in an attempt to heal the schism which split the Roman Church. They were to meet at Nüremberg and Aeneas Silvius was chosen by Frederick III as the only lay members of the brains trust of four eminent theologians and orators who were to represent him at what came to be known as the

Nüremberg Diet. Aeneas saw at once that what mattered to the Emperor
was not who was Pope, but the reunification of the Church. So long as it
was split by schism, the various bishops and the princes felt themselves
independent not only from the Pope, whichever he might be, but also
from the Emperor, who in theory derived his power from the Pontiff. So
long as there were two alternative Popes, each bishop and each petty
sovereign would veer from one to the other according to his own interests, which often conflicted with those of the Emperor. The seed of the
Reformation was already germinating below the surface and, in due
season, it would only need the magic call of Martin Luther's sincerity to
bring it to the fulness of its bloom. Many theologians and—it would
seem—both Popes were unaware of this. Aeneas Silvius, the layman,
sensed it and understood to the full. No theologian, though part of the
Emperor's delegation of which the other three members were
theologians, he was tolerant where doctrinal differences between the
various groups of the Diet were concerned, but he saw in the continuing
schism a danger to his master, the Emperor, and a threat to the universal Church and to friendly understanding between the peoples of
Europe. Though siding with the anti-pope and not the Pope of Rome, he
strove from the first meetings of the Nüremberg Diet to bring about
reunion within the Church and between the Church and Germany, no
matter which of the two Popes might in the end prevail.

Fully alive to the dangers of the situation, he lost patience with the
shilly-shallying of most of the clerics in the Diet, who wasted their talent
in useless disputation and intrigue, when not in fornication. He was no
virgin and he wasn't chaste but he could not abide that ecclesiastics
should violate their solemn vows. He himself would have been much
further on in his career had he taken Holy Orders which had been
offered him more than once. But he did not intend to become chaste and
with equal determination he did not intend to make promises he would
not or could not keep. To him this seemed far more important than most
of the theological arguments that came up for discussion in the Diet. His
impatience with the hypocrisy of many members of the Assembly, as well
as with that he had so often witnessed in Basle, drove him to write a
comedy *Chrysis* in which real people, including himself, are brought
vividly to life and still live for us. It is remarkable that—at the time—
many more people, than those whose failings Aeneas Silvius consciously
depicted, thought they recognised themselves in the play and angrily
voiced their resentment. One of these, much to Aeneas's sorrow, was
none other than Michael Pfullendorf, who had been such a comfort to
him when he had been derided and ill-used at the beginning of his career

in Frederick III's Chancery. Though it seems that Pfullendorf was finally persuaded that he was not one of the characters held up to ridicule in *Chrysis*, he nevertheless continued to criticize the play as immoral and too revealing of weakness in others. Aeneas was grieved because he had never intended to offend his friend. Actually he himself not Pfullendorf, was in a far from favourable light as one of the characters in the play. His is the part of Charinus, the gluttonous lover of a prostitute with whom he eats and makes merry, only to let her go to the arms of another man—a cleric—to make money.

The comedy's open denunciations of ecclesiastical impurity and intrigue go a long way to explain why the original script cannot be traced. Pious priests will tell you that the future Pope Piccolomini destroyed it in a fit of repentance for having exposed members of the Church, harming the Church herself. Though this may be so, it is at least equally probable that succeeding Popes and later ecclesiastics tore up the manuscript in an attempt to whitewash the reputation of prelates and Councils. This assumption seems to be confirmed by the fact that *Chrysis* was never again re-presented to the theatre going or reading public for five long centuries and that the few copies of it that were found to exist were in Prague, the centre of the protestant Hussite movement.

The play is in eighteen scenes. In the first, two ecclesiastics, Diofane and Teobolo, no longer very young, each have an appointment with a different courtesan in a brothel kept by a procuress, named Cantara. Diofane is to spend the night with a girl named Cassina, who is at the moment in the arms of her real lover Charinus[5] and leaves him in a hurry for her tryst with Diofane. Teobolo—on the other hand—has an assignation with the heroine of the play: Chrysis herself, who is in bed with her lover, Sedullio[6], whom she tries to prevent from leaving her. Sedullio, evidently a very practical man, insists on going because Teobolo can give her much more money than he can. But Chrysis is very seductive and, in the end, Sedullio cannot resist and jumps back into bed with her.

Meanwhile the two cuckolded ecclesiastics, in excellent humour, wend their way, conversing, to Cantara's house. Diofane extols the advantages of being an ecclesiastic: "We are not like others who are compelled to have a steady relation with their wives" "Non ut alii stabilem uxorem ducimus" he says in elegant Latin but "Nova in dies, himeneos novos celebramus. Si placet amor revertimur—si displacet, alio flectimus iter." "Every day we celebrate fresh hymens. If the woman we feel attracted to still gives us pleasure, we go back to her. If she displeases us, we switch to another." However, when they reach Cantara's bawdy-house, they find that, this time at least the girls have done their own switching. The spry young wenches are not waiting for them at all. Though the two clerics have no way of knowing it, the girls are still in their lover's arms and enjoying it. Understandably the two churchmen are extremely vexed and vent their angry disappointment on the procuress Cantara; they shout rudely at her: "If it weren't for us, you would starve like the meanest pauper!" to which she retorts tartly "It is not to feed me that you come here. I have pretty bait for you and you will just have to be patient." The outraged priests cannot do otherwise. Diofane is so strongly attracted by Cassina that he bursts into an admission that he cannot do without her. Teobolo tries to stop him for fear Cantara will raise her price. She herself goes on drinking as if she hadn't heard, but smiles.

Meanwhile, Charinus, who, as we have said, impersonates Aeneas, revels in the delights Cassina knows so well how to afford him and to his bliss is added the pleasurable and triumphant knowledge that he has captured the first fruits that another has paid dearly to secure. Aeneas Silvius, poor from his Siena days and still not rich, draws an added satisfaction from reaping golden harvests that others have yearned and paid for. Besides Diofane whom he is cuckolding is a hypocrite and it is this breaking of an oath by a priest that incenses Aeneas. The aim of *Chrysis* is to condemn not whoring but hypocrisy. (Charinus does that and more)—hypocrisy and blasphemy of breaking solemn vows.

However, in *Chrysis*, the priests have paid their money and the girls go to them at last. But the spell of what should have been a happy evening is broken and—instead of love or the pretence of it—there is much bickering. The two prelates try to vent their annoyance on the girls but the two comely wenches know how to defend themselves. Cassina proudly displays her shapely charms and shouts right in the face of the unhappy Diofane, drooling with desire: "Semper novae Kalende, amores novos offerunt mihi". "Each month fresh lovers offer themselves to me."

Brazenly she stamps off, sweeping Chrysis with her, leaving the timid Diofane deeply hurt and the sturdier Teobolo very much annoyed. Needless to say, the two girls repair to Charinus and Sedullio for more lovemaking. When they are satiated, satisfied and drowsy, they at last return to find that the two ecclesiastics—notwithstanding their previous pomposity—are still miserably waiting for them. Reconciliation follows and a pleasant if by this time very sleepy night of voluptuousness. At the end of it, poor Diofane feels the bitter melancholy of it. In a final anguished soliloquy, he expresses the deepfelt conviction that is really Aeneas's and what the play is all about: "Rather than sink to such degradation, better, far better to make no promises, take no vows, remain a layman."

Well meaning, sincere Catholic critics—torn in their conscience between admiration for Aeneas Silvius's honesty and their loyalty to the Church they belong to—have gone out of their way to explain that Diofane—and consequently Aeneas—was merely voicing his disenchantment with sexual pleasure and the disappointment that follows its more shady aspects. Others, including Giuseppe Bernetti, say the whole comedy was an attempt to imitate the Latin poet Plautus, some of whose plays had recently been discovered and are mentioned by Aeneas in a letter[7]. However this does not explain why Aeneas, when Pope, should have destroyed this play while many other of his writings on amorous matters were allowed to survive. The significant fact is that Chrysis shows not ordinary people but churchmen in an indecorous light and it is for this reason that either Aeneas himself or, more probably, his successors tried to suppress it.

Another of Aeneas Silvius's erotic writings, the *Historia de duobus amantibus*, the *Story of two lovers* suffered no such fate and has never ceased to be read. It has been translated into many languages, eastern and western. Significantly in it there are no priests. The hero, under the name of Euryalus, is the great friend and protector of Aeneas in the Imperial Chancery, none other than Kaspar Schlich. *The Story of two lovers* was written a little earlier than *Chrysis*, at the beginning of July 1444, while *Chrysis* was composed at the end of August and beginning of September of the same year. It begins with a preface in the form of a letter to Mariano Sozzini, who, it will be remembered had introduced Aeneas to sex and to girls in his early days in Siena and who had written to his erstwhile pupil asking for a titillating piece of prose that would revive his ageing impulses. In exactly three and a half lines of terse Latin Aeneas bares his soul to Sozzini: "Rem petis haud convenientem aetati meae, tuae vero et adversam et repugnantem". "You ask me for something which is not decorous in my age and is incompatible and repugnant in yours ... Nothing is more shameful than old age that seeks love without virility. Mature women no less than young maidens despise the old. Women love only men who are in the fulness of their vigour. If they tell you otherwise, they deceive you. However all the good you have done me was and is so much that I cannot deny your request, even if turpitude goes with it. Vice and lust prevent you from feeling your old age. So I shall oblige and bring an itch to that old and worn out groin of yours."

He then says he will not make use of imaginative poetry to excite the
senses of his friend but will just tell in prose some events that had
occurred in Siena some eleven years earlier (in 1433). He will use fictiti-
ous names to describe real people. Accordingly he says there lived in
Siena a lady called Lucretia married to a certain Menelaus. The name of
Helen of Troy's husband is purposely chosen both as a compliment to
Lucretia and as a disparagement of the ageing Menelaus on whom
Aeneas Silvius heaps yet more derision as "excessively rich and
unworthy to have a beauty like Lucretia in his home"; that he was the
type "a wife should disgrace with horns as long as a stag's!" Perhaps
recalling his and Sozzini's youthful experiences with the pretty girls of
Siena, Aeneas describes Lucretia as "irresistible and charming" and
with dimples "such that no one who saw them was not moved by a wild
desire to cover them with kisses, passing then on to her delicious
mouth"—"ad morsum optissima"—"made to be softly bitten" while
her tongue roamed softly through her lips tremulously inviting. There
was nothing along her whole body that was not perfect and the beauty of
her face excited visions of magnificence hidden under her clothes.

But if the story was not to become Aeneas's own love story, he felt
compelled at this point to turn to the hero of the piece, Euryalus, who is
the personification of Kaspar Schlich, the gallant friend and protector
who had put an end to the persecutions Aeneas had been subjected to in
the Imperial Chancery. Such was the gratitude Aeneas felt for him that
we need not be surprised when we read Euryalus was unsurpassed in
physical beauty and was favoured in all women's eyes. Lucretia had
magnificent eyes and, in a thrice—"such is the power of an exchange of
glances" that she felt herself faint with desire for Euryalus when first
she saw him. He, for his part, craved at once to have her and—despite
many difficulties, some foreseen, others unexpected—the day came
when he could cry out "Ego te habeo" and possessed her "pugnantem
feminam, quae vincere nolebat" "a lively woman who fought resisting
but yearning to lose". There were more difficulties and they delighted
not only the two lovers but all Aeneas Piccolomini's contemporaries
who read about them and the work was an unparalleled success.
Even today it is probably the most widely read of Aeneas Silvius's
writings.

Part of the thrill lies undoubtedly in that it was written by one who
later became Pope. To some this may be sufficient to arouse interest, but
the writing's chief worth and absorbing fascination lies in that it shows
us the future Pontiff Pius II, as one enlightened, who, not having
accepted the priesthood until he could live up to it in every sense, was

neither a hypocrite nor one of those spiritual leaders, ignorant of the ways of life, unable to understand and feel compassion; not just haughty pity but co-suffering with his fellow beings, in their failings. His Pontificate was free from unbending juridicism—the mere reading of the letter of the law, the severity that lays aside all understanding, allows only supercilious pity and holds that morality is strictly incompatible with the natural eroticism that is a part of love. Had there been more Popes like him, with his knowledge and perception of women's most delicate feelings and ardent desires, they never would have countenanced the subjection of wives to their husband's egoism; the bearing of tens of children, one after the other, only for the pleasure of the man. They never would have allowed their blessing to be given to the marriage of a woman who had been raped and was given no other reasonable choice but yield and live together forever with the man who had abused her. Such husbands, we feel, Aeneas Silvius would have judged as he judged Lucretia's "worthy of horns" and long ones. *Historia De Duobus Amantibus* leaves us in no doubt that he also judges "worthy of horns" those husbands, who with their wealth or influence and power have acquired a wife as mere chattel. Perhaps, had Pius II lived longer, many customs and habits that have so long oppressed women since his day and that only some recent Popes and Statesmen and the force of feminist movements have succeeded in large part in lifting might have been removed earlier. Men would certainly have abused women less— perhaps they might not have pampered some of them so much—but pampering and the domineering it tends at times to arouse, are all unworthy of woman and Pius II knew it and told us so.

Aeneas's next book was *De Curialum miseriis* concerning the vileness and wretchedness of courtiers, completed on 30 November 1444. It describes the terrible conditions in which some courtiers—evidently among them those of Frederick III's Chancery—lived feeding on "meat that is foul, fetid, tasting of smoke and of the charred wood that's mixed with it". It goes into the details of the rest of a courtier's griefs but more than an attack on courtier's conditions it is a severe judgment on the courtiers themselves.

Piccolomini classifies them into three main categories: those who seek what they can never hope to find; those who run after what is harmful to them in the end; those who pursue their objects by the wrong road. To these aims courtiers sacrifice freedom of thought and action— they have no place where they may study at leisure—they are given to intrigue and try to win power by smiling at superiors and by being blustering to inferiors—they judge human and intellectual values by what influential people say and not by their true worth.

   To this evident allusion to Wilhelm Taz and his underlings, Aeneas's persecutors in the Imperial Chancery, Piccolomini now famous dedicated the following end of *De Curialum miseriis*[8].

> "Rumperis invidia, quia carmina nostra leguntur
> Quod tua nemo legit, rumperis invidia"
> "Burst with envy for my poems are read
> And no one looks at yours; burst with envy"
>
> "Rumperis invidia, quod laurea serta feramus,
> Tu non feres Hederam; rumperis invidia."
> "Burst with envy because I wear a crown of laurel.
> What you wear is not even a drunkard's ivy ornament. Burst with envy"
>
> "Rumperis invidia, fidos quod tenemos amicos
> Quod te turba fugit; rumperis invidia"
> "Burst with envy because I have friends who trust me
> While whole crowds flee at the very sight of you; burst with envy."

CHAPTER THIRTEEN

Reunification and the Road to the Papacy

CTUALLY the invective against Taz
was not added to *De Curialum Miseriis* till much later. In November
1444, Aeneas put a hasty finish to the work because a tremendous event,
all important to the whole of Christendom, but particularly to Central
Europe and the Church had occurred. It was to lift Piccolomini to the
highest pinnacles of success and he was aware of the momentous hour
from the start. For the moment it was a great tragedy, but like so many
tragedies, it was to have a chastening effect on people and spur them to
successful effort. On 10 November 1444, a Christian army of Poles and
Hungarians led by the King of Hungary had suffered a disastrous defeat
at Varna on the Black sea. The King had fallen in the battle and the
army had been utterly destroyed but for a few stragglers most of whom
fell prisoner to the pursuing Moslems. Poland and Hungary were left
practically without organized defenders. Austria and Germany were
directly threatened and the menace of invasion lay over the whole of

Western Europe. Frederick III at last realised that this was no time to await the conclusion of the subtle disquisitions and discussions of conflicting interests at the Diet of Nüremberg. He judged that Eugene IV, perhaps because he had given 300,000 ducats to the King of France, and certainly because he had given Naples to the Aragonese[1], was of the rival Popes the one who could call on a larger share of Europe's soldiers. The Church and Europe, both in mortal danger, must unite under him and Felix V must go. It was not an easy decision for Frederick. Many if not most of the Prince-Electors—the feudal Sovereigns who had chosen him as their Emperor and kept him on the throne—were against Eugene. It was not a personal hatred. But they saw in him a Roman Pontiff who would continue the Roman habit of exploiting the Germans by the sale of indulgences and a thousand other means thought up by the cunning Papal environment in the Eternal City; the sort of exploitation that, though no one knew it then and only Aeneas Silvius sensed it, would in the end lead to Luther and the Reformation. The Germans felt that a Pope like Felix V, who had been a hermit, lived far from the Roman Curia and, though not lacking the means, had refused to buy the support of the King of France and not stooped to simony, was more likely to respect their liberties.[2] One might say, they thought him less of a politician and more of a priest. Perhaps too the fact that he had had as his secretary Aeneas Silvius Piccolomini, who knew the Germans and their problems, carried weight with them. Certainly it was a master stroke, typical of the Hapsburgs, for Frederick to choose just Aeneas, Felix's one time secretary, to carry to Rome his proposals for a reunification between Germany and Eugene. Outwardly it would appear as a mark of the Emperor's filial trust in the goodness and mercy of Eugene to send him as peacemaker the man against whom the Pontiff might be justified in feeling animosity because of Aeneas's involvement—however innocent—in the Bishop of Novara's plot to kidnap him a few years earlier[3]. The choice would also create the impression that, by sending an Italian, Frederick was anxious not to antagonise the Roman Curia who had every reason to fear that a German envoy would insist on redress for the many wrongs they had inflicted on German princes, on the people of Germany and even on her Bishops. The Curia and the Pope might think an Italian more malleable, but the shrewd Hapsburg knew very well that he was sending a man who would defend to the utmost the rights of Germany and the Empire, one who was trusted throughout Germany and so would secure the acceptance by the Prince-Electors of the Empire's recognition of Eugene.

On his way to the Eternal City to fulfil his dream of restoring Germany to the Church and the Church to Germany, Aeneas passed through Siena and Corsignano, his birthplace. He was delighted to see his native land again. His artless relatives, who went out to meet him, were on the contrary horrified that he should be going to Rome, to place—as they saw it—"his head between the fangs of Eugene IV" who would certainly punish him for his entanglement in the Bishop of Novara's plot—for his siding with the Council of Basle against Rome's authority and for his having supported and aided the antipope Felix V. But Aeneas was calm and smiling, certain that his mission to reunite the Church, in the moment of the Ottoman danger, was a good and worthy undertaking. He also shrewdly guessed that, in the circumstances, with the Moslems approaching fast, the Pope would go to any length to avoid giving offence, let alone cause damage, to the person who came to him as representative of the Emperor whose armies in Austria, Bohemia, Brandenburg, Bavaria, Serbia and other German States were the only immediate bulwark against the mighty Ottoman onslaught.

Aeneas's kindred wept as he left Siena for Rome but could not shake his confidence. He knew himself to be a good persuasive orator, master of the written and the spoken word, fully capable of presenting well his case.

Finally the day came when two cardinals led him into the Papal presence. Aeneas was still under indictment for having sided with the Council of Basle, but he knelt dutifully, kissed the Pope's foot, then looking straight into Eugene's face, made one of the boldest speeches ever made to any Pope by one anathematized.

"Holy Father, before I deliver the Emperor's message, I shall speak a few words about myself. I plead guilty to having spoken, written and contrived much against Your Holiness at Basle." In equally firm tones he added: "I acted wrongly; I erred. I followed men who were regarded masters of canon law and truth, universities and schools that were against you. When I suspected the misconceptions of the supporters of the Basle Council, I took time to think things out. I did not want to fall from one error into another. So I joined the camp of the neutrals to have time to meditate and come—with God's help—to a well considered decision." After long meditation, he had come to the conclusion that right lay with Eugene: "therefore I rejoiced when the Emperor my master wished to open relations with Your Holiness through me. I hoped to be restored to your favour and here I stand and ask for forgiveness".

The speech took Eugene by surprise. Aeneas was known to be a timid man, more persuasive than forceful, one whom the Pope had thought he would find no difficulty in overawing. And here was this rebel not on his knees but squarely planted on both feet before him, telling him openly he acknowledged him as Pope, not out of reverence to an authority blindly accepted but after careful, independent deliberation. Neither of the two men knew that Galileo would be tortured for far less in a later age, but meanwhile here was Aeneas claiming forgiveness on the basis that he was free to think and even make mistakes, in the matter of papal authority. The Supreme Head of the Church yielded the point and said: "You made mistakes like numberless others. We cannot refuse our forbearance to the repentant."

Aeneas Silvius had won the first round and would soon win another. Eugene thought he had come cap in hand to beg for pardon from the Pope and the Roman Curia, but he soon found himself compelled by the tolerant power of Aeneas's persuasive personality to make concessions and in his turn be humble. He discovered that Aeneas's cogent and clearheaded reasoning, expressed as only a great humanist could express it, left him no choice but to dip his hand into the papal coffers and restore in part at least to the Germans what an avid Curia had deprived them of during the years. German benefices were restored to the thumping tune of 221,000 ducats and all the bishops, who had been deprived of their emoluments for having opposed Eugene at Basle, had the satisfaction of seeing them restored in full. The money-loving Roman Curia understood only too late that the humble Italian, whom they had thought the Emperor had sent as the most likely to win the favours of Rome, was himself dictating the reunification terms in very clear, very beautiful Latin, that allowed of no equivocation, not even by those of papal scribes who were masters at it. Its members whispered little jokes against Aeneas one to the other, but they never raised their voices. The Emperor, who had put as one of his conditions for recognising Eugene that he, Frederick, be officially crowned in St. Peter's, wanted the Pope—they said—to pay in cash not only for the coronation but for the Imperial progress to Rome as well.[4]

Time dragged on and Rome has always counted on time to put another aspect on problems as they slither into the past that dims everything.[5] But Aeneas too knew how to be persistent and the day came—23 February 1447—when Eugene IV lay on his deathbed and the Curials and Barons whispered to each other, outside the dying Pontiff's door through which they were not admitted. But Aeneas at the dying Pope's side got his signature of acceptance[6] on the settlement with Germany. While news of Eugene's demise was dispatched to all lands, to the message sent to Germany, Aeneas Silvius added the brief but telling sentence: "God has reunited his Church."

He had every reason to feel triumphant. Through his clearheaded-ness, courageous diplomacy, mastery of language, he had won over Eugene, once his enemy and left out, literally left out beyond the door, his opponents in Rome. But there is no pride in the way he tells us the facts in his *Commentaries*. His elation at the Pope's acceptance *in extremis* of the German terms stemmed from quite another reason. He saw in the unification of Rome with the North a hope for the future as well as for his time. Not only were there now formidable forces to withstand the Ottoman onslaught but Rome had learnt (or should have learnt) not to make unbridled use of its authority with no regard for others convictions or doubts let alone for worldly and financial ends. Other Popes, beginning with Piccolomini's immediate successor, des-troyed what he had built[7] but, at the moment of Eugene's death Aeneas Silvius the Poet had brought forth a Church that stood united on the basis of conviction not authority. It was not to exist again until John XXIII in this century.

And this was a church that Aeneas felt at last he could give his full allegiance to. On the 4 March, nine days after Eugene's death, certain too that what Goethe called "the peace of the senses" had come to him at last, he embraced the priesthood and received Holy Orders. Two days later, on 6 March, his old friend Parentuccelli, (under whom he had worked in the service of Cardinal Albergati at the beginning of his career in 1433,) became Pope Nicholas V. On 19 March, when the new Pontiff was crowned, Aeneas, now the new priest Piccolomini, carried the Cross before him in the procession of the coronation. They were both humanists, both writers and now that they wielded immense influence over a united Christendom, they renewed their friendship and we need not wonder when we learn that only a month later, on 19 April, one month and fifteen days after Aeneas had been made priest, he became Bishop of Triest. Certainly many of the Curials must have thought of it as favouritism, especially those who had been passed over, but it would have been foolish and unrealistic, to keep the man who had turned a divided Christendom into an harmonious whole, in a rank lower than a canon of Saint Peters or an Apostolic notary. To Piccolomini the writer the Bishopric brought many duties of which he acquitted himself well but also one great balm. He who, in his young Siena days, had had to sit up nights to copy laboriously his friend's books and documents because he had had no money to buy them and later, at Basle and in Frederick's Chancery, had had to write out for himself the copious literature he produced, now at last could make use of ammanuenses to write out and adorn what he wrote. Thanks to this circumstance, before the year 1447 was out, he completed *De rebus Basilae gestis* (Events in Basle) and *De viris aetate suae claris* (Of men renowned in their times) for which he had collected notes over the years, and by Christmas 1449 he was able to send a completely new work, *"De liberorum institutione"* (The education of children) to Frederick III. It was a highly detailed book of suggestions on the education of children sent to Frederick, unmarried and childless, because he had adopted the fatherless Laslo Postumus, King of Bohemia and Hungary.[8]

In 1450, Nicholas V gave back Aeneas to Tuscany by promoting him Archbishop of his native Siena. Most definitely the new archbishop did not confine his activity to governing his archdiocese. Even before formally taking possession of his See, he had to proceed posthaste to Naples to arrange the marriage between the Emperor and Eleonora, sister of the King of Portugal, who had sent a committee to the Neapolitan Court to discuss the matter and could not be offended by delays. Also, when, after forty long days the marriage contract was signed and the new archbishop could at last start his journey back to his awaiting diocese, he very nearly drowned owing to the incompetence of the boatmen who ferried him across the river Liri.[9] He was then sent to Bohemia to compose a quarrel between the Emperor and the local regent who wanted at all costs that the young boy Laslo be removed from the guardianship of Frederick and be allowed to rule over Bohemia at once.

In 1452 Archbishop Piccolomini was entrusted with the task of officially meeting Leonora of Portugal, Frederick III's chosen bride, on her arrival in Italy at the Tuscan port of Leghorn. Aeneas had to wait a long time there. Painstaking as usual, he had arrived a few days early. Not so the Portuguese. They were 104 days late.

The delay did not worry Aeneas. He wrote much and wrote with the happiness that many literary men find in themselves when thwarted and an unexpected obstacle to practical action provides them with the leisure and the time to study and to think. It was now that he finished his *Curialum Miseriis* with the poem that heaps scorn on his opponent and persecutor Wilhem Taz,[10], now quite sunk into oblivion while Aeneas whom Taz had bullied is an Archbishop, a renowned author and diplomat who consorts with Emperors and Empresses.

But at last the Portuguese Fleet appeared on the horizon. However the men from Lisbon made more difficulties. The Portuguese ambassador who was escorting Eleonora to her imperial bridegroom considered it below his dignity to entrust his charge to anyone of lower rank than the Emperor himself. If the sister of the King of Portugal had crossed the sea, an Emperor could cross the land. He stressed that the

Princess had travelled 104 days (how well Aeneas knew it!) so the Emperor might well take the trouble to travel a day or two from Siena and not wait for her there. But no such easy solution was at hand and the argument went on for a fortnight. Finally Aeneas proposed that the matter should be put to the bride and she be asked whether she would abide by her would-be husband's arrangements or by accompanying ambassador's wish and she accepted at once to adhere to the Emperor's plan.

But all Aeneas's troubles were by no means over. As he arrived in Siena escorting Eleonora, he found that all the most comely women of the city had come to to meet the Princess and sing poetical compliments to her. The Portuguese courtiers of the suite saw in this the occasion for ribaldries that outraged the Sienese ladies' sense of propriety and, much offended, not the girls only but even the most worldlyminded and experienced matrons, angrily left and withdrew to their homes. And there was the Emperor coming to meet his bride at the Porta Camollia. Aeneas came forward to heal the squabble and with his knowledge of women and diplomatic experience got the girls back into the street to acclaim Frederick and prevailed on the Portuguese to keep quiet.

From Siena the bridal pair proceeded to Rome where, on 19 March—three days after the celebration of the marriage—Pope Nicholas crowned Frederick and Eleonora Emperor and Empress. After many festivities, the imperial couple, now in every way officially blessed by the Church, went on to Naples where Alfonso of Aragon, the bride's uncle, was King. Needless to say, there too there were comical incidents. It appears that—while the Court and the people of Naples gave themselves up to celebrations, Eleonora of Portugal, though wedded to Frederick, had not yet become his wife. Frederick, a ponderous personality, wanted the marriage to be consummated in Germany. But the maiden grew desperately unhappy and believed that her bridegroom would always be indifferent to her and that she might as well have gone into a convent. She expressed her views with displays of temper and tears to her husband, to her uncle Alfonso, to the Court. Everywhere she found sympathy and Alfonso intervened with the young Emperor. In vain. The King tried again. No success. Finally Alfonso actually begged Frederick to consummate the marriage. The situation was getting out of control. The Neapolitans were taking offence that the Naples sky, Naples bay, Vesuvius in flames, aroused no thought of eroticism in Frederick. They began to say that he must be homosexual or, worse, someone addicted to some secret unmentionable vice. The ladies complained he was being limitlessly brutal with a poor, innocent girl, who only claimed what was due to a bride between the sheets.

At last the Emperor ordered a bridal bed to be prepared. In accordance with German custom, he made Eleonora lie on it in the presence of their host—the King of Naples—of notabilities of the Court and of Eleonora's maids of honour. Then Frederick climbed into the bed himself. The maids of honour shrieked. Some made as if to flee from the room. Others held their hands spread over their eyes, but it is not clear whether their fingers were held as close together as they might have been. We know for certain that Alfonso insisted on staying until it was all over and he could vouch that the marriage was at last a real marriage.

When, soon after the Emperor and Empress returned to Germany, they found the country in a state of turmoil. Many of the princes, though they had agreed to a reunification of the Church, thought the Emperor had gone too far when he had sworn "obedience" to the Pope. They saw in it a danger of a renewal of Roman exploitation and authoritarianism at the expense of the north of Europe. In a rough and ready way they treated both Pope and Emperor with contempt. Aeneas too, who had been the instrument of reunification, came in for much criticism and brusque treatment. In the winter of 1452, he was one day in council with the Emperor, when, suddenly, one of the Electors, Prince Albert of Brandenburg, rushed into the chamber, abusing everyone loudly and shouting he cared not a fig for Emperor or Pope. Aeneas, though not directly attacked, felt it his duty to intervene with civility and said: "It is a common fault among princes, brought up as they are among their inferiors in rank, always ready to agree with everything they say, that when finally they find themselves among their equals, they suffer no reproof; fly into rages; lose their self control if anyone disagrees with them". Aeneas's "*Historia Federici III*" goes on to tell us that "Albert took Aeneas roughly by the shoulders and pushed him out of the room, shouting: 'Are you a prince that you think yourself my equal?' " Aeneas, locked out, went round by a corridor and entered the hall by another door and said: "Some electors are no better than Saracens." They rely on swords not on civilized exchange of opinion. The *Historia Federici* does not tell us what happened next. We know however that Aeneas, undaunted, went on travelling through the whole Holy Roman Empire in an attempt to rouse the people against the Ottomans, who once again were nearing. Constantinople fell. Not long after, Nicholas V died. In 1456, the next Pope, Callixtus III, who had passed Aeneas Silvius over in a first consistory, created him cardinal. All the Princes of Germany—including Albert of Brandenburg sent him congratulatory letters. When Callixtus died Aeneas became Pope Pius II, on 3 September 1458.

The very day of his crowning, after the magnificent ceremonies at St. John the Lateran, when he narrowly escaped death among the rough crowd of Romans who fought with drawn swords for the horse he had ridden in the Coronation procession, Pius, meticulous in his duties as always, set down in detail what he considered was to be the main task of his Pontificate: the defence of Europe from the Moslem invasion. It took many hours and—as he sat up into the night—his prose took shape. Though he didn't bother to polish it, when he passed it on to his literary friend, Campano, it was found to need practically no change. His policy decision was also immediate. He would call a conference of the rulers of the West to discuss and plan the contribution in arms, men and money each and all would be called upon to make for the crusade. To make it easy for everyone to come together and to stress his absence of authoritarianism, the congress would not be held in Rome but he would go to meet the other participants in Mantua, half way to northern Europe. It would not be an easy journey for him—he suffered from the stone and the perpetual gout he had contracted in Scotland—but he would make it. He wanted to create a novel image of the Pope. Not a ruler who pronounced orders or anathemas, but a friend who would go forward arms outstretched towards the world not just for fleeting visits but for a more or less permanent stay if need be.

When the Romans learnt of his decision, the *Commentaries* daily kept up to date, tell us they were greatly distressed because they realized they were going to be deprived of the business the presence of the freely spending Curia and the easily fleeced pilgrims denoted. As they had done often on similar occasions and would continue to do for centuries after Pius II, they maliciously raised doubts as to the Pope's sincerity and judged of his honesty by their own lack of it. Some asserted bitterly that the Pope had no intention of stopping in Mantua but intended to transfer the papal See to Germany. Others that he would pretend illness and stop in Siena to enrich his native city at Rome's expense. From Pius's *Commentaries* we learn that "women went wailing through the streets—children were taught to utter blasphemies—men cursed and threatened,"—such was the extent of the material benefits that—one way or another—the Pope's presence brought to Romans at all levels. At the Papal Court, they went to all lengths to get him to renounce his plan. They came up with pretended credits in the attempt to deplete the papal coffers. He paid them off, urgently wanting to be away. Then came hypocritical concern for his health. How could he in his condition stand the hardships of the way in the frightful winter, across the frozen Apennines? To these arguments was added a feigned anxiety for the Church itself "Who will protect the patrimony of St Peter? What of the papal State? The instant you have crossed the border, all will be at each other's throats." they said. But the Pope answered, serene as always: "If Divine Compassion permits that which you fear, I would rather see the Church despoiled of all her temporal goods than jeopardize the Faith in whose defence the congress has been called." They then went back to urging his gout, an affliction which would make it impossible for him to travel. Openly contradicting them, he began the journey to Mantua on foot going at night from the Vatican to the shrine of the Virgin at Santa Maria Maggiore to pray for protection on his undertaking. Only after long prayer did he make his way to the Milvian bridge and the road to the north. Again some Romans tried to detain him and Aeneas— always so calm—for once lost patience and retorted: "I am suffering from the stone. Don't make my journey longer than it need be. I am off." But the journey was arduous and, as it progressed by stages, first one of the cardinals of the retinue then another dropped out. Others followed their example and rushed back to the comfort of their palaces. Pius himself took a few days off to rest at his native Corsignano.

We don't know whether he had decided long before to make of Corsignano (a small medieval town) a Renaissance jewel or whether it was a sudden impulse. But it may not have been mere coincidence that he had in his train, the greatest city planner of the Age: Leon Battista Alberti.[11] Rebuilding Corsignano was not easy. The rectangle that was to become the central square was bound on one side by the splendid medieval palace of the Aldermen which had to be preserved and at the other end by the church of Saint Francis which must not be touched. In front of the Aldermen's palace, restricting the building site still further ran, in beautiful curves, Corsignano's medieval main street, which Alberti wanted to save at all costs because he saw in it the perfect artery of the perfect city. On the opposite side, across the building area, was the sternest obstacle of all: a precipice falling away into the valley. In this limited space of 300 by 130 feet, the Pope wanted no less than: a palace to be erected on the site of his father's modest home and a cathedral to be dedicated to the Assumption. Despite the room they were bound to take they were to enframe a square as spacious as possible.

Leon Battista Alberti proposed the work be entrusted to Bernardo Rossellino, native of Settignano near Fiesole, who had collaborated with him in the building of the Palazzo Rucellai in Florence and had some notable monuments to his credit: the facade of the Misericordia at

Arezzo; the monument to Leonardo Bruni in the church of Santa Croce in Florence. He had also been employed by Nicholas V in the first attempt to build a new St. Peter's. Alberti provided the main ideas. Rossellino applied them in practice. Both agreed that, in honour of Pope Pius, the new town would be called Pienza.

Rossellino accomplished the miracle and fixed in stone the vision that had been Alberti's and Pius's. The Pope wanted a spacious square and there wasn't room for a spacious square. Rossellini gave the area the shape of a trapeze widening out towards the cathedral so giving the square the impression of being wider than it actually is. To make it appear yet more ample, the cathedral was not built to occupy the whole of one side of the square, but is flanked—to the right and to the left—by visions across the Val d'Orcia to the hills beyond. The square has been described as "150 feet, stretched into what looks like infinity by Rossellino's genius". On the right of the square and enclosing it is the Piccolomini Palace, a perfect Renaissance building, with gardens and windows looking out over the Val d'Orcia. In one of the upstairs rooms the large beams in the ceiling do not run from wall to wall. They dovetail into each other in mid-ceiling forming four P's, which stand for Pope—Pius—Piccolomini—(of) Pienza.

Another of Rossellino's difficulties was that Pius sensing death not far off, was urging him to hurry as fast as he could. And there was Rossellino with a landslide where the cathedral was to rise! But—amid untold difficulties—he built a base and reinforced it—and in less than three years he accomplished the miracle. But for the bell-tower, the cathedral was built. The whole of Pienza was completed in 1462. It is a unique town and the cathedral with its spacious gothic windows, admitting an exceptional abundance of light, is most unusual in Mediterranean climes. Monsignor Aldo Franci, the erudite canon of Pienza, says Pius was influenced by the memory of churches he had seen in Graz and Wiener Neustadt. The churches of Austria and South Germany are full of light. However it is difficult not to recall Aeneas's own words in the first book of the *Commentaries*, when describing his travels from Scotland to London, he wrote about York cathedral saying it was memorable "for its chapel so full of light, whose walls of glass are held by extraordinary pillars." The same words could be used to describe Pienza cathedral, the church on the continent of Europe most reminiscent of York Minster.

But Pius could not indulge his delight in planning the city to his own name that winter 1459. He hurried on through Tuscany, dragged himself over the snowclad Apennines and at last, on 27 May, arrived in

Mantua, accomplishing a journey far more arduous than circling the globe in an aeroplane today. A bitter disappointment awaited him: of the Kings he had invited only a few had responded and sent representatives to the Congress. It was the bitterest moment of the long journey he had undertaken to shorten and lighten theirs. He exclaimed: "The loyal Hungarians are suffering many disasters. Once they are conquered the Austrians, then the Germans, then the Italians, then the whole of Europe may be vanquished. Turks do not hesitate to die for their Faith. We feel deeply ashamed that Christians are indifferent to theirs."

He remained in Mantua for a time to no avail. Back in Rome he tried to comfort himself by writing. He completed his *De Germania*, *De Europa*, and his own History of events wherever they happened and description of where they occurred, *Historia rerum ubique gestarum locorumque descriptio*, a copy of which Columbus was destined to take with him and follow part of its precepts, on his first journey to America. But even the delight of seeing Pienza completed and holding a joyful fiesta there left him a broken man. He died at Ancona on the Adriatic at ten o'clock in the evening of 15 August, the feast of the Assumption of Our Lady, to Whom he had dedicated the cathedral at Pienza. It was the year 1464 and he had gone to Ancona to witness and bless the departure of a christian fleet that was to go to the support of Skandenberg, the Albanian Leader, who had succeeded in halting the Mahometans. The fleet did not come over the horizon to assemble and never departed for the East. Aeneas Silvius the Poet and Pope Pius II died. When recently the people of Pienza asked that his remains be brought to their own— which is also his—cathedral at Pienza from his tomb close to the Chapel of Saint Andrew in Rome's St. Peter's, the tomb was found to be . . . empty. We have his books. We have Pienza.

CHAPTER FOURTEEN

The Passing of the Golden Age

HE tolerant Pontificate of Pius II and the joyful early years of Lorenzo de 'Medici's rule in Florence were the peak, the culmination, the Golden Age of the Italian Renaissance. It was the season in history when Pope, ruler, man in the street and peasant of the countryside in Tuscany, were freed from prejudice and—though with varying degrees of perceptiveness, were released from oppressive superstition. It was a time when man felt really free to examine and observe, reason and learn through his own personal experience and was no longer compelled passively to accept notions, imparted to him by others however authoritative and strong.

Pius II and Lorenzo de'Medici, these two pillars of this glorious Age, on which the foundations of modern western civilization rest, were, as we have seen, two men completely different in character and in the circumstances of their lives: Lorenzo, impetuous, of lightning speed of thought and decision, tempered by, sometimes uncannily accurate judgement. Pius II, on the contrary, prudent, meditative, plodding, learning from a long list of mistakes and overcoming adverse fortune. On the one side, Lorenzo born in a position of power, trained to rule, with a city and a State—(and what a State!) thrown into his lap when he was twenty. On the other side, humble Aeneas Silvius raised in straitened circumstances, working his father's fields forced to borrow books and copy them if he wanted painfully to learn something, worked his way up through patience, setbacks, continuous toil, to a position of influence through service, persuasion, the use of talent not forcefulness nor an innate ability to command. He seldom appealed to his own authority, even when he held the Papacy.

Whenever danger threatened, Aeneas retired momentarily to marshal his thoughts and organise his exceptionally persuasive powers and use them to advantage to carry conviction through the strength of argument and the music of the well turned phrase.

Lorenzo de'Medici, though also able to cajole and compel with the spoken and the written word, addressed alike to enemy or friend, is equally apt—when he judges it best—to force an immediate conclusion by driving his fist or his sword into his opponent.

Aeneas—through immense difficulties—finally swayed the decision of a Church and an Empire and gave both a moment of greatness, unhappily destroyed by those who came after him. Lorenzo led the city which was the flower of Europe and was the source of its civilisation.

Both in their different ways—knew how to unite men of opposed opinions and contrasting interests and passions. Looking at both, one is at a loss to decide which is the more likeable: Lorenzo, the superman good at everything, (except at perceiving smell and digesting his food,) or Aeneas Silvius Piccolomini, modestly plodding uphill and through quagmires, always deeply humane and profoundly human. Perhaps it was all as it should have been: Lorenzo de' Medici, the splendidly magnificent, the exciting temporal ruler. Pius, the true spiritual leader who knew the frailty and the temptation besetting those he must lead. Both believed with true conviction in the power of poetry and the music of prose, in the immense value of civil exchange of opinion. Both had the same vision of tolerant progress and saw with a clearness all the more astounding considering the times they lived in, the distinction between the spiritual and the temporal power. Both were honestly, deeply persuaded that the encroachment of one on the other could only spell ruin to both. Their other great common characteristic was the ability to read other's minds. No matter if Aeneas addressed Pope Eugene IV or Lorenzo spoke to King Ferrante of Naples, the listeners fell captive to their arguments and it was they—not the listeners though they might be more powerful—who set the course and reached harbour.

After them, darkness descended. In Rome, Pope Paul II, as we have seen, brutally destroyed the tender plant of tolerance and free inquiry. In Florence, Lorenzo's son, Piero, grew up bigoted, incompetent and incurious, resembling more his Roman mother with her feudalism and rigid religious notions, than his father with the flights of his mind into freedom.

It is true that—after Paul II, the torturer and persecutor of humanists and after Sixtus IV, the villain who built monuments only to his personal or his family's glory, we do have in Rome what are generally referred to as "The great Renaissance Popes": Julius II, Leo X, Paul III. But even Leo X, though Lorenzo de' Medici's son, no longer belongs to the true Golden Age. He encouraged the arts and poetry and music and drama, but he was more of a Maecenas than one who himself inspires the Muses. Though tolerant as his father had been, he did not insist on tolerance in his collaborators, not even in those to whom he gave precise and definite directives. We have seen how Pius II knew how to lead the Curia prelates where he—not they—wanted. Leo on the contrary did not find it in himself to rebuke Cajetan when Cajetan quarrelled with Luther, and the rupture of Christendom, which Pius had successfully prevented in his time, became and still is a reality.

In the secular sphere too and in Florence herself, we have a lapse back into medievalism with Savonarola, a fall into sheer wickedness with Benvenuto Cellini,—however beautifully and imaginatively he clothed it. We drop into scepticism with Machiavelli, whose literary excellence is not used to bring to light a work of art, but to secure a post, wangle a favour. Machiavelli, whose writings about the Quattrocento (fifteenth century) are pure Quattrocento, showing that he understood to the full the spirit of that epoch, in the following century, took up his pen only to assert himself as a politician, not to widen and spread understanding. And the paradox is that, while he wrote his *"Prince"* and his *"Discourses"* in an anguished endeavour to get back into politics and stooped to change the early spirit of his *"Historiae Florentinae"* to get into the good graces of Pope Clement VII, he failed dismally, in both instances, in his twisted design. He was not reinstated in governmental office in Florence and, when he actually interrupted his *"Historiae"* to carry out some menial task in an attempt to please Clement, he just didn't please him. He forgot to seek literary perfection as he had done when telling the story of Lorenzo de' Medici. He sought only the favours of the Great and did not get them. He forgot the Medicean Golden Age and his *"Historiae Florentinae"* contain the damning sentence "Wise men know that proficiency in letters is less important than skill in the use of arms"; the very opposite of what Pius II maintained both as Aeneas Silvius and as Pope and he united a church and an empire and built a city, while Lorenzo De' Medici would certainly have put letters higher or at least on a level with arms. Machiavelli, on the contrary, brilliant though he was, did not influence the mass of his contemporaries, only the tyrants and the bullies. He had later repercussions—abominable repercussions—on the generations that followed—on the despots of what is called (and is not) the late "Renaissance" and on those of the modern Era, on Mussolini, Hitler, Stalin and others. Machiavelli commands attention and admiration because he was "modern" a precursor of today's alienation and discontent. He was not a genius of the Renaissance. He does not belong to the age of forbearance and enlightenment. He lacks the qualities that marked and made great Lorenzo's and Aeneas Silvius's Golden Age.

Another great historian and author, Guicciardini, who was almost a contemporary of Machiavelli, makes it very clear that times had changed in his epoch from the Renaissance's heyday, when he says "Don't believe those who preach liberty with fervour. Nearly all—probably everyone of them—has his own particular interest in mind. Experience proves that, if they thought for one moment that they would personally be better off under a tyranny, they would rush under its wings." Reading these words, we cannot help our minds refusing to focus on Lorenzo's and Aeneas's Renaissance and wandering instead to twentieth century extremism and poltroon government men.

According to Nikolai Rubinstein, even the freedom-loving poetical Poliziano fell a victim to the decay of Renaissance ideals that set in, after Lorenzo de' Medici's death. Rubinstein says that Poliziano, after proclaiming in the Laurentian Era that Florence owed her foundation to Julius Caesar or the free days of Republican Rome, later, under Piero de' Medici, reversed his theory and claimed to have found a document that proved Florentia to owe her origin to Augustus and the Empire. In other words, the creation of the city had been merely a step in Augustus's grand design for extending his rule over the whole world.

We know that Poliziano was far from being a brave man and it is most unlikely he would have persisted in a theory if it caused him to lose favour with the anti-republican Piero. Nevertheless one may feel doubts concerning Rubinstein's appraisal of Poliziano on two counts: the most recent archeological research has definitely established that the Florence of the Roman republican era was no city but merely a camping

ground, used by the Romans before attempting the climb north across
the Apennines or as a resting place on the return southward. Professor
Guido Morozzi, the Architect who has directed practically all the recent
archeological work in Florence and particularly underneath the
Cathedral, writes on page 113 of the book on his and other's findings[1]
that the aspect of Caesar's original Roman colony on the Arno river was
rudimentary, archaic if not actually rural. There are none of the powerful Roman foundations that come to light all over Italy, Europe and the
Middle East. Instead it appears that pebbles, fairly large pebbles, obviously taken from the river where there was no need to quarry them,
were simply carried to the campsite and dropped in the mud of the
marshy ground. At most an attempt was made to glue them together with
clay taken from that into which they had been dropped. There was no
concrete used anywhere. Though cautious Professor Morozzi does not
state it openly, all points not to a permanent settlement but to a halt; a
resting place on a travelling route. Another theory could be that the
remains that have come to light are the foundations of rustic buildings
used by Caesar's retired veterans, who cultivated as best they could the
surrounding countryside before moving elsewhere. This too does not
point to the founding of a city. What does denote the creation of an
established colony is the extent of walls of durable brick and mortar that
have been found to the north of the cathedral, round the site where the
temple stands and under it. The type of brickwork uncovered is typical
of the first century of the Empire and not of republican Rome. So it
would seem that Poliziano had really found documentary evidence of
these remains that have only recently come to light thanks to Morozzi
and the interest of two successive Archbishops of Florence: Cardinal
Florit, famous for his abnegation in relieving the victims of the great
flood that hit Florence in 1966 and Cardinal Giovanni Benelli, a man
reminiscent of Pius II, with an all embracing European mind.

The remains uncovered point to the early "Florentia" being no mere
imperial city but an agglomeration through which Greeks, Armenians,
Parthians and others travelled on their way to and from Northern
Europe and—halting for a space, brought Florence Christianity and her
inborn civilisation. This would explain why Florence cathedral, when
first built, was dedicated, not to any Roman Saint as would have been
the obvious choice if Florence had been a Roman city, but to Santa
Reparata, a Martyr put to death in Asia Minor, which was then Greek.
Certainly the Florentines, with their speed of thought and calculation,
their will to work and their appreciation of all that is gracious and
beautiful and fanciful, resemble the Greeks far more than they do the

Romans and it remains a mystery why the Florentines of the Renaissance—including Poliziano—turned somersaults in an attempt to establish a Roman origin to the City of Flowers, when they could have drawn their classical models from the Greeks and felt themselves the heirs of Greek not Roman freedom.

Whether Poliziano did or did not stoop to authoritarianism in the general decadence of the Renaissance after Lorenzo's death, it is regrettably certain that another eternal poet, Ludovico Ariosto, who brought the Italian language to a degree of perfection correctly judged unequalled, did, however protestingly, bow and scrape to the powerful and mighty. In one of his *Satires* he complains, perhaps only metaphorically, that he had to take off his master's boots and spurs:

> "Agli usacci, agli spron (perch'io son grande)
> Non mi posso adattar per porne o trarne"

which can be rendered with "I cannot adapt myself (since I am great) to bad manners nor to putting on or taking off another's spurs."

The actual unlacing of boots and spurs may well have been one of Ariosto's figures of speech, but there is no doubt that his master, Ippolito d'Este, a rough and ready soldier who had ecclesiastical Orders and a cardinal's hat thrust upon him at the age of seven for political reasons, never treated Ariosto the way Lorenzo Il Magnifico would have done. When the poet presented him with the first copy of the "*Orlando Furioso*", Ippolito the cardinal, son of Duke Ercole I de'Este, could not have shown himself more illbred and contemptuous.

Ariosto read to him the verses in the third Stanza, with which he dedicated the Orlando to him:

> "Piacciavi, generosa Erculea prole,
> Ornamento e splendor del secol nostro,
> Ippolito, aggradir questo che vuole
> E darvi sol puo' l'umil servo vostro"

"May it please you to accept that which is all your humble servant can offer you, o generous son of Duke Ercole, ornament and splendour of our century." Ippolito looked at him out of irate eyes and spat out the following words: "Wherever did you get hold of such trumpery?" Poliziano would have left in a huff. Ariosto continued humbly to serve the cardinal, though he complained bitterly in private: "If just because you give me twenty-five escudo three times a year and argue about the sum every time you pay me, you think you have the right to keep me in chains making me your slave, compelling me to sweat and fear, I would rather face indigence''. But the verses in which Ariosto expressed all this were never carried to Ippolito. Ariosto, the poet of heroic knights, the writer of tales of chivalry and honour which were to charm whole generations and perhaps will never cease to charm, kept his tantrums against Ippolito very carefully hidden and continued to serve him and, when at last they parted, sought and obtained to enter Ippolito's brother's service. It was only after he was dead, that one hundred thousand copies of his poem were sold all over Europe.

After Ariosto, who reached a degree of perfection in the Italian verse which many believe to have been and to be unsurpassed, there is a further decline in the Renaissance spirit. Torquoto Tasso—however exalted the poetry he has left us—was understandably far too fearful of the Inquisition, not to be careful at all times meticulously to avoid anything that might expose him to its horrors. Despite occasional moments of rebellion, he definitely belongs to the modern and not the Renaissance Era, for all the charms, the wit, the poetic flights of the *Gerusalemme Liberata*.

Part III

FLORENTINE

CHANCELLORS

OF THE

RENAISSANCE

Dies mei velociozes fuerūt cursoze. fugerūt
et non viderūt bonum: pertransierunt quasi
naues poma poztantes. sicut aquila volás ad
escam. Job. viiij.cap.

209. Woodcut on frontispiece of a book PRINTED IN
SALUZZO, 1507. Biblioteca Vaticana.

CHAPTER FIFTEEN

Coluccio Salutati

HE main causes that brought about the downfall of the Renaissance are sadly evident. On the one hand, the obscurantist currents in the Church of Rome, fearful of the rise of new thought and independent spirit of inquiry, did their utmost to reverse the progress made under the tolerant and enlightened Pius II. On the other, temporally-minded Popes, like Sixtus IV, saw in the rise of strong and free republics a limit to their worldly power and those who should have been spiritual leaders joined with the princes of this world in extinguishing the flame of free thought and free scientific research. Where Popes and princes encouraged the arts and discovery as some of them certainly did, their motive was their own glorification not the search for beauty and for truth. Under them, the painter, the sculptor and the poet became mere servants not revered creators. One of the most striking examples of this haughty spirit was that of Cardinal Raffaele Riario, by then recovered from his fright during the Pazzi conspi-

racy and perhaps wanting petty vengence on a Florentine. He sent the
great Michelangelo daily to eat among the lowest menials. Certainly the
freedom of the Renaissance republics did not reach all classes, but, for
the first time since Athens, the intellect was free and the lowest underling
was incomparably better off than a medieval serf. What had brought
this about? What had made man feel he was master of his destiny and
need not rely only on outside help?

Many factors contributed to this. All are valid and all may be dis-
puted but one circumstance cannot be denied. It was in Florence that
the Renaissance first took shape and it is there it reached its peak. At a
political level, the Renaissance began when the conviction grew in Florence that the highest offices of the Republic must be entrusted to literary
men and Florence based her prestige on the concise and literary expressions of her Chancellors, which gave polish and clearness to the
business acumen on which Florentine power rested.

The Chancellor's style and the substance of what he wrote must
convey the feelings, aspirations and convictions of the Florentines and
their passing moods at all levels of the people. And in Florence we find
the whole people, the humble workers of the lower Guilds as well if not
as much as those of the wealthier Corporations, in some way taking part
in city government. It would be absurd to compare the way Florence was
run to the system secured by universal suffrage, but it certainly pro-
longed the method of government of the medieval Comuni or city state,
at a time when Papacy and Dukes were giving rise to and forcing on
others the tyrannical State. As Hans Baron writes[1] the threats to Florentine liberty of Popes and Dukes had the effect of stirring the Florentines,
to a strenuous defence of their freedom. This determination to be free
was voiced to perfection by the Chancellor, Coluccio Salutati. He had
become Chancellor in 1375 three years before the uprising of the
Ciompi, the lowest paid workers in the textile industry, whose insurrec-
tion secured with Medici support, the overthrow of the oligarchical aristocratic families of Florence, for a while at least.[2]

During the rebellion, the government had momentarily tottered. The
high offices of the State became vacant through the flight of the aristocrats to their defensive strongholds in the country while many of their
city palaces were in many cases gutted and set on fire by the insurgents.
The authority in those troubled days rested almost entirely on the
Florentine Chancellor, Coluccio Salutati. The Chancellor's was the only
office that might be considered permanent, though it was renewed by
yearly election. All other posts changed hands in fast rotation. Most
offices lasted a few months only. A Priory only eight weeks and even the

term of the Gonfaloniere of Justice, the Magistrate responsible for public order, was only sixty days. Salutati was the only official who remained in office throughout the Ciompi rising, which some have described as the most significant of the Age and it seems impossible to deny that the gradual establishment of peace was largely due to him.

Coluccio Salutati's name is not widely known outside Italy. Born the son of fugitive, not even possessing the right to call himself a Florentine citizen, he attained to the most influential office in the Florentine state and held it for thirty one years. He provides one of the best illustrations of what heights a man of literary excellence could reach and what power he might wield in Renaissance Florence, despite accidents of birth and formidable handicaps.

When Salutati was born on the 16 February 1331, his father Piero had been compelled to flee from his native Stignano in the Val di Nievole near Lucca, because the faction, opposed to his own, had won a resounding victory. Piero Salutati had found refuge in Bologna but had found it impossible to take his expectant wife with him across the Apennines. However despite his defeat, since he was a good soldier, he found ready employment under Taddeo de'Pepoli, Bologna's ruler. Coluccio was born in his father's absence, back home in the Val di Nievole. According to Berthold Louis Ullman,[3] the tragic circumstances of his birth had their comic side. The child's mother and her mother in law had a violent quarrel as to what name the boy should be given. Finally they named him after both his grandfathers, the mother's father and the mother in law's husband and he was called Lino Coluccio. He soon dropped the Lino.

When the baby was only two months old, his mother joined his exiled father in Bologna and took Coluccio with her. The family were together for ten years until 1341 when the father died. The ruling Peppoli family continued to protect the Salutati and young Coluccio, the first of ten brothers and sisters, four of them shortlived, studied to become a notary, hoping—one day—to earn a living. He was of an exceptionally inquiring mind, always asking questions and engaging in discussion. He took an interest in everything, pestering his teachers and starting disputations on all sorts of problems.[4]

It would be a mistake however to think the young Salutati was a freak. Alfred von Martin sums him up as a typical representative of the cultural transition of his day.[5] One who reflects and makes known to us the thoughts and convictions of those around him, who saw in him the best of their number but not one fundamentally dissimilar from themselves. He was a leader who did not have to issue orders because he governed by winning the people's consent. Actually he went a little further and many of his contemporaries must have known it. By crystallizing in exquisite language and with an orator's vigour what they hazily were already convinced of, he kept them from wavering in the dark hours when enemies or pestilence threatened Florence, so that Gian Galeazzo Visconti, Duke of Milan, when desperately trying to conquer the city and destroy her liberties, found himself saying of him: "A thousand cavalrymen wreak less damage to the enemies of Florence than Coluccio's pen!" This was all the more extraordinary in that—before he reached the Florentine Chancellorship—he had never been in high office anywhere and his life had been mostly rather ordinary.

At twenty years of age he had left Bologna, a full-fledged notary thanks to the patronage of the Pepoli family, and begun practising as an obscure country registrar in the villages of Stignano—Pescia—Empoli and Montecatini, (its fame as a watering place was to come later). His main tasks were recording births, marriages and deaths, contracts, and acting as Court Clerk. Official correspondence had to be conducted in Latin. He had however much time on his hands and put it to good use reading the classics of antiquity, as well as the then emerging ones of the new Tuscan tongue: Dante, Petrarch and Boccaccio. He was soon composing Latin poetry himself and corresponding in Latin with kindred spirits all over Italy. But in 1366 he married a girl from his native Stignano and found, as he wrote to a friend quoting Cicero that "one cannot serve a wife and philosophy at the same time". In other words, he needed more money. And so after seventeen years, he found himself compelled to place his knowledge at the service of more strenuous and remunerative duties. It was the end of 1367 when, after trying unsuccessfully to obtain the Chancellorship of the relatively large town of Perugia—he managed to secure the same post only in the smaller, less important municipality of Todi. The only future the modest appointment offered was the chance, because Todi is near to Rome, of possible employment at the Papal Court. Salutati tried his best to take advantage of this but with little success. Because of popular unrest in Todi, he lived in constant fear. In his Epistolarium I—46 he writes: "During the day and through the night I am apprehensive and worried and fear possible revolutionary upheavals." Nevertheless this must have been a good experience and rendered his task easier when later, in 1378, he was to govern and hold Florence through the Ciompi rebellion. But in Todi he felt himself a mere functionary, not one of the people, and their fights were not such that he could share or understand, so, after just two unhappy months, he sought a position at the Vatican. Inexperienced, he made the mistake of choosing as one of his mentors a great friend of his, Giovanni Boccaccio who, undoubtedly a very great man, was not in vast favour with ecclesiastics. Results were disappointing. So Salutati wrote to the Papal Secretary, Francesco Bruni. Bruni promised him nothing and did nothing. So, in despair, Salutati wrote to Boccaccio again insisting that he was ready to "go to Rome and begin at the bottom" rather than eke out a small income and face the danger of unrest at Todi.

Alas, when he reached Rome, after waiting eight long months, he discovered they had taken him at his word. Either because they were unable to discern his worth or because they wanted to exploit him and leave higher places for less worthy men, they put him at the very bottom of one of the lowest offices and—as the seasons went by and the second year followed the first—he came to realise he would never be promoted. In the splendid Vatican halls where men laboured for a pittance he bitterly learnt the truth that Alfred von Martin tells: "One must speak to the Great not with the heart but with the mouth only. He who tells the truth must succumb." He approached one of the cardinals and—lavish in his praise—wrested from him a recommendation not for a higher post at the Vatican (even a cardinal could not go counter to the sinecures and favouritisms there) but for the office of Chancellor in the town of Lucca, not far from his native Stignano.

He took up his new post in 1370 and Ullman gives us the cheery news that, after so many hardships, he was given Lucchese citizenship and, for the first time in his life, an assistant. In other words, this was, at last, an important post. In his new-found happiness, he composed his "De Vita Associabili": "Of Social Life". It illustrates the importance for the cultured man to put his culture to use in active and practical life.

But this happy period was shortlived. Strife among Lucchesi factions prevented his being reappointed after his first year in office and, towards the end of 1371, his wife died. She had borne him a son who was then less than a year old. From what he wrote much later, we learn his views on love and women. In spite of his humanism, he shared with some of his contemporaries the old asceticism of the Middle Ages, which died hard even in his enlightened epoch. He made a sharp distinction between love and the calls of the flesh. Love was a virtue. It was in the heart and in the head. Sex was in the senses. The purest love was that for sons and daughters, followed by the love for friends. That for the woman who held the rank of wife came last. She had an undisputed right to complete faithfulness, to care and to the warmth of affection. Respect and deference were her due but not love. If any existed it came from the physical desire for her. It was most exceptional that marriage should occur between two kindred spirits. This side in the choice of a partner was completely left to chance. This did not mean that friendship could not in time develop within the married couple but it was given no opportunity to be tested or even to grow in the smooth-tongued artificial period before marriage. Judging by the way the Renaissance developed, Salutati's notion was definitely rooted in the Middle Ages not in his own times. It is not very different from the distinction Dante made between his idyllic love for Beatrice and that for his wife, Gemma Donati, whom he left without any great regret and not a line of verse, when he went into exile. In the Renaissance once it reached its flowering, wives fared better than that in their husband's hearts and minds, even though husbands, and at time wives too, may not have had Salutati's strongly moral sense that "to a wife absolute faithfulness is due". Even if the men of the Renaissance at its height indulged their physical appetites with their amours, they kept their affection and the fulness of their devotion for their wives. Cosimo de'Medici was a perfect husband to Contessina de'Bardi. Piero Medici, the Gouty, worshipped his Lucrezia Tornabuoni, whom all in Florence held to be on the same spiritual and intellectual level as men and Lorenzo—however many loves and amorous escapades he may have indulged in—held his wife in the greatest honour not as a mere childbearer but as companion, despite the fact that her intellectual interest and outlook for the children was completely different to his. Salutati would never have countenanced such a difference in his wife. With respect to women—though in nothing else—the cobwebs of the Middle Ages still clung about him. Considering this, we may be surprised to learn that after his wife had been dead a few months only, he married again. The explanation is simple. He had been left with an infant son on his hands and needed someone to look after it.

He didn't stop long to brood over as to how she should be, but followed his first impulse and rushed back to his native Stignano and there he found just the girl he was looking for and married her. After a lapse of time and after she had dutifully borne many children not a few of whom died, she won also his affection and in the end—despite his tenets—his sincere and tender love.

At the time he married her, he was practically right where he had started years before. He had worked for many years—he had held public office and his output of Latin epistles and poems besides being copious was definitely of the best and there he was; right where he had been at the beginning: a notary at Stignano.

But fortune soon smiled on the new couple and they never looked back. First Coluccio was chosen as Segretario delle Tratte—Secretary of

Municipal documents no longer in Stignano but in the city of Florence itself. Then—at last—in April 1375—his grand opportunity arrived. He was appointed Chancellor of the Florentine republic. It was a post that required yearly confirmation but Salutati was elected and re-elected to it, again and again, without interruption for thirty-one years—through wars, pestilence, famine and political upheaval, right up to when death came to him at his Chancellor's desk on the radiant morning of the 4 May 1406. The secret for this exceptionally long tenure is simple: he was the first in the long line of Renaissance men in public office who truly represented the spirit of their contemporaries.

Salutati achieved this by the way he exercised his office and in his writings. Like so many in his day, he composed in verse and prose and although the presence in his time of formidable literary rivals such as Petrarch and Boccaccio, whose works lived on after their death, have caused Salutati to be for centuries forgotten, in his day it was his vibrant prose that made Florence respected by friends and feared by enemies. It was he who established the principle that Florence to be great and exercise an influence must have—at the head of the Republic's Chancery—a man of outstanding literary skill. From Florence this tenet spread to the whole of Italy and then throughout Europe. Though Petrarch and Boccaccio were greater than him, it is he who was the first to embody the conviction that knowledge and literary ability must be of practical use or lapse into empty scholarliness. The way the Florentines rewarded him with lifelong high office, once they had discovered his qualities, seems to indicate that this ideal was also theirs.

His office was truly important. Lauro Martinez[6] tells that the post Salutati occupied was one of the most highly paid in the Republic. "The legal advisers of personages in public office drew a monthly salary of two florins. The Chancellor normally drew 40 or 50. As if this were not enough to show how much the Florentines valued the office, from Coluccio Salutati's letters we learn that—in his case—he drew a salary of 100 florins every month as well as an allowance of 40 florins for the hire of an assistant. Martinez points out that "In all the Florentine domains only administrative posts in Arezzo, Pistoia and Pisa (all of them trouble spots) entailed salaries higher than that of the Florentine Chancellor."

However the real prestige of Salutati's office lay not so much in the money it brought him as in the power it placed in his hands. All the secret paperwork connected with the drawing up of the lists of candidates for public office came under his scrutiny. In other words, he knew—months in advance—who might next come into the various posts. Further, his long term of office provided him with the unique experience

which only continued, unbroken association with the secret affairs of the
State could bring and it was natural that those newly elected to government posts should turn to him for advice and guidance. This discreet
participation in the State's affairs became open and public when the
Signoria could not reach a conclusion as to what to do. Then the Chancellor was empowered to speak and even suggest possible solutions and
explain precedents. In short it was the Chancellor who, one way or
another, assured the continuity of Florentine policy. He could do this
better than any man because of his unrivalled knowledge of the records
of previous meetings and discussions, records of which he was the
keeper and he saw to it that they be kept properly in concise, clear and
literary language that could be referred to and quoted in any instance
and be clear to everyone so that particularly those newly elected to office
could readily understand their purport. Salutati also saw to it that the
phrasing be given an elegance that would prevent it from becoming
tedious. No one had achieved all this so well as Salutati and his renown
spread to the whole of Europe bringing distinction and prestige to the
Florentine republic. It is not surprising that after he had been re-elected
to his Chancellor's office for the twenty-fifth time, he and all his relatives and descendants were granted Florentine citizenship.

The parsimonious Florentine however never increased his original
salary of 100 florins plus 40 for an assistant. But other emoluments went
with the office. Authenticated copies of the Republic's official ordi-
nances had to be paid for when it was a private person or firm which
requested them and the Chancellor got a slice of what was paid. The
same applied to passports—safe conducts—permission to carry certain
weapons—certificates of good conduct and many other documents.
Judging by Salutati's expenditure, particularly what he shelled out for
ancient manuscripts (by the end of his life he had collected about a
thousand) his additional income must have about quadrupled his salary.
By the time he had reached his later years, he had accumulated considerable wealth and it was honourable wealth. He never accepted bribes
or even gifts and always observed the discretion his office required.
Documents in the State Archives in Florence tell of his rigid honesty[7]. So
does an incident which occurred in January 1382. In that month, one
Iacopo di Bartolomeo publicly accused Salutati of treason but as
Demetrio Marzi[8] writes: "So well known was the honesty of the man who
dedicated his whole days to his work in the Signoria Palace that the
accusation went unheard and the accuser ended by confessing that he
had invented his charges."

Honest work was rewarding in Renaissance Florence and, by the end of his life, Salutati had a fortune amounting to 8,000 to 9,000 florins. According to the system of taxation then in force, property was capitalised on a 7% basis, that is to say that the annual income from land and buildings was taken to be 7% of what the land and buildings were worth. Salutati's tax return in the last years of his life reveals an annual taxable income of 600 florins. That is the amount he was taxed on but Florentine legislation permitted him to deduct from his total income his house rent—any debts he might owe—and 200 florins for each member of his family, which at one point numbered ten people so he could deduce in his declaration 2,000 florins from his annual income on this score alone. By evaluating Salutati's earnings on a 7% basis less allowances his property must have been conspicuous and he was definitely among the 2% richest Florentines.

Salutati had fully earned this reward. The Chancellorship of Florence had been a very important post when he first took it over. But, by the time he had occupied it a few years its moment had increased immeasurably, and Salutati had become essentially the Foreign Minister. And it was just carrying out his task as Foreign Minister that Salutati excelled as a Renaissance writer, who directed his talents not to the production of a masterpiece nor to imaginative abstractions but to the active work of everyday, which, in his case, was service to the State. He did not write an epic poem but framed powerful epistles, admired alike by enemies and friends.

He was confronted with formidable difficulties from the beginning of his Chancellorship. Pope Gregory XI back in Rome from his exile in Avignon, cast covetous eyes on Tuscany and invaded Florentine territory. The result was a war that lasted three years and was outrageous for the many instances of perfidy on the part of the invaders, mostly mercenaries. Desperately, the Republic fought. Its troops battled under two standards. One, the city's, the other, a banner on which a single word stood out embroidered in gold: "Freedom." A reduced Council of eight members, ironically called the "Otto Santi", the Eight Saints because one of their duties was to dispossess Church property, ran the affairs of the State and supervised the conduct of the war, but it was the Chancellor who had to draw up the instructions to military leaders in the field and write almost hourly to the Confederate cities of the Florentine Republic. It required great qualities of persuasion and much versatility to deal with different minds. Salutati felt a not unjustified indignation against the enemy, an indignation which had first taken root in him when he had served and been exploited in the Roman Curia. With his insight into the affairs and twisted way of thinking at the Vatican, where each man was not only out for himself but determined to outdo and possibly destroy his rival, he succeeded in arousing disaffection among the population that were subject to the Pope. Then came what appears to a devout Catholic, such as Salutati was, the most terrible of punishments: excommunication. To Salutati it was a moment of extreme anguish but it is remarkable that—filled with horror at the censure— divided between his duty to his Church and that to the Republic he served—he did not have a second's doubt. There couldn't be and there mustn't be an encroachment of spiritual authority into the civil sphere. The clerical attempt to crush the people's liberty by resort to spiritual weapons must be resisted. The Chancellor was definitely not alone in reaching this conclusion. The words he wrote in missive after missive embodied the views of the citizens of Florence, who, reading what their Chancellor wrote, recognised their own thoughts in his phrases.

We have already said that prudence was one of Salutati's chief characteristics and, even in this moment of dire stress—he showed himself prudent. The Church was formidable—all the more so because he believed in it. Taking a long view, he did not meet it head on, as he would have done a worldly enemy. He first of all tried to show beyond doubt that the Florentines were innocent of the accusation levelled against them that they had taken up arms against the man Catholics consider God's Vicar. Salutati wrote: "Florence aims only at preserving her liberties from the attacks of the foreign mercenaries that the Pope has called to Italy."

But excessive prudence was soon shed and Salutati did not hesitate to write unpalatable truths. To Francesco Guinigi—Papal Legate at Lucca—he wrote: "We are well aware that the Papacy is formidable, but to us liberty is most dear. We cherish it all the more when it is edged about by a thousand dangers. We would not change it for a slothful servitude however blessed (by ecclesiastics). However great the peril, we shall counter force with force and show that the liberties of Florence may be threatened but not easily destroyed. God will judge the People's Cause and in His Mercy will protect our freedom and those of our children and of our children's children."

This letter tells us that, on reaching the Chancellorship, Salutati shed the cobwebs of medievalism that had hung about him in his youth. Entrusted with the duty of expressing the feelings and convictions of the Florentines, he emerges as a Renaissance giant.

The German historian Gregorovius, in his *History of Rome*, says of Salutati: that his "Patriotic epistles, springing from the indignation in the breast of a great thinker and written in the name of a powerful

Republic, are greater than Petrarch's declamations and querulous writings. The scandalous abuse of the Sacred for temporal ends was what aroused Salutati to the highest wrath."[9]

In the end, Florence won the war and secured her freedom. Salutati could turn to the peaceful pursuit of recording orderly government operations. It did not last long because the Ciompi agitation broke out. When Salutati had governed Florence through the disturbances, financial difficulties began to loom threateningly over the State. In consequence of the Eight Saints war and the rebellion, the public debt had soared. It went on soaring[10] until, in 1387, five years after the rising and seven after the war, it stood at more than 150 000 Florins. These were anxious days for the Chancellor. Debt might spell bankruptcy for Florence and an end to her trade and banking, endangering her liberty. The Chancellor found it necessary to start his working day at dawn and carry it on till late, very late, into the night. As if this were not enough, there came the threat of a Visconti invasion.

The Visconti, the Milanese ruling family, were strong believers in government by force and right of conquest, and had conceived the idea of making themselves rulers over the whole of Central Italy down to the borders of the Papal States. They argued, not without logic, that this would put an end to the factional strife between one small republic and another, between town and town and even between the clans and classes in each town or city. The strange paradox about Salutati is that he recognised, in his treatise *De Tyranno*, the validity of the Milanese argument. He even composed some epigrams "on Caesar the Conqueror, Augustus, Constantine the Great" presumably meant as captions to the portraits in Palazzo della Signoria[11] of these protagonists of One-Man rule. But his love of freedom proved greater than his appreciation of order at the cost of servitude. When Antonio Loschi, Gian Galeazzo Visconti's Chancellor, hurled against the Florentines what was then called an "Invective", (an official document to illustrate the reasonings behind a government's or a tyrant's action), Salutati answered with a powerful "Invective" in his turn. In the case of Loschi's Invective, Professor Eugenio Garin aptly says it was a sort of propaganda manifesto in the service of Viscontean expansionist policy. Salutati, in his reply, set out to rebuff Loschi point for point. To the Chancellor of Milan who had written haughtily: "We shall soon see the fortitude you boast of in defence of your vile freedom", Salutati retorted: "You have had ample and very good occasion to see (in the war of Eight Saints against Gregory XI) with what gallantry and self reliance the Florentines defend their liberties, which they prize highly but you call vile because you have never tasted them. How could you in fact know of freedom, you who have been at all times the lowest of menials? There is nowhere else in Italy or any other country a freedom such as the Florentines enjoy under the rule of law. It is so precious that you and your Duke can't begin to understand the richness of its worth."

The war proved bloody by the standard of those times and devastatingly expensive for Florence. Nicolai Rubinstein tells us that the cost of hiring troops which had amounted to 300 000 Florins in 1388, had soared to 750 thousand by 1391, and, by 1406, when the Florentines were at last victorious, they had spent something like 10 million Florins, not counting the ransom money to Kings and Princes to keep them from entering the fray on the Visconti side. Rubinstein explains that all these payments became possible only through an unprecedented flow of capital from the private into the public purse.

But the troubles of the Republic and the need of a firm but friendly hand at the helm of the State were by no means over. A pestilence struck Florence. Stern Salutati—at his post—refused to consent to his wife's desperate pleadings that she be allowed to take their children to safety away from the city. Salutati deemed it his duty to share the anxieties and—if God so willed—the sufferings of the poorest among the Florentines. He conceived it was the least that he, his wife, his children could do, since they had been granted the happiness and honour of becoming citizens of Florence. Two of Salutati's sons died of the epidemic. One of these was his favourite, Piero, who—he had dreamed—might one day in the future be chosen by the People to succeed him in the Chancellorship. Though heartbroken, Salutati remained, active, at his post. Then came the great news! Gian Galeazzo Visconti had himself caught the plague and, without their leader, his troops were in full rout northward. At last Florence was safe. With peace, trade would pick up again somehow. Debts would be repaid. The future looked hopeful. It was May and the scent of irises and roses wafted down from the surrounding hills to caress the City of Flowers, Salutati slumped down, dead at his working desk, his job completed.

CHAPTER SIXTEEN

Leonardo Bruni

HE next of the Florentine Chancellors to achieve greatness and contribute to the greatness of the Renaissance was Leonardo Bruni. He reached his exalted position in quite a different way to that which had raised Coluccio Salutati.

Leonardo Bruni, born in Arezzo in 1370, had to fend for himself when young and there is no indication of anyone whatever supporting him, while he studied in Florence. All we know is that he did have some relations who lived in the Tuscan capital and it must be assumed they helped him financially from time to time. Unlike Salutati, who, as a small town notary, lived a tranquil life of study for many years, Bruni was compelled from his earliest age to learn all the ruses necessary to earn his next meal. He learnt so well that he ended up far richer than Coluccio Salutati. The son of an impoverished pharmacist in Arezzo, a defeated and dependent town, in the last twenty years of his life, Bruni was known to be one of the richest citizens of the capital of Tuscany.

From Martinez[1] we learn that Bruni, when he reached old age, was the owner of five farms in the countryside round his native Arezzo and of two others, close to Florence. He had a palace in Florence and one in Arezzo; a villa at Fiesole and another near his native town. Martinez tells us further that—"his remaining assets—the largest part by far— were divided into commercial and financial investments and good firm Government securities. These last were valued at 3835 Florins. His cash deposits were spread over thirteen different accounts and amounted to 7445 Florins." Beside being exempt from taxation on his Chancellor's salary—as Chancellors always were—Bruni could and did claim other exemptions. While occupying his post, besides his normal Chancellor's work, he also compiled what to all intents is the best political history of Florence up to his time. It is not certain whether he did this on com- mission from the Florentine Signoria or not, but Donald J. Wilcox says[2] in a footnote that Bruni was granted exemption from taxation on "significant dates in the writing of the *Historiae Florentini Populi*. The first in 1416 (just about twelve months after he had started writing the *Historiae*). The second in 1439, when the first nine books were formally presented to the Signoria."

Lauro Martinez states that only six other persons in Florence claimed this sort of exemption. Bruni solicited it on a permanent basis. Both Wilcox and Martinez agree that so much is clear from "his two identical pronouncements in 1427 and in 1433" in both of which he claims to be exempt from the payment of taxes: "I protest that I do not intend nor consent to depart in any way from the provisions of the agreements I have come to with the City of Florence. According to these agreements, I was granted the privilege, a privilege that I intend to enjoy and hereby request it be observed, that I be immune from taxes. I neither intend nor consent that my wealth be included or written down in the taxroll."

This may seem in sharp contrast with the stern and meticulous tax declarations of Coluccio Salutati. However it would be hasty to leap to the conclusion that Bruni was less upright. For all his literary talent, Salutati did not produce a monumental work such as Bruni's *Historiae Florentini Populi*. The research, the thought, the careful weighing of facts lavished on it, entail a work that goes far beyond Leonardo Bruni's duties as Chancellor. His history is no mere account of facts. It gave the Florentines the foundation on which their spirit of liberty still rests; the basis from which Florence led the world in creating the yearning for individual and collective freedom after the Middle Ages. To be sure, Bruni was not the first to put this ideal into words but his mastery of language was such that what had been an intuition and a feeling became first a vision and then reality. Bruni certainly did not create the ideal. It had existed before and been voiced by Salutati. It had been acted upon on the ramparts in the desperate struggles against the Popes and the Visconti, but it was Bruni who found for this ideal an historical justification. It is uniquely illustrated and explained by Hans Baron.[3] He says that Bruni, with Dati and others less skilled than he in handling language, was the pioneer of a new outlook. Rome, as Bruni saw it, owed her greatness "not to her Empire, but the days when the life of the citizen of the Respublic Romano had found its fulfilment in active participation [of the citizen] in his Commonwealth."

It also came as a novelty to the Florentines, who had proudly accepted the theory that Florence had been founded by Caesar or Augustus, to be told by Bruni—as Hans Baron says—"that Italy and, in particular ancient Etruria, had been covered with independent city-states and that much of this flowering life was subdued by Rome's ascendancy but rose again" after the collapse of the Empire. It also must have thrilled the Florentines and made their hearts beat faster to learn that Tuscany had been originally a country of civic freedom and this explained why the Tuscany of Bruni's time was "the region of the greatest city states and the strongest lovers of freedom."

Bruni's work struck so powerful a chord in the hearts and minds of his contemporaries that, far from insisting that he pay his taxes, they provided him with funds (tax-free) to pay for someone to translate his work from Latin into Italian. They were rewarded by the excellent translation by Donato Acciaiuoli[4] of the *Historiae Florentini Populi*, completed in 1473. Bruni's great feat certainly cannot lower the heights Coluccio Salutati reached. On the contrary by giving Salutati a long established—if forgotten—historical basis for Coluccio's and Florentine greatness, it made its ideal spread to Europe and beyond.

Bruni was not Salutati's immediate successor in the Florentine Chancellorship. A series of circumstances, not least his ambition to make his way in the world, had driven him to leave Florence before Salutati's death, and take a post in the Roman Curia. So, when the prestigious office of Florentine Chancellor became vacant at the end of Salutati's life, the man elected to succeed Coluccio, was not Bruni, but one of the dead Chancellor's closest collaborators: Bernardo Fortini. After a short six months in office, Fortini too died. The choice of the Florentines now fell on Ser Pietro da Montevarchi. He stepped into the Chancellery on 28 December 1406 but, four years later, decided to retire to a monastery. This time, the Florentines anxiously appealed to

Bruni to come back from Rome and Bruni rushed back to the city he had once loved and called his own. His pay as Chancellor ran from 29 December, 1410.[5]

His personal circumstances when he took up office were quite different to Salutati's when he had become Chancellor. Salutati had been more or less at a loose end. Bruni, by contrast was on the first rung of a ladder that promised to raise him to eternal fame. The Church of Rome was then in the throes of one of her frequent squabbles between Popes and Antipopes, and Bruni's eloquence and literary ability was such that he and others had entertained reasonable hopes that his wise and clear counsels might prevail. He would have gone down to history as the man who reunited the Roman Church at a time when three different Popes contended for the tiara. It would have been an enticing prospect to anyone but the magnetism of the call from Florence proved greater and, after what must have been an anguished soul search, Bruni left Rome and its Curia to its troubles and took up the Chancellorship. He didn't stay in it for long in this his first tenure of office. Only a short three months after his appointment, three Popes of Rome, [only they were not all the sames ones as three months previously] were contesting each other's right to the Papacy, each claiming it for himself. And once again, the possibility that it might be he who would set things straight, would put an end to schism and forge a Roman Church united and triumphant, winning him renown for all posterity and beatitude for his soul forever, enticed Bruni back to Rome. However, between Popes and Antipopes, even the stalwart pen of as great a writer as Leonardo Bruni could not at that time bring unity to the Church, and, by 1415, he was back in Florence.

Understandably the Florentines did not immediately offer so volatile a Chancellor, as Bruni had proved himself to be, the same post again. But fully appreciating his probity and highly cultivated mind, they gave him an office in the Florentine Municipality. Then—after twelve years—in 1427—came his second Chancellorship. Though nowhere near as great as the difficulties Salutati had had to face on entering office, the problems that confronted Bruni required perhaps a subtler understanding, and a more pliant mind. Salutati had had to hold out and win against the Visconti and the Pope, both overt enemies. Bruni was called upon to re-establish Florentine dominance on the confederate cities and towns of Tuscany, which had manifestly or underhandedly yielded to the enemy.

Lucca was one of these. The Lord of Lucca, Guinigi, had actually sent 700 lances to fight on the side of the Milanese, and the Florentines were not unnaturally incensed at this behaviour by a town, bound to them by a treaty of alliance. However a large section of the people, tired of war, might have let the Lucca case slide, had it not been that Lucca had set a dangerous precedent that might well be followed by other allied towns should Florence find herself in difficulties in a future war. Bruni was one who advocated peace but was overridden and a Florentine army laid siege to Lucca on 28 February 1430. Lucca appealed for help to the Duke of Milan, but he, grown wise after two wars that had seen the Florentines undefeated, left Lucca's plea unanswered. Lucca, in despair, turned to Genoa for help and on the 2 December 1430 the Genoese defeated the Florentines on the banks of Lucca's river: the Serchio. The Lucchesi—drunk with victory—began inciting all the other allies of Florence to rebellion. A letter, accusing the Florentines of having massacred unarmed people in Lucca, was sent to Leonardo Bruni, Chancellor, who replied:[6] "Before I make full answer, I would like it to be clear that I am not one of those who approved the war against Lucca. I wish to state categorically that—before the People of Florence decided to wage it—I disapproved of this conflict, not because I considered it unjustified but because I believe all wars are accompanied and followed by so much harm and so much damage and other great upheavals that one cannot but hold war in horror. But, once the Florentine People had taken their decision to join battle, it was my duty and the duty of every citizen to accept and agree fully with that which the City had deliberated." Bruni then rebuts Lucchesi claims that the help to the Milanese had been sent not by them but by their Lord Guinigi, whom they had subsequently ousted from power. Bruni's rebuttal points out that cities or states who lose their liberty through sloth cannot escape entirely the responsibility for the actions of the tyrant they have allowed to take power. In the case of Lucca, there seemed to have been no protest whatever at the despatch of 700 lances in support of the Visconti. The impression was that the Lucchesi had sought the goodwill of both sides in the war, uncertain as to which would win it.

Pisa too had gone over to Gian Galeazzo during the war but her case, though far more damaging to Florence than the loss of Lucca, was different. It was not her benevolent Signior, Gambacorta, whose palace still adorns the Arno's southern bank in Pisa, to go over to the enemy. Gambacorta had been murdered and the man who had murdered him, not a Pisan, had called in the Milanese to control the mouth of the Arno river and Florence's natural western outlet to the sea.

Florence succeeded ultimately in re-establishing her predominance over both towns and this was due, in no small measure, to Chancellor

Bruni's ability. It was not a greater but a subtler task than the one Salutati had been called on to fulfil. Coluccio had fought and won for the liberty of all men against tyrants. Bruni, as great a lover of freedom, found himself compelled to limit for a time the liberty of action of faithless allies in order to ensure the ultimate freedom of all Tuscany. It is all the more remarkable he achieved this, while spreading with his literary works—the *Laudatio*, the *Dialogi*,—above all, the conviction that it is when all citizens are free to run for office or in other ways take part in the state's daily life, then the nation is at its greatest. Bruni was certainly not the first to think this out. Strangely he had been preceded by one Ptolemy of Lucca—the town whose liberties Bruni found himself compelled to circumscribe after the Visconti war—but it undoubtedly was Leonardo Bruni who popularised the idea and made it a fundamental conviction of every Florentine. From Florence it spread to other cities, to other States, to Europe and finally the world.

It explains the great respect in which he was held by his contemporaries. His monumental tomb in the church of Santa Croce in Florence, stands testimony to how much he was revered. It is a masterpiece by Rossellino, the artist who built Pienza for Pius II. The visitor can approach it by the side door half way up Santa Croce's right wall. On it lies the full length marble figure of Leonardi Bruni, clasping in his hand the *Historiae*, the *magnum opus*, which gave the Florentines their solid basis for their sense of freedom. Below the figure is the inscription: "Postquam Leonardus evita migravit, Historia luget—eloquentia muta est—ferturque Musas tum graecas tum latinas lacrimas tenere non potuisse." "After Leonardo migrated from his life, History mourns and eloquence is silent—it is related that the Muses whether Greek or Latin could not restrain their tears."

CHAPTER SEVENTEEN

Poggio Bracciolini

N the long line of humanist
Chancellors of the Florentine Republic, who, beginning with Coluccio
Salutati, placed their talent and their scholarship first and foremost at the
service of the State and of the People, there is one notable exception:
Poggio Bracciolini. While Salutati was the stern functionary devoted to
his duty, who defended with his fortitude and pen the Republic and
liberal thought in their moments of greatest peril and while Bruni, not
only ran the Republic's daily business in a period when the greatest
subtlety was essential, but provided with his *Historiae Florentini Populi*
the foundation on which Renaissance free convictions rest, Bracciolini,
on the other hand, paid so little attention to the calls of his office that it
was found necessary to flank him with a second functionary to carry out
all normal business, while he devoted himself entirely to learning, collecting or arranging the documents of antiquity he had discovered, polite
conversation and the enjoyment in every sense of his wife, the beautiful

Vaggia de'Buondelmenti, whom he had married when he was fifty and she eighteen. He had previously had a mistress who had borne him twelve sons and two daughters.

Despite this laxity in his office, the Florentines treated him well. Though not all his wealth came from what the Republic of Florence paid him, he was, by the end, extremely rich. He had gone to Florence from his native village of Terranuova, not far off in the valley of the Arno, with only five 'soldi' in his pocket in 1390 but, when he made his last tax declaration in 1458, his net taxable assets amounted to 7000 florins (5000 fls in various banks—970 in government holdings—his real estate was valued at 2500 florins but he paid tax on 1030 only because the houses used by his family, including his illegitimate children, were tax-free). Lauro Martinez in his enthralling book *The Social World of the Florentine Humanists*, masterfully sums up the figures of the steady growth of Bracciolini's assets through the years with the words: "Owing to lucrative affiliations with the Roman Curia, his humanistic connections, his commercial acumen and his Florentine friendships, Poggio managed to raise his family to the economic level of the city's oligarchical households." It might be added that, even when he married the beautiful Vaggia in her teens, she had come to him, not as a waif to a rich old man's arms, but as a young woman from one of the noblest families in Florence and a dowry of 600 florins.

But even this spectacular accumulation of wealth was, like the Chancellorship of Florence, only a secondary manifestation of his abilities. His chief contribution to the civilization of the Renaissance and of the world lies in his having discovered, after the long Middle Ages, numberless forgotten documents of antiquity, buried deep under the dust in monasteries in Switzerland, Germany and France, and elsewhere. It was because of the renown that all this brought him and the honour that it brought the city that the Florentine Republic, ever sensitive to humanistic values, was more than willing to pay him emoluments for offices he did not fulfil but adorned by his mere presence,[1]. It reached a point that even Poggio—moneygrabbing and shameless as he appears to have been—thought it was too much and in 1458, at seventy eight years of age, he retired from office. It was a magnificent ending to what had been at first a desperately hard climb, comforted only by study and by writing, mellowed by a keen sense of humour. After his earliest period of indigence in Florence, during which he nevertheless managed to study and had as companion and intimate friend the equally penniless Leonardo Bruni, he moved at the age of 23, to Rome and became Apostolic Secretary to Pope Boniface IX. The Reverend William Shepherd,

whose *Life of Poggio Bracciolini* (Florence 1825—Liverpool 1837) is
the most comprehensive account of Poggio, says "The appointments of
pontifical secretaries were not splendid" and adds that young Bracciolini "acknowledges that he had frequent recourse to literary pursuits
to beguile the anxiety caused him by his narrow circumstances".
Besides, literary pursuits were fashionable and opened doors that might
have otherwise remained firmly closed to a mere young secretary. With
his sense of humour and vivacity, he soon became a fashionable young
man in literary society and, when Boniface IX died, and Poggio had
been in Rome only about a year, the new Pope confirmed him in his
office of Apostolic Secretary. He was to hold it for a succession of
Pontiffs. His duties ended by taking him to the Council of Constance
(1414—1418) which had, as its main object to combat what were termed
in Rome "the heresies" of the Hussites of Bohemia.

Poggio, a free-thinking liberal of the Florentine school though not
actually born in the Tuscan capital, did not take doctrinal differences of
opinion very seriously and his first concern on arrival in Constance was
to try and find out if there were ancient manuscripts of classical authors
in the neighbourhood. He was appalled at the lack of interest of the
Council fathers in this matter. The Swiss too at that time appeared not
greatly aware of the glory the possession of ancient manuscripts would
bring them. They were bitterly to regret their lack of interest when they
re-arranged the magnificent library at St Gallen. By great perseverance
and indefatigable search, Poggio managed to gather what amounted to
rumours and, following these up despite the hard winters and the
difficulties of communications in places, he did find what he wanted.
Shepherd does not mention that Poggio, in his search, was assisted by
another great Tuscan Humanist, Aragazzi of Montepulciano, with whom
he was to quarrel later. Possibly assisted by Aragazzi, in 1416, Poggio
crowned many discoveries of valuable documents, when he unearthed at
St Gallen a complete copy of Quintilian, which lay deep in the dust of a
cellar. It was a work that all Humanists hankered after and his best find
so far. For long years afterwards, Poggio was known in St Gallen as the
"Dokumenten Dieb" the documents thief.

Leonardo Bruni, when he received news of the discovery of Quintilian, wrote enthusiastically to Poggio: "It will be your glory to have
restored to the present age the writings of excellent authors, which have,
until now escaped the searches of the learned. Your labours and diligence and the success of your undertaking earn you the gratitude not of
our generation only. It will be recorded in the distant future that these
works, whose loss to mankind had been lamented for so long, were

recovered through your industry and talent.'' No one seems to have said it, but it may be possible that the Florentine Republic's later generosity towards Poggio may have been due to this appraisal by Leonardo Bruni. Anyway, Bruni ends his missive with concrete offers of immediate monetary help should Poggio require it for his continuing searches.

The quest went on but it was not the only concern that kept Bracciolini away as much as possible from Constance and the Council. He was no enthusiast for the science of theology and considered that, rather than discuss subtle points of doctrine, it was far more important for someone like him, who was not a theologian, to help and contribute to widen the knowledge literary men had of the ancients.

However one could not study the whole time. Never one to neglect his own amusement and relaxation, Poggio took long leaves of absence from the Council for reasons other than the researches into antiquity. In the year 1415 (one year before his discovery of the Quintilian manuscript), the Council of Constance was passing judgement on John Huss, who had been inveigled to the Council with a safeconduct and a promise he would return safely to Prague after discussing his differences with Rome. Instead, as soon as he arrived in Constance, he was taken into custody and imprisoned. He avowed his intention of either vindicating the correctness of what he believed or retracting anything they could honestly convince him he was wrong in believing.

It would perhaps be hazardous to venture the opinion that Poggio Bracciolini, knowing he lacked the theological knowledge to form an opinion of the rights and wrongs of Huss's case, decided to stay away from Constance altogether. The fact is that he did stay away and was still away when Huss was sent to the stake. The official reason he appears to have given for his absence was that his health had suffered both through apostolic work at the Council (not that he had really done much) and through his long travels in search of literary treasures (these had certainly been exhausting). He went for a rest to the town of Baden, well known already then as a Kurort: a place of healing. He enjoyed himself there immensely as he says himself.[2]

"Every circumstance relating to the medicinal springs is so pregnant with delight that I frequently imagine that Venus, with all her attendant joys, has migrated here from Cyprus. The frequenters of these waters observe her laws with very great devotion .... The baths are altogether thirty. Of these, two are public and are frequented by the lower orders of the people. The males and females of all ages are separated by a simple railing. It is droll to watch decrepit old women vying with magnificent, breathtaking maidens in exposing their charms to the gaze of men, and entering and coming out of the water far more than one would judge necessary. The private baths are common to males and females separated by a partition. Nevertheless, in these partitions, there are low-set windows, through which the members of the opposite sex can not only see but also touch each other and converse.

"Above the baths, there is a kind of gallery on which people stand to watch the bathers and talk to them. As the ladies below go in and out of the water, they offer to the view of those above not inconsiderable portions of themselves .... Many of the baths have a common passage for both sexes, a circumstance which frequently provides the occasion for interesting meetings, as the men, issuing from the water, wear only a pair of shorts and the women's delightfully thin linen dresses are slashed on both sides revealing the neck and breasts. I really believe there are no baths in the world more efficacious in promoting the propagation of the human species. An innumerable multitude of all ranks come to this place not only to improve their health but to enjoy life. These baths are the resort of lovers and their mistresses .... Many ladies, not only throughout Germany, but in other nations as well, feign sickness merely to have an excuse to come to this watering place ... (many) come adorned with apparel so beautiful and costly to seem more fit for a wedding than for a cure. As for the males, you meet here with abbots, monks, friars, priests who often live with greater licence than the rest of the company. These ecclesiastics, forgetting the gravity of their calling, bathe regularly with the ladies and often, rush forward—quite unnecessarily—with an offer to re-arrange an unknown lady's hair and smooth for longer than is needed the silken ribbons which adorn it. All people here concur in banishing sorrow and courting mirth. It is astonishing that—with so many people of such varying dispositions—no dissension or hard feelings ever arise. There are husbands who, seeing their wives courted in a lively manner and spending evenings alone with strangers, are neither disturbed nor rendered uneasy. Jealousy that elsewhere causes so much misery is unknown here. How pleasant and unlike are the manners of these people compared to ours! I often envy the serenity of these Germans and execrate our perversity including my own. We are always after what we have not got and we mar present joys by a dread of the future. These people content themselves with little and so enjoy their days in mirth and merriment."

But to this lighthearted opinion of his fellow beings, Poggio added an estimate of strongest disapproval when, on his return to Constance he saw with his eyes what the Council fathers of stern Roman Church were doing. They had burnt Huss alive, and now they were all out to get the

Martyr's closest friend Jerome of Prague. Jerome—when Huss had been about to die, alone in the claws of the Council—had, as William Shepherd tells us "found himself bound in honour to repair to Constance and administer assistance and comfort to Huss in his last hours." Immediately after his friend's death by burning "alarmed by the violence of spirit which raged against all reputed heretics, Jerome fled". The Council, viewing with suspicion his friendship with Huss, sent him an order to appear before them. Rather naively, Jerome asked for a safeconduct. In the case of Jerome, the Council was more honest than it had been with Huss and they let him know that for him there would be no safe-conduct. Shepherd says that "Justly dreading the consequences of appearing before ecclesiastical dignitaries, whose morals and principles he had so often branded with infamy, Jerome set off to make his way back to Bohemia" and put as many miles as possible between himself and Constance. He had apparently not reckoned with what the lack of a safeconduct meant for one accused of heresy. It meant that he was "Vogelfrei" as free as a bird that can fly whither he will but is everywhere open to the shafts and the net of the hunter. He was soon arrested and brought in chains back to Constance. It could be that he lacked the heroic fortitude of Huss but more probably the fate of his close friend, a formidable threat as he mulled it over, during the long days and the longer nights in prison, may have made some doubts loom in his mind as to the correctness of all his views. In any case, on the 15 September 1415, he read in open Council a recantation of what he termed his "errors." He expected to go free but was detained in custody "to purge his soul in penance for his past sins". While he was meditating on and regretting his past, new accusations were raised against him and new articles of impeachment were formulated. Against these, he decided to defend himself. He appeared before the Assembly on 26 May 1416. Poggio was present and he sent the following letter to Leonardo Bruni, who had been his friend and companion in the Curia, but had now returned to the freedom of Florence.

"Soon after my return from Baden to Constance" Poggio wrote "Jerome of Prague, accused of heresy, came up for public hearing. The purport of my present letter is to give an account of this trial.

"I never heard anyone pleading a case, especially one on which his life depended, approach so closely and perhaps rival the eloquence of the ancients. It was astonishing and marvellous to witness with what clear choice of words, cogency of argument and conviction he replied to his adversaries."

After this very favourable appraisal of Jerome, of his culture and honesty, Poggio, who was a devoted son of the Roman Church, a firm believer in the Pope and his authority and laid no claim to a knowledge of theology, adds in his letter: "So impressive was Jerome's peroration, that it must be a subject of grief to everyone that a man, so noble and excellent, should have strayed into heresy. On this important point, the extent of my knowledge is such that I could not possibly pass judgement on so vital a matter and so I will acquiesce in the opinion of those who know more than I do. However I cannot prevent myself from entertaining serious doubts about it, in my mind. What I do know from my notarial studies and practice of the law is that the legal procedure followed in the trial was most unjuridical and illicit. Jerome was never allowed to speak in defence of himself. He was told he must restrict his answers to replying to the objections of his judge."

Poggio Bracciolini goes on to quote the words of Jerome of Prague, who exclaimed at one point: "What gross injustice is this? For long days and endless months, while I lay in filth and fetters in your prison, you have been listening to my adversaries and slanderers. Now you refuse to listen to me for a single hour. You seem to have prejudged my case and perhaps to have condemned me in your minds. Be careful, beware: you are not God. You are men and—like all men—liable to error, subject to imperfection. You must guard against it. We are taught to believe that this Assembly is the light that must guide the world. You are endangering its credibility if you fall into error. For the sake of the Council and the Church, do all you can to avoid this happening. I, who am pleading for my life, am a man of little consequence. I am ready to submit to death which must come sooner or later. But let not the collective wisdom of so many eminent men, to whom entire nations look up to for guidance, be proved wrong through the violation of the laws of justice."

Poggio says: "These and many other observations he made with great eloquence and held the floor though often interrupted by murmurs and clamours, scandalous in a Court of law.

"Despite his pleading, it was decreed he should first answer the charges brought against him. The heads of accusation were read out to him. The skill and judgement with which he replied were incredible. He said nothing that to me appeared unfit for a good man to say. If his real sentiments accorded with what he said, he seems to have been very far from deserving death. In fact to someone who is not a theologian, his principles did not appear to provide sufficient ground for the slightest offence. It seemed to me that some of the judges shared this view and that, as the trial went on, the number of those favourable to him was increasing. But then he was asked what he thought of John Huss. Without hesitation he spoke well of him, his erstwhile friend who had been committed to the flames for heresy. Many of those present, who had hoped that Jerome would escape death, cried out in distress because they knew that by taking the side of a convicted heretic, he had inevitably slipped into heresy himself. When the judges made this clear to him, Jerome proclaimed he entertained no principle contrary to or hostile to the Church's structure. He only bore testimony to the abuses of the clergy and the pride and wealth of some prelates. The resources of the Church should be mainly intended for three ends: to serve the poor, to help strangers and, after that, to erect churches necessary and essential to the faithful. Good men resented that they be lavished on harlots, entertainments and splendid garments.''

Poggio Bracciolini tells us too that he marvelled at Jerome's knowledge of the Scriptures and memory when Jerome, who had been confined for months in a black dungeon where he could not read, quoted word for word and without the transposition of a single pause, many learned writers in defence of his opinions including arguments by more than thirty Doctors of the Church.''

But by his staunch stand in defence of John Huss, Jerome of Prague had sealed his own fate and Poggio Bracciolini tells movingly the scene of his end:

"Jerome stood undaunted when they fastened him to the stake. No stoic suffered death with greater unconcern. When the executioner began to kindle the fire behind him to spare him the sight of the flames, he shouted: 'Light it in front of me for, had I feared death, I would not be here'. When the blaze enveloped him, he intoned a hymn and it continued to reach us for long through the flames and the smoke. Socrates did not drink the hemlock as Jerome submitted to the fire. So perished a man exemplary in every respect except in the erroneousness of his faith.''

This manifest interest in a victim anathematized by the Church alarmed Leonardo Bruni for the danger it represented to Poggio himself. On receiving the letter, which spoke so clearly of Bracciolini's feelings, Leonardo hastened to write back: "You seem to give a more ample testimony to the merits of heretics than I would wish for your sake. I must advise you to write on such subjects more guardedly.'' He added that such things as the burning of Huss and Jerome would not happen in Florence, but, were the Florentines to try to defend liberty of opinion as far as Constance, they would be beaten and lose their own liberty also. Coluccio Salutati—the great defender of freedom for everyone—might have answered differently and composed one of his invectives even if it meant sending his own children to the stake. His and later Lorenzo de'Medici's was the clearest perception of the division there must be between things sacred and profane. But Leonardo Bruni and Poggio himself had been long years in the Curia; they suffered the heartrending anguish of the countless multitudes, who saw that killing innocent men was wrong but, in their total acceptance of the authority of the Church, suffered the mental and soul searching torture of trying to reconcile her doctrines with her deeds, and , frankly, could not make up their minds where justice lay.

Poggio, for his part, would not stay in Constance. He set off almost immediately after Jerome's death to find solace to his torment where he knew he'd find it: in the search of ancient documents. He looked for them in the monasteries of Northern Europe. But leaving Constance and its Council was not enough. Mindful perhaps of Leonardo Bruni's warning that he might have compromised himself over Jerome of Prague and might do so again were any hint of his feelings inadvertently to escape his lips, he made up his mind to stay away from the Curia for as long as possible or long enough at least that the memory of his stand at Jerome's trial might have grown dim.

Extraordinarily enough, this decision brought him rich rewards and the discoveries of ancient documents he made in consequence were the beginning of his rise in fame and wealth. Only a few months went by and in the same year 1416 in which he had laid hands on the Quintilian—as we said earlier in this chapter—he ferreted out the first three books and half the fourth book of Caius Valerius Flaccus's "*Argonautica*". More discoveries followed in January 1417. A few months later, in the spring, he traced down the "*De rerum Natura*" of Lucretius. A few months more and, in the summer, at Cluny in France, he lighted upon no less than eight of Cicero's orations. There is a French saying in the Burgundian dialect: "Partout ou le vent vente, l'Abbé de Cluny a rente." "Wherever the wind breathes, the Abbot of Cluny makes an income out of it." This was certainly true of most of Cluny's Abbots from the moment the monastery was founded and endowed by the Duke of Aquitaine in 910 down to Cardinal Mazarin in the seventeenth century. Mazarin never went near Cluny, but, like many others, clung to the title of 'Abbot of Cluny' for the large income it brought him. But when Bracciolini visited the Abbey in 1417 and spotted Cicero's eight speeches, it appears the Abbot of the day for once made nothing out of it. Perhaps he didn't realise the worth of the discovery—perhaps he never knew Poggio had alighted on the *Orationes*, since he himself had never suspected their existence. It is impossible to trace the wily reason-

ing of the astute Tuscan Bracciolini undoubtedly was. Poggio himself
was certainly fully aware of the money he might make out of his findings
and had no qualms of conscience about it, since it was he who had
brought them to light from under the centuries of dust where their
custodians had left them neglected and forgotten. If any worry he had, it
was at the thought of the hundreds of other precious documents that
must have gone lost and decayed through the indifference of those who
should have been their caretakers and treasurers. That he was aware
that he had collected a hoard worth a great deal of gold, becomes evident
when we learn that he let word go round that—after his long years of
service in the Curia and because of his literary achievements—he felt he
was entitled to promotion and higher pay. In his days of indigence, he
would never have dared make such a claim, terrified then of losing the
little he earned. But now he must have felt himself out of the financial
woods, and he raised his price. He found the Pope (the newly elected
Martin V, a strong authoritarian) a non-taker for the time being. The
new Pontiff replaced Poggio, who was clamouring for more money, with
Poggio's friend, Aragazzi, who, being a monk vowed to poverty, could
accept no money at all and so cost nothing. This led to a break between
Poggio and Aragazzi who had been friends and searchers after documents together.

Perhaps Poggio was not as unhappy at this as he pretended:
Aragazzi would no longer be a possible witness to further priceless discoveries and second: Poggio himself may not have been distressed at
being, for a time at least, removed, far from Martin V, who, being a firm
asserter of the Pope's supremacy was necessarily an antihussite and this
to Poggio, after seeing the fate of Jerome of Prague, and Bruni's warning spelt danger.

Besides he had had an invitation from none other than Cardinal
Henry Beaufort, Bishop of Winchester, great uncle of Henry VI of
England. Poggio may have hoped for a great deal from Beaufort—whom
Shakespeare has immortalized in his Henry VI as an unscrupulous,
scheming, powerhungry, intriguing prelate. But Bracciolini was doomed
to disappointment. The cardinal, who had promised large emoluments,
gave none and, worse still, Poggio found out with dismay that the
English at that time, what with the wars in France and their dynastical
quarrels, had little time for the study of humanism.

Nevertheless, in England as everywhere else, Poggio soon dedicated
himself to the task he found most congenial: the quest for ancient documents. He rummaged in every likely spot with infinite pains. We have
little news of his findings, if any, but it would seem as if he met with

disappointment because he abandoned the search and set to, diligently, to learn the customs of the English. Then an offer reached him from the Pope in Rome. We would be welcome to take up his post of Apostolic Secretary again and at a much higher salary. It was the spring of 1423. He accepted and, back in his office, he seems to have felt far more sure of himself than when he had been in papal service earlier. He lashed out caustically at the corruption of the Curia and no enmity he aroused or reproof he brought down on his head could silence him. When, in 1429, a plague broke out and Pope Martin, with his Court, moved from village to village, always one jump ahead of the epidemic, for once Bracciolini found he could not search for documents. No one was allowed to leave the Pope's entourage and risk coming into contact with the plague and becoming a source of infection to the Court. But Poggio could not be kept from humanism. He set himself to writing. His subject was the Pope's most obvious vice: avarice which he condemns in the circuitous way so prevalent even now in the Roman Curia. He begins by dealing not with avarice itself but with the affection of some preachers. "So many of them do not preach with a view to doing good but merely to display their eloquence. They are not so anxious to appease spiritual anguish as to win the applause of those who hear them. They learn a few phrases by heart and utter them indiscriminately before the most different types of audiences. They discuss recondite matters, soaring through a scale of words utterly beyond the understanding of the uninitiated, leaving the distressed widows, the ignorant and the fools who deserve to be saved, utterly as they were."

Poggio goes on to declare: "It is difficult to decide whether squandering or avarice is the predominant sin of our time." He then attacks a particular branch of the Franciscan Order who had rejected their Founder's vow of poverty as applying to monastic communities and asserted it applied only to individual monks. The monasteries in question had accumulated and were amassing money and property.

As a result Poggio Bracciolini incurred the anger of many of the richer monasteries, but Martin V stood by him and entrusted him with the task to draw up a papal decree to prevent the building of new monasteries until all irregularities had been remedied. Some communities disregarded the decree and began to raise new buildings despite the ban. Poggio informed the Pontiff—as it was his duty to do—and the Pope immediately directed the Bishop of Fiesole, in whose diocese the first unauthorized monastery was being erected, to stop the work at once. A large number of monks and other ecclesiastics rose in anger against Poggio who calmly replied that it surprised him that friars should always want to erect their monasteries in the pleasant districts—Fiesole for example—where there were already Bishops and many priests. He had already criticized some monks as "slovenly, hypocritical vagrants, who, under the pretext of the religious life, do no work and make their pretended poverty and contempt of worldly things a mighty source of gain." They should retire to isolated places where they would not be tempted by riches.

The freedom with which Poggio writes of and tries to correct the vices not of individuals only but of all categories is astonishing and proves to what heights of authority he had risen in the Curia through his sincerity, frankness and his remarkable literary ability. When Martin V went to his reward, and Eugene IV was deposed by the Council of Basle, Poggio, as much a firmly convinced Catholic as he was a frank critic of the corruptions of the clergy, remained faithful to Eugene in the Pope's darkest hours. He had to pay for his steadfast devotion, when he was caught by the mercenaries of the condottiere Niccolo' Piccinino, whose plan had been to capture Eugene IV himself.[3] Poggio was renowned and people interceded for him. One of the first was the Prior of Camaldoli, the hermitage high up in the hills of the wild Casentino,—a proof that good and holy monks had appreciated and approved Poggio's condemnation of their richer confreres. The Count Guidi of Poppi also begged for Poggio's release. But the mercenaries wanted ransom money and Poggio had with him no valuables only manuscripts of great worth but that meant nothing to rough soldiers. Disgusted, they finally set him free, and Poggio reached Florence with his booty of literary treasures collected through years of search. With the sale of a copy of Livy it provided him with enough money to buy a villa in the Valdarno. Here was peace at last and security and comfort. Bracciolini settled down to enjoy them. He had a collection of 2500 volumes and documents, remarkably large for his era.

On 19 January 1436, he married the very beautiful and very young Vaggia di Buondelmonti, having first dismissed the mistress who had borne him twelve sons. Despite the fact that the malicious Niccolo' Niccoli called him a fool for having chosen "the career of the cuckold" sometime after the marriage, Bracciolini wrote of Vaggia: "Such indeed is her beauty that I cannot but reflect on the disparity of our years. However I determined to make her my own and I do not repent of my resolve. So much does she rise every day in my esteem that I hourly give thanks to God, Who has so bountifully provided for my comfort and satisfaction, that there is nothing I can wish for in addition to his present mercies." Vaggia was never unfaithful to him and bore him more sons.

And to the Reverend Nicholas Bilstone, Archdeacon of Winchester in far off England, Poggio wrote: "Though declining in the vale of years, I have ventured into matrimonial union with a young lady of great beauty and endowed with all the accomplishments proper to her sex. I thank the Lord for having bestowed on me more than I ever had the right to hope."

The next step upward was the Chancellorship of Florence and the freedom of writing practically without minding tedious official business, thanks to the reverence of the Florentines for literary men of Poggio's value.

He died while working on the greatest of his works: *The History of the City of Florence* from the war with Giovanni Visconti to events in the year 1455. It was the 30th of October 1459.

PART FOUR

FORERUNNERS

OF THE

RENAISSANCE

Luigi Pulci, *Driadeo d'amore*, frontispiece

CHAPTER EIGHTEEN

Dante

HE fountainhead of all Italian litera-
ture is known to all: Dante Alighieri. He was poet, theologian, scientist,
politician and soldier but, of all his qualities, the one he prized most and
excelled in, was the ability to string words together so they would not
only be clear in their meaning but would never be forgotten and, with
them, his own name would be eternal. He achieved the immortality he
yearned for through showing that the language used in common speech
could supplant Latin both in poetry and in prose if handled well.

He had his faults too and they were grievous faults. They stemmed
from his inordinate pride that made him churlish from his infancy,
supercilious when not downright unbearable, in his adult years, except
at times when he wanted something. But then he sometimes turned on
those who had helped him. He appears to have stood aloof from other
children from his earliest years. In all the great mass of his poetry he
never mentions his father, whose name was Alighiero and of his mother

all we know is that her name was Bella, family unknown. Yet Dante appears to have pined for someone who should address him as "my son". No one, it seems, ever did and it is only when he came to compose the *Divina Commedia* that he could at last place the longed for word "son" on the lips of three personages in his poem, beginning with Adam, the father of us all. The other two were: Cacciaguida, an ancestor and the third, Brunetto Latini, his teacher from 1274, when Dante was nine years old. It was a memorable year for Dante not only because he came under the tutelage of Brunetto who introduced him to Latin, French and Provençal, but because he met the girl who was to arouse the flame of poetry in him: Beatrice Portinari, who was only a few months younger than he. She did not speak to him. Neither did he address her a single word but the moment stood out in his thoughts for ever. It kindles the anger of Dantologists to say that the rising of the poetic strain in the little boy may have been due as much to the fact that Brunetto Latini had begun teaching him as to the sight of little Beatrice, not yet in her teens. It certainly is possible that little Dante may have felt some sexual urge, of whose nature he was not yet conscious when he saw the girl but that somehow it released itself under Brunetto's teaching. Strangely in the Commedio, Dante puts his master among the homosexuals. None, not even his worst enemies, have levelled the same epithet at Dante however.

So it seems probable that Dante channelled what must have been to him the strange and perhaps frightening call of sex into the vein of poetry that was in him and that Brunetto Latini drew from the little boy. Some Dantologists suggest that the emotion that Beatrice aroused in Dante, the motherless little boy, was the longing for a mother's care, such as he had known only in the first few years of his otherwise solitary life. They point to—as proof of this—that Beatrice was to become in the *Commedia* the personification of motherhood and of a mother's guidance. At first sight however, it would seem more probable that such a feeling, if it ever existed in the little boy, was likely to be aroused by a woman a little older than Beatrice's nine years. Giovanni Papini[1] in his *Dante vivo* says that the real root of Dante's poetry grows in the nostalgia the lonely child felt for the companionship his parents did not or could not give him. Anyway, Beatrice was a fancy in the young boy's mind but Brunetto was the living teacher who taught Dante the rules of versification and what to versify about.

Nicola Zingarelli, who wrote what is probably even today the most comprehensive life of Dante,[2] tells us of what turned out to be a little less ethereal coming together of Dante and a girl: his marriage to Gemma Donati when he was only just twelve years old. All that it had in common with Dante's love for Beatrice is that the two young people did not make love, at least not until several years after their marriage. More than a wedding it was a marriage contract, by which the young couple promised to become man and wife when they reached maturity. What Gemma got out of it we don't know but for Dante it was a great leap upward in society. He left an orphaned family and a stepmother anxious to dedicate herself to her own children and have him out of the way.

Gemma Donati's family were among the most powerful in Florence and one of the richest. He quickly took up their habits, particularly hunting and falconry. Zingarelli confirms that "judging by his many accounts of hunting scenes, one is justified in thinking that Dante had direct experience of the sport and especially of falconry". He describes falcons in *Paradiso* XIX, verse 34 and in *Inferno* XXII verse 130. He also re-lives in forceful verse proper hunts and the stalking of the wild boar and of wolves. He became so well acquainted with archery that he was one of the first to describe the threestringed bow, which was a complete novelty then. He also took up the arts of war, as was the custom of the dashing young men he now consorted with. He practised running, jumping, throwing the dart, riding with the spear and sometimes fought mock battles with them. He did not neglect his studies however. On the contrary, in 1279—two years after he had been admitted to wealthy company through his marriage contract with Gemma Donati—a way suddenly opened for him to climb and shine and outrival all the young bloods in Florence in the art he was best at: writing verse.

It had become the fashion of elegant young men to compose what we would now call "avant-garde" poetry. It did not simply mean producing verse in Italian instead of Latin, the language that had been used by poets throughout the Middle Ages. It meant writing with a clear, concise style free from academical affectations and pedantry. Attempts at writing Italian verse, some of them successful, had been made in the Sicilian kingdom of Frederick II Hohenstaufen and a little earlier by St. Francis of Assisi and Jacopone da Todi. But the poetry written in the Sicilian school was very highly stylised and conventional as befitted an Imperial Court, while St. Francis's and Jacopone's was confined mainly to ecstatic religious wonderment. The young blades of Florence introduced a completely different type of poetry. It had to be in language understandable to everybody and current with the people without losing any of its musicality and rhythm. It had to be in the language of everyday not that learnt in academies or practised in particular schools. The greatest test of its worth was not whether the learned approved of it but whether the people in the streets, the workman at his work, the woman at her laundry or cooking would memorise it and recite it to lighten the hours and days. Far from mystical raptures and fawning praises of Emperors and Kings, the Tuscan language was destined to become the "lingua franca" of the Italians, the "dolce stil nuovo".

The "stilnovisti", creators of a new style did however adopt a type of poem—the sonnet—that had made its first apparition in the Sicilian school, but they gave it a new lilt. Dante whose poetical nature craved for recognition threw himself with relish into the new fashion, but, though he wrote better than most, was not immediately appreciated. But he persevered and at last—in 1283—he again met Beatrice. It happened in the street and the encounter gave him the boost he needed to leap into renown. By this time, Beatrice was married and must have heard of Dante as a man of fashion and a budding poet. No longer restricted by the custom that severely forbade young unmarried women to address men in public—let alone a fop such as Dante now was—she greeted him. Dante tells us this proved a moment of "boundless bliss." But, however great the elation that Beatrice aroused in him at this their second meeting, he was extremely quick to make good use of it to advance in the estimation of the cultured and widen his circle of influential friends. Still fluttering with delight at having met his lady and heard her voice, he composed the poem that was to make him famous.

> "To every captive soul and gentle heart
> Before whose sight may come the present
> words
>
> Be greetings in Love's name . . .
> Joyful to me seemed Love and he was keeping
> My heart within his hands, while on his arm
> He held my Lady, covered o'er and sleeping;
> Then waking her, he, with my flaming heart
> Did humbly feed her . . .[3]

Having written his verses, Dante did not sit down to dream of Beatrice. In his future poems, she was to be in turn goodness, theology, mother, wisdom, the one to guide him to visions of Eternal Bliss but, at the moment, she was most definitely and prosaically the ladder he was determined to climb to win recognition and success. In effect, he did not send his poem to her as might have seemed natural, nor to the Donati who appreciated him already as much as they ever would, but to Guido Cavalcanti, the leader of the "Stilnovisti" whose criticism, in matters poetical, was universally accepted as law. Cavalcanti replied with a poem of his own, full of praise and unbounded admiration[4] and Dante found himself suddenly numbered among the Stilnovisti and a close friend of their leader. A few felt differently, some roused by envy, others to anger but Guido Cavalcanti goes down to history as the first man of talent to have recognized the worth of Dante's poetry and to Cavalcanti goes the merit of having helped Dante to develop his genius.

Very soon Dante took him as a model in all things—in the arts of war and those of culture, in sport and in merrymaking but above all in poetic feeling. Cavalcanti composed about forty sonnets and ten ballads and in one of them listed what were to him the most beautiful things in the world: the beauty of women—the tenderness of love—armed horsemen—the song of birds—amorous conversation—early morning in spring—meadows in flower. But to him and to Dante the beauty of women surpassed and summed up all beauty. The two young men however had different conceptions of their love for a woman. To Dante, Beatrice in the end became ethereal indistinguishable from goodness, virtue, blessedness. To Guido, women were women. He sang many a verse to his idol Monna Vanna but also took her to spend the night in one of his villas. This Dante never dreamt of doing with Beatrice, also because, while Monna Vanna was willing, Beatrice though pleased by the admiration of a young poet of growing repute, was definitely not. She was prone to laugh at him. She laughed openly whenever he tried to rouse her envy by flattering another.[5]

But, except for this attitude towards the female sex, Dante followed Cavalcanti in everything. Accordingly when in 1248, Cavalcanti was elected member of the Council of Florence, Dante's mind too turned to politics. He was only nineteen and not eligible to any post but he began revolving political matters in his mind. Convinced that his best poetry would always be that dedicated to Beatrice, he stopped or at least put a brake on his wenching. He was helped in this by the arrival in Florence of a Franciscan monk of Provençal origin, whose name the Florentines had italianised to Pietro Giovanni Ulivi. From the monastery of Santa Croce, the friar pleaded for a return of the Franciscans to their original poverty, to evangelisation through the example of a devout interior life. Ulivi's preaching and his writings were condemned during his life-time and, when he was dead, Pope John XXII had his ashes scattered to the wind. But the friar had many followers and Dante was one of them. Sometimes openly, more often in secret, he remained faithful to the ideals of the friar. Nevertheless at about the same time he consulted the works of Ahmad Ibn Muhammed Ibn Kathir, an Arab scientist in Spain and also became engrossed in Hippocrates, Galenus and other medical authors. He sat up late at night studying philosophy and science by the light of a feeble taper and his eyesight began to fail, so that he says "the stars became blurred and only through long hours of rest in the dark" were his powers of vision restored.

Cavalcanti was not at all pleased with what he considered his friend's excessive seriousness but fortunately an event occurred that brought the two friends together again. They were both cavalrymen. They both went to war together against Arezzo on 11 June 1289, on the stretch of flat ground known as the field of Campaldino, high on the hills between Arezzo and Florence. The Aretines were the first to attack and Dante himself was unhorsed and in danger of losing his life. Of Cavalcanti we have no news but he was part of the troop under severe pressure. It was Corso Donati who came to Dante's help and saved him. Dante continued the battle on foot and suddenly found himself confronted by none other than the enemy commander, the great Buonconte di Montefeltro himself, towering above him on his huge horse. Dante aimed straight at Montefeltro's throat and gashed it open, no mean feat for a poet just unhorsed. Buonconte's mount carried the dying condottiere off and Buonconte's body was never found. All we know about his end is Dante's fanciful tale in the *Commedia*. According to this account, the condottiere, fleeing in the general rout, found his way to the river Archiano and dismounted to bathe his wound but, weakened by the loss of blood fell into the water. Actually the Archiano is much too far from Campaldino for a wounded man to have reached it on a horse. But in Dante's imagination that is where he fetched up and died. Worried lest Buonconte's soul be damned in hell and he be responsible for this, Dante has him repent for his misdeeds and says that as he fell into the water he crossed his arms over his breast in the sign of the Cross. Satan then unleashed a storm over the Casentino hills where the Archiano rises and the flood, rushing down the river, unlocked Buonconte's arms. But, just as the prince of darkness was about to gather up the condottiere's soul and drag it to hell, the Angel of Mercy appeared and saved it. This worry over Buonconte's fate once he had died, (a worry that is not evident in Dante concerning far worthier people), is definite evidence that the poet did in effect kill Buonconte at Campaldino.

We next find Dante taking part in the assault on Pisa that followed soon afterwards and there he heard of the fearful punishment inflicted by the Pisans on Count Ugolino della Gherardesca, shut up in a tower with his two sons and no food so that, in the end, he ate his two children's dead bodies.

At about the same time, news came from beyond the Apennines of the violent death of Paolo and Francesca da Rimini. So in a relatively short space, Dante was offered dramatic subject for the poem on which the reputation of the Italian language rests.

Then, just as Dante seemed on the way to every success, and he had become a respected philospher, an admired poet and was fresh from military victories, the blow fell. On 8 June 1290, Beatrice died. The living presence that had kept Dante in a state of poetic and religious fervour was no more. He was distraught. Nevertheless he tells us in the *Commedia* that when finally he came within sight of Beatrice in Paradise she looked on him reprovingly for having found consolation with another lady after her death. However his little escapade, if escapade there was, did not last long and Beatrice was soon overpoweringly present in his mind, no longer as the vision of a human being but the personification of philosophy itself. As for his love life, he fulfilled his youthful promise to marry Gemma Donati. The number of children they had appears uncertain. According to some authors, they had as many as nine but the only ones we are sure of are two boys, Pietro and Jacopo, and a girl, who was to become a nun and call herself Sister Beatrice.

Dante at this point seemed to be settling down. He still wanted to follow Cavalcanti in political life but, to aspire to public office, one must belong to a guild, and practice the trade or profession that that guild represented. Dante chose the guild that was easiest to enter: that of the Apothecaries. He also practised as an apothecary and became acquainted with all the most loathsome diseases of his time, which he describes with great dramatic effect in the *Commedia*. He knew all about the smells and dirt in the hospitals of the malarial districts in the Val di Chiana, in the Maremma and in Sardinia. He knew about the frenzied itch of those afflicted by leprosy who end by tearing their skins. He could tell the symptoms of dropsy, which becomes one of the tortures he witnesses in his journey through the Inferno.

After all this medical experience, he was at last called to the office of Prior of the city of Florence. Little did he know that he was to look back on this Priorship as the beginning of all his woes. Actually the city was already in turmoil when he took up office on 15 June, 1300. There were two factions at war with each other: the Blacks, led by Dante's cousin by marriage, Corso Donati, and the Whites, led by his close friend and fellow poet: Guido Cavalcanti. The first had provided him the ladder to climb socially and had saved his life at Campaldino. To the other he owed his renown as a poet.

To avoid further fighting in the City, the Priors, of whom Dante was

one, exiled the two leaders. It has been said and written that Dante
showed great moral courage and devotion to civic duty as Prior when he
contributed to exile both his kinsman and his friend, to each of whom he
was immensely indebted. Others, among them the great Giovanni
Papini hint that he had grown jealous of Cavalcanti and resented his
verses being read and admired as much as his own. From the point of
view of their poetic quality, Dante was right. Compared with the sublim-
ity he himself had reached by 1300, when he was elected Prior, Cavalcanti's poetry might rightly be considered much inferior. To a personage
of Dante's pride it may well have been extremely irksome to hear Cavalcanti continually judged on the same level as his own.

Papini explains that the underlying jealousy arose from other
causes: "Guido certainly applied himself to study, but only as an
amateur, in the hours of leisure left over from amorous adventures and
political intrigue." One might add left over by frequent street fighting
when—on occasion—he had nearly been killed by Corso Donati and had
tried to kill him in his turn. To Dante, on the contrary, poetry and
philosophy were serious business. He had dedicated himself to the
acquisition of knowledge from the time when he was a boy and was
determined to become an erudite, one knowledgeable in all fields. He
followed Corso's falconry and Guido's dancing not only because he may
have enjoyed them and for their social value to him, but because he
wanted to learn what they were all about. His real business was writing.
To Cavalcanti, verses were just a way to relive his pleasures. To Corso
Donati they were just something to read or listen to. To Dante, who was
not anywhere as rich as they, it proved insufferable to hear the other
two, who lacked his poetic powers and widening erudition, treated as if
they were as worthy as he. There is certainly no indication that he made
the least attempt to help his friends when the Priors banished them. All
seems to point that he concurred to add to the severity of the punishment inflicted. Moreover the degree of punishment in each case was most
unjust and we do not hear of Dante raising his voice against this bias.
Corso, the victor of Campaldino, was a military and political strategist
of the first order. He was the most violent of the two accused. Cavalcanti, on the other hand was the fun-loving Leader of a party, which was
moderate, at least by comparison to Donati's Blacks. And what did
Dante do or at least what did he allow the other Priors to do?

He gave his consent to sending Corso to Citta' della Pieve (the Castello della Pieve) a healthy spot close to the border with the Papal
States. It was a matter of weeks before Corso, bribing or killing putting
to flight his custodians, was off at a gallop southwestward, towards

Rome, where Pope Boniface VIII was only too happy to afford protection to a Florentine, who might well, if helped by the Church and her Allies, become one day ruler of Florence, vassal of the Pope, and bring the tumultuous but wealthy republic into the fold of the dependencies of Papal Rome.

Guido Cavalcanti on the other hand, irascible but fundamentally less dangerous, who never would have sold the Florence of the Stilnovo to anyone, was confined in Sarzana, the perilously malarial district close to the mouth of the Magra river. The other Priors may or may not have known what they were doing. But to Dante, the apothecary, who had practised medicine, seen people die of malaria it must have been clear. He had full cognizance of what he was exposing Guido to, with his connivance at least. In his sublime poem, the *Commedia*, he portrays the ghastliness of the sickness showing he knew it well. In his list of malarial areas, he mentions Sardinia, where he never went, but is ominously silent about Sarzana, which he knew and whose number of syllables and accentuation would have fitted the verse just as well. Why? Was it perhaps remorse for having sent his erstwhile friend, his benefactor, who had launched him on the way to fame and loved him dearly, to a pestiferous zone in the months from July to September, the period of the year which he, Dante, knew to be the season when malaria is at its worst and most dangerous? Dante was no longer Prior when a more compassionate and just body of magistrates allowed Guido back to the city, only to die of the malaria he had caught at the Magra.

Meanwhile in Rome, Corso Donati was perfectly well and was having no difficulty in persuading Pope Boniface that the Whites, Cavalcanti's party, were enemies of Papal power. Not so his own party, the Blacks. Were they to come to power and he become the city's ruler, Boniface and future Popes could all count on Florentine support. What Donati was actually doing was selling Florence to the Pope.

But the Pope, though more than willing to make full use of Corso Donati, decided to resort also to someone more powerful to crush the Florentine republic. He induced Charles de Valois, brother of Philip the Fair, King of France, to cross the Alps and make an attempt to "pacify Tuscany." Corso Donati and the whole Black faction were to collaborate with Charles. The first step in this "pacification" was that Corso personally rushed back to Florence to meet Charles and "began sacking the city and setting fire to all the houses and properties of the Whites, among them that of Dante Alighieri". Dante was lucky to be out of Florence. He had been sent posthaste to Rome, as part of an ambassadorial mission of three notables, in an attempt to persuade Pope

Boniface that he could count on the Florentine Whites should he help them to resist the French King's onslaught on Florence, which, in their artlessness they never dreamt had been instigated by the Pope himself. It was a mission doomed to failure from the beginning. Dante might consider himself fortunate that—in travelling towards Rome to carry it out—he had not run into Corso Donati who was journeying the other way. He realized this when he reached the Eternal City and was able to weigh to the full the Pope's real intentions.

The meeting of the poet and the Pontiff was one of the most moment-ous of all ages. It certainly marks one of the most solemn hours in Dante's life and in the history of the fourteenth century. Both men were stubborn to the point of foolhardiness. Each considered himself above the other. Boniface because of his office, his wealth, the support he could command from mighty princes. Dante, (well aware that the Republic he represented had not sufficient strength to withstand the Pope and the French,) counting on what he knew to be, and was, his own higher intellect. The Pontiff representing the crushing might of the Roman, based on force, the recourse to outside help and when necessary to superstition. Dante standing alone for Tuscan wiliness and swiftness of mind. Dante had caused the death of his best friend. Boniface had imprisoned his Predecessor and let him die of want. It was a fight without an immediate conclusion: within two years, a soldier, Sciarra Colonna, in the service of the King of France to whom Boniface had appealed to help destroy Florentine freedom, slapped the Pope so hard with the back of his hand, an insult greater than had ever been hurled at any Pope, that Boniface, in his impotent rage, suffered a mortal stroke. Dante by then was wandering in exile, he too helplessly storming against his enemies. But, in the end, it was the poet who won and Boniface owes his renown not to what he accomplished as Pope and politician nor to having caused the death of another Pope, but to Dante, who, in the *Inferno*, puts him to burn in Hell.[6]

The sentence banishing Dante was passed on January 27 1302. Forty days later the sentence was increased to one of death by fire should Dante be found anywhere on Florentine territory.

Free from public office, having shed all his friends, Dante devoted himself, with venom almost, to collecting facts and searching out the innermost meanings of theology and philosophy, so that he could hurl them in imperishable verse against his enemies. It gave his poetry and prose a force that it would have lacked otherwise because he was not by nature the type to reach his highest composing madrigals. He felt himself and was to many the Vengeance of the Lord. But the Lord's vengeance also fell on him.

After many wanderings,[7] to the Court of Verona, to Padua, to Trent, to the Castle of Romena[8], then later to Ravenna, the guest of Guido da Polenta, the city's ruler who entrusted him with a diplomatic mission to Venice in 1314. Like all Dante's diplomatic missions, it was a fiasco. So little did the Venetians rate him that, when he began addressing the assembled Council in Latin, they roared with laughter at him and told him, who had composed Latin verse and written Latin prose that people had marvelled at, that he must get an interpreter because his Latin was un-understandable to them, it was so bad. Fuming, shaking with rage, Dante addressed them in pure Tuscan, the language of the *Comedy*. They laughed all the more; cried that his accent and expressions were incomprehensible to them. They, who had Ambassadors and spies all over the known world, who exchanged thoughts with Tartars, were just determined not to listen to his arguments and kept up the pretence of not understanding what was to become in time the recognised model of the Italian language. If he would speak to them, he must speak Venetian. He went back to Ravenna and his poetry, which was the mission he never should have departed from. But Guido da Polenta, benign and friendly, very full of admiration for him, persuaded him to take on yet another diplomatic mission in 1321. This one too was to the Venetians and again they would not listen to him. When he begged the courtesy to be granted to travel back to Ravenna by sea on a Venetian ship that was going there ... they laughed him to scorn and told him that the ships of the Serenissima were not for such as he. Humiliated, the great Poet undertook the journey by land through the deadly malarial swamps of Comacchio. It was July, just about the same month in which, twenty-one years previously, Dante had connived in sending Cavalcanti to catch malaria in the marshes of the Magra river. And now his turn arrived to catch the disease. He died of it on the 14 September. Justice appeased, he must have learnt at last that Christ is not only the severe judge in the medieval sense, nor merely the One theologians tell and philosophers try to explain, but the kind co-sufferer with mankind to win forgiveness for all women and all men.

Because of this, Dante's great gift to the world, the proof that the vernacular, of whatever language, could, if properly used, substitute Latin and make it possible for everyone to acquire learning, covered up and erased his many faults from the memory of men and the day of death 14 September 1321 is a memorable date for all mankind.

CHAPTER NINETEEN

Petrarch

ITALIAN poetry did not die out nor did it know a pause in its development with Dante's death. Within a few years, the torch that had fallen from Dante Alighieri's anguished hand, was in the joyous grasp of Francesco Petrarca, a completely different poet and person. A keen extrovert, he loved life, made friends easily and was faithful to them and they to him throughout his life. Above all, he looked on political and ecclesiastical office not as a duty or as an honour, but merely as the means to provide himself with a comfortable income that would give him ample time and pleasant surroundings in which to pursue his studies and compose his poetry and his prose. These he judged to be of far greater benefit to mankind than the fulfilment of the humdrum duties of a post, however exalted. His interest in politics, barring a brief period, was scant and when—exceptionally—he grew concerned about them, it was the poetic fantasy, the grandiose epic of the past that rose up in his imagination rather than the reality of his

troubled times. He never yearned for rank, but only for the benefices
that went with it. If—as he found—neither custom nor law supplied an
erudite literary man with an income sufficient to make him independent
of financial worries, he would secure—he decided—perquisites in any
way opportunity afforded and was in turn, canon, archdeacon, librarian and sometimes all three together, though he was much attached to
his mistresses and had illegitimate children. This did not prevent him
from taking Minor Orders, without the slightest compunction, provided
an income, not too much work and no preoccupation whatever went with
them. Unlike Dante, he did not suffer inwardly in the least for being
compelled by circumstances to live away from Florence, so long as he
had enough money to travel where he liked or live in villas of his choice.
Far from shunning society, like Alighieri, he loved to shine at Courts.
Dante had always aspired to be crowned poet in Florence and it had
been denied him. Petrarch, on the contrary, had the laurel offered him
twice over: once by the City of Paris; then, almost simultaneously, by
the Romans. He chose to accept it only on the Roman Capitol, because
his mind was filled with a belief in Rome's grandeur and, more practically, because being crowned in the Eternal City would give him greater
fame and a renown more durable, since he wrote in Latin and Italian.

Where Dante woke every day in gloomy despair and in a rage, Petrarch opened his eyes each morning on a world he loved and which he
expected to give him an added zest of life. The tears, sighs and sorrows
he describes so aptly and with such art, are mostly in his pen and his
imagination practically never in his heart. He spent his days happily
with friends or deep in study which he enjoyed just as much. His first
friend was a certain Guido Sette, his contemporary, whom he had
known when both were tiny tots of only seven years of age. His next
bosom crony was Giacomo Colonna, whom he came together with when
both were studying law at Bologna University under a renowned jurist of
the day, Giovanni d'Andrea. As is the way of the world, d'Andrea had
taken a lively interest in the young nobleman Colonna, and the young
patrician had taken Petrarch with him to see the Professor. Although
Petrarch turned the conversation from juridical matters for which he
had no liking to literary questions in which d'Andrea was by no means
proficient, they all three made friends. In subsequent visits too, Petrarch could not resist trying to assert his superiority in literary matters
over the other two and it is a remarkable proof of the charm of his
personality that he did it in such a way that never was there the slightest
dent in the intimacy the three had come to feel for one another.

The trio only broke up when Petrarch, on his father's death, gave up

legal studies and went to Avignon. He and Giacomo Colonna were
together again not very long after. Colonna was by that time Bishop of
Lombez in Gascony though he was only twenty-seven, and very much
dedicated to his duty. Petrarch too had changed but in quite a different
way. He no longer was the student wholly addicted to literary pursuits
but, together with his brother, who later was to become a carthusian
monk, wasted many hours in combing his hair, adjusting his dress and
choosing the tightest shoes to make his feet look dainty. Dobson tells us
the two brothers "not very expert in the use of hot irons, in their efforts
to shape their curls, often burnt large blisters on their foreheads. In the
street, their chief worry seems to have been that the wind would ruffle
their locks, or some animal, not too clean, might rub against their
delicately perfumed clothes."[1]

The fact is that the two brothers had both fallen deeply in love. Of
Petrarch's brother's girl all we know is that she died very young. But of
the lady who aroused the passion of the great Poet himself, we know
practically everything except, strangely enough, who she really was.
Petrarch sang of her to the end of his days but never revealed her
identity in writing. She is commonly believed to have been Laura de
Noves, who had married Hugh Marquis of Sade whose descendant was
to acquire fame for quite different reasons. Some authors think she was
Laura Colonna because Petrarch and the Colonna family were always
close friends. But then Laura—whatever her family name—was
definitely not a close friend of Petrarch and it is reasonable to suppose
that her father and brother had she been a Colonna would have somehow intervened with their friend Petrarch to stop him pestering her
because he most definitely pestered her. "I run after her everywhere,
but she flees from me like Daphnae fled Apollo"Petrarch tells us and in
fact Laura treated the poet with the utmost contempt as soon as she
became aware of his passion. She avoided him pointedly before people
so everyone should know how distasteful his approaches were to her.
When, at a party, the popular Petrarch, who made so many girls swoon
with longing, walked in, Laura would rise and leave, however exalted
the host and the other guests might be. Hugh de Sade, her husband
whom she had told at once, forbade Petrarch the house. She is known to
have been an ever faithful wife and, in an attempt to avoid Petrarch's
harassment of her, she took to always carrying a veil whenever she went
out; when she saw Petrarch in the distance, she would quickly throw the
impenetrable veil about her face; the same happened when Petrarch
walked in at any public function she also was attending. All he had was
the vision of a thick veil with a pretty coronet of diamonds perched on

top if it—a beautiful sight undoubtedly but not enough to satisfy an ardent young man who made no secret that he desired her carnally. Perhaps it was because of this veil that Petrarch described Laura as gloriously fair with very dark eyes (unless we are to assume she was a peroxide blonde).

Umberto Bosco sees in Laura symbol of the poetic laurel crown that Petrarch longed after even in his youth. She then became the personification of poetry itself once the bard had won his crown.[2] One way or other she was always a symbol, according to Bosco. But then why a Muse with eyes of a colour in contrast with her hair?

Perhaps no study of Petrarch's early love-life is so accurate as that of Arnaldo Della Torre's.[3] He inclines to think that Petrarch had his first sexual experiences in puberty. This view was strongly contested, only a few months later by Enrico Sicardi,[4] a priest, who appears earnestly convinced that Petrarch, throughout his life, was one of the chastest men of his period. But Sicardi has no very plausible explanation for what Petrarch himself says in his *Secretum* a sort of diary of his innermost feelings which he wrote in later life. In it Petrarch states most clearly that, with adolescence, he lost the virtues which had been strong in him in infancy. According to Della Torre, Petrarch had experienced love—we don't know how far he went—with Bolognese girls of good family when he was at Bologna University but then, when he walked past the block on which rested a head, all that remained of one of his friends, who had tried to abduct a girl of a prominent family and had been caught in the act by her brothers, he thought better of it.

He determined to resist becoming emotionally involved but to vent his understandable youthful passion on girls of easy virtue, unlikely to cause trouble afterwards. He seems to have succeeded until he met Laura in Avignon. There is no doubt that then, whether she were woman or symbol, his emotions became immensely involved. Had Laura been only a symbol why should Francesco Petrarch curl his hair, wear the tightest of shoes and the most elegant attire and accompany his brother on his love errands? Far more likely that a young man full of passion would produce the poetry he did produce, not to express symbols but to clothe his natural desire in sentiment and gentle thought. His longing for Laura was always thwarted. When their paths crossed in the street, she always made a point of going over to the other side or, if it was at all feasible, she turned down some alleyway where it was impossible for him to follow her without the risk of her escort dealing with him. The memory of the young man beheaded in Bologna invariably stopped him from following her.

But Francesco Petrarch had a very high opinion of himself and continued to be extremely persistent, though he never got anywhere with his Laura. Unable to satisfy his passion, he vented his sentiments in fine poetry until he managed to convince himself that his enforced chastity, where Laura was concerned, was something to exult over: the mainspring to higher poetical effort and, since he was never modest, to success. Undiscouraged by her contemptuous refusal to allow him anywhere near her, he just turned her contentedly, rapturously even, into a vision. His true Laura was no longer the living beauty concealed behind the veil but the laurel tree whose leaves would one day—deservedly as he knew—adorn his brow. He was convinced of it, though for the moment, he had to content himself with just sitting long and often under laurel trees. To Laura de Sade's infinite annoyance, one of her favourite walks was lined with them and she had to give it up. He doggedly went on composing poetry in their shade, delighted with his verses and himself.

In 1330, a new period of his life opened and it turned out to be one of his happiest. The friend of his Bologna days, Giacomo Colonna, now Bishop of Lombez, invited him to his diocese in Gascony. "He begged me to go" wrote Petrarch "when he could have ordered me" and it was not the authority of the Bishop but the call of a friend that the poet obeyed. At Lombez, he found two other friends who were to be spiritually and intellectually very close to him as long as they lived. They were: the musician Louis Sanctus de Beeringen,[5] a Belgian and the young Roman nobleman, Lelio Stefano, a literary philosopher. The meeting was important: with de Beeringen, Petrarch began what was to be his confirmed habit throughout his life—that of consulting a musician before approving his sonnets in their final form. With Lelio Stefano on the other hand, Petrarch relived in his fertile imagination the glories of Rome's classical past. This greatly increased his proficiency in Latin on which he prided himself. Bishop Colonna on the contrary tried to encourage him in what was already Petrarch's real mastery of the vernacular.

This continuous improvement of himself was marvellously congenial to the self centred poet. It also led to an advancement in his fortunes and to seventeen decisive years in his life. On the recommendation of his friend Giacomo, he entered the service of Cardinal Giovanni Colonna, just as the leaves were turning brown. His rank was to be that of chaplain and the emoluments most handsome. During the long seventeen years in Cardinal Colonna's service, there is no record of his ever having exercised the simplest ecclesiastical function. In fact, to begin with, in 1333, he asked for a long leave of absence, with pay naturally, and it was granted him at once. His friend Louis Sanctus de Beeringen had often told him about the libraries of Belgium and particularly those of Liège and Aachen. So off went Francesco to Belgium. But not directly. He went by way of Paris. With the usual haughtiness, that his contemporaries and posterity forgave him and forgive him because of his evidently exceptional charm, he described the French capital as "more insufferable than Avignon even". But, at Liège, he discovered two of Cicero's speeches. He does not mention, in his Epistle Senile XVI, I, the exact place[6] where he came upon them but provides the following haughty details: "I copied one of these speeches and found a friend to transcribe the other. It is entirely through me that Italy came to know of these masterpieces." He adds superciliously: "Is it not laughable that in so renowned a city we should find ourselves compelled to waste time and wrack our brain to find some ink?" When, at last, he ferreted some out, it was only very little and what incensed him more was the colour: saffron! a bright yellow! Louis Sanctus de Beeringen, without whose advice Petrarch would never have traced the document he had found, does not seem to have minded the unkind quip about his city. He merely asked: "Was not the glory of finding two of Cicero's orations by Cicero worth the effort of looking for some ink?"[7]

From Liège, Petrarch wandered through the Ardennes where a war was in progress. He took no notice of the clash of arms and instead wrote poetry by running brooks, while birds chirruped overhead or he imagined they did. Finally he got back to Avignon. Laura by now had definitely become only a poetical inspiration, so Francesco Petrarch took on a mistress in the flesh from whom he had two children: John, born in 1337 and a girl, Francesca, in 1343. He found his pay as chaplain was no longer sufficient to keep him in the comfort he was used to, now that he had a family to feed, a mistress to amuse, himself and his friends to entertain and his children to educate.

At this point, a sort of contest seems to have started between Petrarch and his friend Louis Sanctus de Beeringen as to which of the two would secure more ecclesiastical emoluments. Family or no family, Petrarch was made Canon of Lombez on 25 January 1335. Promptly Louis Sanctus became Canon of Saint Donatien at Bruges, though he had already been appointed Master of Ceremonies and Music & Entertainment to Giovanni Cardinal Colonna, to whom Petrarch was chaplain. Petrarch got himself appointed Prior of St. Nicholas at Migliarino near Pisa where he never went. Louis Sanctus secured the Canonry of St. Aimeé at Douai. Petrarch riposted by becoming Canon of Parma. By 1347, the two contenders were still neck and neck, but five years previ-

ously in 1342 Louis Sanctus had become Master of Music at Saint Dona-
tient with the obligation to reside there. Not to be outdone, Petrarch had
his son nominated, at the age of ten, cleric of Florence cathedral, after
he had been legitimized.

While this race for office (or emoluments) had been going on, Petrarch had not been the whole time at Avignon acting as chaplain to
Giovanni Cardinal Colonna. He had been very active with his own poetry
both Latin and Italian. In 1337 he had visited Rome where he was
received by the Colonna as one of the family and shown the curiosities
of the city and the traces of ancient monuments which then were not yet
uncovered. Because of this visit, Petrarch became almost obsessed with
the grandeur of Roman history and classical literature. Back in Avignon, he retired to the mountain village of Vaucluse where he acquired a
villa, which was to be his haven. He drew his salary as usual from
Cardinal Giovanni Colonna but abandoned fashionable dress and his
conversation was limited to that with country folk. He wrote: "It is
easier to accustom oneself to plain diet than to luxury." He underwent a
period of spirituality and began to realize he must turn his thoughts to
God and wrote his imaginary *Dialogues* with St Augustine in which
the Saint expresses dour words on Petrarch, and his conduct.

But spiritual yearnings were not the real reason for the poet's decision to leave Avignon and seek the tranquillity of Vaucluse. Rome had
made a terrific impression on his imagination and he decided to write a
Latin epic—nothing less than a masterpiece that would outshine Virgil,
such was his conceit. He would give it the title of *Africa* because he
meant to write of Scipio Africanus and his victories. It was never completed but it brought Petrarch a poet's laurel crown and a coronation
in Rome.

The invitation to accept the crown he was longing for reached him at
nine in the morning of 1 September, 1340. It was followed by another on
the afternoon of the same day. The first was from the University of
Paris; the second from the City of Rome. He opted for Rome. Coronation day was to be Easter Sunday, 8 April 1341.

There are many accounts of this coronation, many of them embellished by the enthusiasm of those who wrote them, but the ceremony
must have been one of the most impressive the city had witnessed in the
last thousand years. For once the Colonna and the Orsini had laid aside
their quarrels. The assembly gathered early in the morning. Trumpets
blared as crowds converged on the Capitol. The streets were strewn with
flowers. The windows filled with ladies sumptuously dressed, who vied
with each other to shower perfume on Petrarch as he passed. He was

preceded by twelve young men of the most prominent families in scarlet dress. Petrarch himself wore a robe given him by the King of Naples. Then followed six notables in green and finally the Roman Senator Orso dell'Anguillara surrounded by his Council. In his own account of the event, Petrarch says with many a flourish "Orso, a tower of eloquence, crowned my brow with the Delphic laurel amid the applause and festive cries of all the Romans. Stefano [Colonna, father of both Giacomo and Giovanni Colonna the cardinal in whose service Petrarch was] was so lavish in his praise of me that I blushed. At the end of the ceremony, we all descended from the Capitol and went to the basilica of Saint Peter, where I hung my crown before the altar in gratitude to God."

Among those present at the coronation was Cola di Rienzo. He was just one of the crowd that day but was destined to become soon, for a space, ruler of Rome. Petrarch and he would meet and correspond and inflame one another with a dream destined to come to nought.

For a moment, Petrarch was the more realistic of the two. He left the Eternal City forthwith, certain that the enthusiasm of the Roman populace would turn to derisiveness in a few hours. He proved an excellent judge of character but he had not really imagined what would happen to him. Soon after he had passed the Flaminian Gate (Porta del Popolo) to travel north, he was robbed, captured by brigands and held hostage until a ransom was paid.

This mishap, which should have shown him the true nature of the Romans, plunderers of the Etruscan traffic on the Tiber river long before they rose to be an Empire and destroyed earlier civilisations, should have cured Petrarch of his illusionary dreams concerning the Eternal City. But dazzled by the memory of his own coronation as a poet, he went on living under the delusion that Rome would one day become the leader in civilisation and culture and would attract again the world's great poets and writers as she had once attracted Virgil from Mantua, Livy from Padua, Horace from Venosa, and others from far away parts inhabited by her conquered peoples.[8]

Largely because of this mirage, Petrarch's coronation marks the high water level of his happiness and practically ends his contribution to the spirit of the Renaissance. After the magnificent ceremony on the Capitol, he meddles in politics, lives in daydreams, and gradually sinks to the level of a Courtier and a servile Courtier at that. Unlike the true men of the Renaissance and some of its precursors, Petrarch lacked the "common touch". He despised the large masses of those who were neither rich, nor noble nor influential and, as if that were not enough, he had the greatest contempt for writers who used the common language;

the vernacular, the vulgar tongue as he called it. A comical supercilious-
ness flies out from his comments of Dante and Boccaccio, who wrote
mostly Italian in preference to Latin. It is all the more ridiculous in that
Petrarch's Latin, had he only known it, was definitely not of excellent
quality and most certainly far inferior to his own Italian. He may have
had an inkling of this when he finally scrapped his *Africa* the work
that had won him the poet's crown and was in Latin. Perhaps for the
same reason, he also abandoned another Latin work *De viribus illustris*. But whether he realised it or not, it may well be that his pretenti-
ous, futile dreams of rivalling Virgil and Cornelius, only ended by
depriving posterity of some of the exquisite verse and prose in the tongue
which he called vulgar but which he knew and handled so well.

But even in his decline, he oozed charm. His foolishness, his egotism
and his pomposity seldom gave offence and, throughout his life, he
rarely made an enemy.

Immediately after the coronation, unwilling to go back at once to
what he considered the drudgery of his service with Cardinal Giovanni in
Avignon, he dallied with a newfound friend in the delightful aristocratic
city of Parma. His new acquaintance was none other than Azzo da
Correggio lord of the beautiful city, who obliged him with a castle in
which to spend the summer. When the days grew shorter and the warm
breezes turned to cold winds, Petrarch moved to a little house not inside
the city itself but on its edges, so that he could be alone to dream and
work in comfort at his poems and—should the whim take him to seek
company—all he had to do was to take not many steps and be in town.
But in these idyllic surroundings, the first great sorrow of his life struck
him: the news of the death of his close friend and patron, Giacomo
Colonne, Bishop of Lombez. However, Petrarch's reaction was merely
to continue dallying in comfortable Parma. When after months and
months of waiting, Cardinal Giovanni Colonna, from whom he was still
drawing a salary as chaplain, summoned him back to his duties in
Avignon, Petrarch complained bitterly; "I am being compelled to venture over the Alps, before their treacherous snows have melted. I am
being forced back to (Avignon) the infamous place which is the lair of so
much evil." He secured for himself an archdeaconry in Parma
cathedral, but back to Avignon he had to go. However when, on arrival,
he discovered that both Lelius and Louis Sanctus de Beeringen were now
in the Cardinal's service, his vexation turned to sheer delight at being
with his friends again.

It did not last long. The dreams of Rome's grandeur that his coronation had caused to swell even more in his mind, made him enter politics

and he was definitely no politician. Events were racing towards revolution in the Eternal City. A deputation of Romans led by Cola di Rienzo arrived in Avignon to persuade the Pope to hold Jubilee in 1350 in Rome, and so give official recognition to the new popular government Cola had set up after toppling the Roman nobles. To perorate his case more cogently Rienzo asked that not he alone but also the Poet Laureate address the Pontiff. Rienzo's speech turned out to be far better than Petrarch's but even it failed to win the Pope's approval for the new government. After this fiasco, the Pontiff, to get Petrarch's mind off revolutions and revolutionary governments, decided to send the bard to Naples to take possession of the Neapolitan Kingdom, then vacant because the rightful sovereign Queen Joan was still a minor. Petrarch failed again though from his own point of view, he occupied the time of his stay in Naples most usefully, visiting the surroundings particularly the places described by Virgil, whom he intended to emulate and surpass. Finally, because a storm and an earthquake had terrorised him, he abandoned his mission. But his troubles were not over. On the way back to Avignon the discomfited diplomatist was attacked by robbers and barely escaped with his life. It is no wonder that, when at last he reached his destination, he retired to his villa at Vaucluse for a little peace. He also asked Cardinal Giovanni Colonna, who had showered benefits and courtesies and love on him to release him from his service. The Cardinal, perhaps a little tired of his unpredictable whims, embraced him and bid him farewell.

At Vaucluse, during the Lent of 1347 Petrarch was lifted almost to heaven by the news that reached him: Cola di Rienzo had been proclaimed by the Roman populace ruler, sovereign almost, of Rome. He wrote at once a long missive to Cola and in it we regrettably find Petrarch's only real act of disloyalty to the Colonnas who had raised him and fed him for so long. In his letter to Cola, he describes the Colonnas as of "German origin and therefore utterly unworthy to be numbered among Romans." Then on 20 November 1347, he set out for Rome full of hope for an imagined restoration of Roman authority over Europe that never materialised and is never likely to. Count Cipolla[9] thinks he wanted Rome's power established over the whole of Italy at least. Another author says: "In 1347 the poet resolved to return to Italy and witness in person the reawakening of the Eternal City, helping with his advice the glorious enterprise of the Tribune (Cola di Rienzo)."

Then Petrarch's exultance was subjected to the coldest of showers. On reaching Italian soil, he learnt that Rienzo had killed several members of the Colonna family and had even cast into prison the head of the

Colonna clan for having dared to criticize him for wearing dress far more costly than that of any prince, while, at the same time, proclaiming himself the humble "Tribune of the People". When he heard of this petty outrage, Petrarch felt all his old loyalty to the Colonna family surge in his breast again. He sat down and wrote to Cola: "Splendid was your rise, Nicola, but it is easy to fall into Avernum. You do not base your powers of government on the Roman People but on the worst possible portion of it." He ended his valediction with the words "Flecto iter" "I turn another way."

It was the sad finale to Petrarch's dreams of reviving Rome's greatness through a popular rising. Dejectedly he went back to his little house in Parma.

Once there, he hoped to form a little community with some of his friends and even offered them the use of his town house, should they find his little villa on the outskirts insufficient to hold them all in comfort. It was not to be. Two of the members of the proposed literary community were waylaid by brigands and killed and, rather than expose others to a similar fate, Petrarch gave up the idea.

There is no point in following all the Poet's wanderings to Verona and Padua and elsewhere but, after three years, he was on his way to Rome again, not to stir a revolution this time but to attend the Holy Year 1350. This journey is memorable because, nearing Florence, he met Boccaccio, who had rushed out to meet him before he reached the city and, before anyone else could, invited him to stay with him as long as he liked. Kindly Boccaccio was to obtain for Petrarch the full restitution of the properties the Florentine authorities had confiscated from his father in the times of Corso Donati. He also obtained for Petrarch a post of professor at Florence University but Petrarch, ungraciously, declined it and, on his return from Rome, went back to Avignon where he stayed over two years, wandering between it and Vaucluse. Though he never regretted them, Boccaccio was soon to have weightier reasons to lament his acts of kindness to Petrarch.

When the poet returned to Italy early in May 1453, he took a decision which hurt and shocked Boccaccio deeply and incensed each and every Florentine. He accepted the invitation of Giovanni Visconti, Archbishop and tyrant of Milan, inveterate enemy of Florence, to enter his service. Visconti's offer was couched in courteous terms but Petrarch's consent to it put the poet right out of the ranks of the writers of the liberal Renaissance to which he should have belonged. Instead he became a courtier.

Thomas Campbell[10] says the poet's new abode in Milan was beautiful with an imposing view as far as the distant Alps. It was in a quiet street near St Ambrose and, since Petrarch complained there was no garden, he was granted the full use of that of the cathedral. Petrarch seems to have preferred all this to his lost liberty. To Boccaccio who was particularly severe towards the man he had taken so much trouble to reinstate in Florence and provide with his father's capital, Petrarch gave only inconsistent answers. He wilfully pretended to misunderstand the vigorous protests of other Florentines, who deprecated that the poet, who had sung of freedom and posed as its lover, should have become the slave of a tyrant, who united in his person the ecclesiastic with the secular power and made all Italy tremble with his plans of reducing the whole country, and especially the Florentine republic, under his sway. Blandly Petrarch assured them in his reply that they need have no worry for his safety. He was no slave. He was free, he told them. But it was not the danger of his being imprisoned that they had feared but his loss of character—the fact that they would henceforth have to despise him as an opportunist. Finally Petrarch, torn between shame and the impossibility of breaking his engagement with the powerful lord of Milan, gave an answer that was both absurd and despicable. He asked his friends how did they think it was possible for one man to resist the demands of so powerful a master as Visconti. With this, he sank to the depths of ingloriousness in the eyes of the Florentines and of Boccaccio in particular. And it was all for nothing. He soon found that serving the Lord of Milan was no comfortable sinecure such as he had been used to. He had to appear at all feasts and show himself as one of the adornments of the Milanese Court to visitors of consequence. The first of these was Cardinal Albornoz, a famous soldier from the province of León in Spain, who passed through Milan on his way to subdue with the sword the lands the Pope lay claim to in Northern Italy. Petrarch outdid himself in servility, on this occasion. He—who had sung of glory and freedom—insisted on being one of the outriders who went out to meet Albornoz before he reached the city. As if that were not sufficient, claiming that the dust the group raised was too much for him, he went ahead of the cavalcade and was the first to find himself face to face with the redoubtable cardinal. With a gesture that would have drawn long laughter from the freedom-loving Florentines, he doffed his hat, backing his horse, the animal's neck well arched as if it too were curtseying. Unfortunately he had not noticed that—at the back of him—was an escarpment, down which went the hindquarters of his mount which lost its footing. But here the poet's undoubted charm came into play. With great dexterity, he gave the horse its head and, though he had to dismount quickly, the animal did not roll on him and crush him, and, after a moment, he was back in the saddle without help from anyone. The poet's equestrian ability and his smiling composure through it all, won the heart of Albornoz and Petrarch was able to ask him for several favours while his visit lasted.

Giovanni Visconti, Lord of Milan, died in October 1354 but even that proved an occasion for Petrarch arousing laughter at his own expense. He had been told to deliver the valedictory oration. Well versed in speaking, he started admirably, but then, in the middle of his peroration, the Court Astrologer suddenly rushed forward announcing that the moment had arrived, which the stars indicated as the most propitious for passing materially the insignia of power to the Archbishop's successors, the dead man's nephews Matteo Barnaba and Galeazzo. There were some protests and much laughter at the interruption, but—in any case—the effect of Petrarch's speech was spoilt.

It is no wonder that—by this time—Petrarch wanted to shake himself free of the Visconti. He thought an opportunity had arrived when, shortly after, Emperor Charles IV, wishing to be crowned in Rome, crossed the Alps southward with an escort of only 300 horsemen. Petrarch hailed him in an enthusiastic missive: "You are no longer merely the King of Bohemia but King of the Globe, Roman Emperor, true Caesar." For the moment however the true Caesar was prosaically detained at Mantua by a severe frost. It did not prevent Petrarch from rushing to him. His charm, despite his inconsistencies pleased the Emperor, who asked to see the work Petrarch was believed to have finished *De viribus illustris*. Always quick to make the most of any occasion, Petrarch explained that, in the arduous service of the Visconti, he had had no time to complete it and that he needed leisure to work in peace. But Emperor Charles offered no residence, no emolument, no post entailing little work and an ample salary. Further attempts by Petrarch in the days that followed brought the same result and he thought better of it than to leave the security, however irksome, the Visconti provided him with. He congratulated himself on this decision, when Charles arrived in Milan, greeted with a show of homage but made to stand and watch the march-past of one of the mightiest armies of the era: 10,000 foot, burgher companies well-mounted and magnificently armed. Compared to the force the Visconti could count on, the Emperor's 300 horsemen looked puny. Charles realised this and, pleading he was tired, tried to leave the window where they had stationed him, but they put Petrarch by his side to converse with him and be witty and keep up the simulation that all was courtesy. It was not the only time Petrarch was given a similar task. In fact, a year later, in 1356, after

Charles IV had been to Rome, had been crowned and was back home from Italy, the Visconti told their poet laureate to hasten to Prague, the imperial capital, and somehow dispel what must certainly be the Emperor's deep displeasure at the way he had been intimidated in Milan. Full of contempt for Charles IV, Petrarch went to Prague and, certain he had fulfilled his mission, when he returned to Milan told his masters they need have no worry; the Emperor would never attack them. But his ornate speech was interrupted, not by an astrologer this time, but by the far more disturbing news that the Emperor's Vicar in Italy had attacked the State of Milan and was advancing on Milanese territory. The Visconti upbraided Petrarch very roughly for the groundless assurances he had just been giving them and the vain supercilious poet realized too late that he was no match for the monarch he had so haughtily despised.

As if to add mockery to injury soon after a diploma reached Petrarch from the Emperor himself awarding him the title of Count Palatine. The Visconti suspected it might be Charles's way of rewarding the poet for having unwittingly helped the imperial attack on Milan through his artlessness in politics. It is not certain this was so but then Charles's dour humour seems never to have been fully appreciated. What is positive is that, from that moment, the Visconti practically ceased to avail themselves of Petrarch's services. Far from upsetting him, this delighted him immensely. Free from Court functions and assignments, he dedicated himself to what he should never have left; his writing and his friends. In October 1359 he was able to welcome in his Milanese home Giovanni Boccaccio, who had forgiven and forgotten the wavering and grovelling of his idol, now that that idol had gone back to writing.

The friendship with Boccaccio was renewed in 1363, after Petrarch had fled a pestilence that had broken out in Milan two years earlier and had retired first to Padua then to Venice. His mind bent on death he offered the Venetian Republic to become the heir of his priceless and abundant library. By way of thanks, they assigned him a magnificent residence, the Palazzo Molin on the Riva degli Schiavoni popularly known as 'Two Towers'. Here he received Boccaccio, the faithful admirer of his writings and Boccaccio stayed with him for three months. It was their last meeting and Hutton says: "The greatest prose writer in the Italian language and the greatest story teller in the world considered himself of no account beside the pedantic lover of Laura.[11]" Petrarch does not seem to have noticed anything extraordinary in Boccaccio's praises. Though Boccaccio was indigent and he was wealthy, he never once, throughout his life made any return for any one of Boccaccio's valuable and numerous presents: a volume of the *Divine Comedy*, painstakingly copied by Boccaccio himself; several Latin works of great value. He merely said that it was despicable of Dante to write Italian and not Latin. Hardly an appreciation of Boccaccio's laboriously worked over present.

It shows Boccaccio's humility that, after he had gone home, he sent his supercilious idol his *Decameron* for appraisal. The aged bard wrote to the great prose writer: "I have run over your *Decameron*. On the whole, from a cursory glance, it gives me pleasure. The licentiousness in it is excusable since you wrote the book when you were young. I did as most readers will surely do. I read attentively the beginning and the end and skipped through the rest. However your description of people is truthful and pathetic."

Soon after Petrarch was found dead in his house at Arqua', not far from Padua to which he had moved from Venice. They found him in the morning at his writing table, his forehead on one arm resting on a book he had been reading, one of Virgil's, the poet he had dreamt he would surpass. It was 19 July 1374.

CHAPTER TWENTY

BOCCACCIO

ETRARCH'S disparaging assessment of Boccaccio's talent as a writer was utterly wrong. Not many years went by that in England, Germany, France and Spain—practically the whole of Europe—Boccaccio's name was spoken and the *Decameron* was translated into many languages. Great writers,—Chaucer in England, Christine de Pisan in France, Juan de Mena and the Marquis of Santillana in Spain,—could see no better way to glorify their respective languages than to follow in Boccaccio's—humble and hungry Boccaccio's—footsteps. It is a sad reflection on Italy that there, in Boccaccio's own native country, recognition came only later. It was after seventy to a hundred years and more that "his subjects were taken up with delight by Bernardo Accolti and Machiavelli."[1]

In the seventeenth century, some 300 years later, the powerful, self satisfied and triumphant Roman Church of the Counter-reformation saw in the modest man from Certaldo a danger to itself yet realized it could not obliterate his masterpiece. It made the laughable attempt to divert all interest from the *Decameron*, by expurgating it. With fervent and ill-directed zeal, the Church of Rome ordered the amputation in all Boccaccio's writings "of anything that might be considered harmful to the reputation of the clergy." But what does that prove down the years, even to our day? It demonstrates that the *Decameron*'s structural and linguistic perfection, its liveliness, its human values, cannot be denied. As if this truth did not speak for itself, a note in the censored version says that "the work of expurgation has been carried out with due consideration for the fact that, in this writer, what one must pay attention to is the linguistic value. To look for subjects of laughter in his writings can arise only from base incontinence".

A few years later, church criticism of the *Decameron* went further. It extended to its content and its style. The longwinded and affected Italian writers of the day, most of them long forgotten, dared define Boccaccio "artificial, faulty in syntax and grammar, most definitely plebeian". But Hauvette[2] says: "Boccaccio knew what words and phrases to put into the mouths of common folk, in the language form they express themselves best."

That is Boccaccio's great achievement: the characters he describes belong to all classes and they really live. Unlike Petrarch whose experiences were limited to the upper spheres of society:—to Popes, Kings, Dukes and Princes, at times an Emperor and always a cardinal or two,—Boccaccio did spend his youthful years in the brilliant Court at Naples but was also in daily contact with the poorest and later he was practically a pauper himself so he knew poverty and the poor both from observation and experience. He knew what pestilence looked like and what hunger could turn human beings into. He knew the lowliest workers and the thieves, the have-nots and the whores and from Boccaccio we learn exactly what they were like in his day, how they lived and loved and felt, how they suffered and how they had fun and what that fun was and, reading Boccaccio, they re-live and breathe. To suppress Boccaccio is to suppress the truth of life as it really is. Yet this is what people aimed at for 300 years and Vittore Branca tells us that the century of enlightenment brought only a slight change in the fortunes of Boccaccio's masterpieces and that it was not until the nineteenth century that "interest widened on both sides of the Alps and the whole of his writings, those best known and also his youthful literary production, were gone into with great diligence."[3] As a result, the *Decameron* came to be considered "the highlight of an artistic development at the confluence of cultural with popular currents." That was Boccaccio's pride had he

lived to see it. He was the first to bring a popular content to erudition
and thereby opened culture to the people and led the way to what was to
be the major achievement of the Renaissance: the raising of the common
man.

Boccaccio was interested in poetry from his early youth but his
father, a practical man, wanted him to become a merchant and sent him
to Naples to learn a merchant's ways. Throughout his life, Giovanni was
to suffer from an inferiority complex because he considered he had lost
six years that should have been devoted to classical studies and to literature. It is perhaps because of this complex that, despite the unique
powers of his imagination, most of his early works were based on humble
imitations of stories drawn from the classics of antiquity or from
medieval minstrels. One of the most imaginative authors of all times
dared not, for a span, commit his fantasies to paper and his pen followed
the well-tried path of those who had gone before, even when recounting
his own personal experiences. It seems incredible, but not unlike
Shakespeare even when our Boccaccio talks of nymphs and fauns that
Ovid or some other genius of antiquity had created (or copied from the
Greeks) one suddenly realises Giovanni is relating his own experiences
and thoughts and that the people he writes of talk and move and act like
the real people of his time. He was in continual contact with them from
behind the counter of the Neapolitan branch of the Bardi Bank to whom
his father had entrusted him and under whose care he was meant to
learn the mysteries of finance and trade. He does not appear to have
done so. He developed instead those powers of observation and human
understanding that were in time to make him the greatest story-teller of
the world though not a merchant.

His father had been a wealthy Florentine merchant, an associate of
the Bardi Bank, which practically dominated the Neapolitan Court
through the large loans it granted to the King and nobles. As the son of
an associate of so useful and generous a creditor, Giovanni was admitted
to the Court. In 1363 he was to write: "I lived from my early years to the
ripeness of manhood in Naples among young noblemen who, though of
gentle blood, did not disdain to frequent my house which was as splendid
as my possibilities allowed."

We must be thankful for this short piece of Boccaccio's autobiogra-
phy since his relations with the Society of his times present a problem.
Authorities on the subject are divided into two schools, each opposed to
the other and each holding passionately to its own conviction. There is
the older school of those who believe that Boccaccio's works are, in
allegorical form, an embellished account of the author's own life:- of his

feelings and experiences and of his loves. If that is so we have little difficulty in following Boccaccio's bonds with his contemporaries.

But a more modern school, led by two most eminent experts, Vittore Branca and Giuseppe Billanovich[4] refutes the earlier theories and contends that Boccaccio's prose and poetry, aflame with love and passion as it is, is mostly wishful thinking. His words, realistic enough in their description of passion, loveplay and delightfully releasing climax, according to this school, represent what he wished had happened not what did, in point of fact, occur. This conviction is based on the circumstance, certainly true, that there are no documents or tales, other than Boccaccio's, to corroborate what he says. Followers of the old school contend with equal assurance that there could not be corroborating written evidence of secret love affairs.

Authorities disagree even over the date and place of Boccaccio's birth. The traditional view is that he was born in Paris, out of wedlock, of a girl called Jeanne or Jeannette, whom his father Boccaccino abandoned to marry a Florentine, Margherita de'Martoli. In the *Filocolo*, his earliest major work, Boccaccio, describing his infancy, made up the following metaphor: "One day, when I followed in my untrustworthy father's footsteps into our home, I saw before me two fierce bears, their eyes burning with longing for my death."

If the old traditional school is right, the meaning is clear. Giovanni knew of his father's betrayal of his mother Jeanne and feared the deadly hate of his stepmother Marherita and of her son, Francesco.

Where did they live? Where was the home that to Giovanni appeared as a snare? Some say at Corbignano, a pretty village close to Poggio Gherardo near Florence and Settignano (where Boccaccio was to place the first three days of the *Decameron*).[5] There is indeed a house there that, with much discretion, is shown to the visitor as "The House of Boccaccio." But the interior has been renovated and all that remains of Giovanni's times are the walls. A dark-eyed, dark-haired beauty, who lives on the top floor, is, naturally enough, among those who feel certain that Boccaccio lived there. Through the village runs a stream, called the Mensola; on the other side of the hill is the river called Affrico. Henry Hauvette who is a firm upholder of the biographical nature of Boccaccio's early work, calls attention to the fact that in the *Ninfale Fiesolano*, Boccaccio tells us of a nymph, whose name is Mensola who loves and is loved in turn by the shepherd Affrico. Their love excites the wrath of the goddess Diana, Mensola's protectress, and the nymph dies of grief. In despair, Affrico kills himself. Death brings the lovers together again through a metamorphosis not dissimilar to many of

Ovid's. They are both changed into streams, whose waters mingle when both—flowing down—reach the Arno river. The Affrico is a sizeable stream but the Mensola is little more than a ditch and—unless Boccaccio either lived at Corbignano or at least went there very often—it is unlikely he would have known of its existence.

The natural beauties that surrounded him at Corbignano and the grace of his father's town houses in Florence did not dispel young Giovanni Boccaccio's fear of the two "bears" Margherita and Francesco. He was desperately unhappy until, in 1323, he was at last on his way to Naples where his father had decided he must work at the Bardi bank and learn a trade.

Of that journey he wrote an account that certainly was not autobiographical but a figment of the imagination. He says that after travelling some ten days and having avoided Rome which was known to be infested with robbers, he fell asleep on his horse, just as he was nearing Naples. In a dream: "there appeared to the eyes of my mind a girl most beautiful under every aspect, pretty and graceful. She was dressed in green and gave me a joyous welcome. She took me by the hand and kissed me and I kissed her. 'Come' she said 'here you will find happiness.' "

It seems very unlikely that a ten year old, such as Boccaccio then was, should have had such a dream but there is no accounting for the romance that breathes on those who see Naples for the first time. Whether it smiled to him from afar or not and whatever his expectations, Naples with its beauty, with its girls, its youth, its music and its songs gave him all that his heart desired. Hutton tells us that "he entered with gusto into the gaiety of what was certainly the gayest city in Italy". And in the *Ameto*, Boccaccio says: "Like the other young men around me I gazed on the shining beauty of the women of this land." Even the most sceptical of Boccaccio experts will allow that this at least is a truthful account and not imaginative figment. Two of the first girls he courted he calls Pampinea and Abrodonia, obvious pseudonyms. They are described in the *Filocolo* as "white dove" and "dark raven". They were not the object of deep passion whether they were real or visions of young Boccaccio's imagination. Whether the future writer's relation with them was fanciful or genuine, neither satisfied for long the ardours of a youth who was both sentimental and sensuous. The "white dove" soon found herself abandoned for the "dark raven" who, in her turn, betrayed Boccaccio. Real or imaginary, neither girl left a mark on his life. Finally on Saturday before Easter day, on 30 March 1331 he set eyes on the one he was to love and worship and make eternal so that her nickname "Fiammetta" is known even today in every continent.

He had gone to church at ten in the morning, the fashionable hour. His intent was to look at the girls and mix with the young men rather than to devote his attention to the service. The church was the elegant one of *San Lorenzo of the Franciscans* and he was to write in his "Ameto": "I was listening to Holy Mass ... there appeared to my eyes a beauty wonderful". What delighted him further was that, under the perfect curve of the eyebrows, he could discern and gaze upon the two most roguish eyes he had ever seen: "Due begli occhi lucean, si' che fiammetta": "Two beautiful eyes shone like brilliant flames"). And he gave her her still famous nickname in that moment. When she changed her place, he changed his position to one by a pillar where he could see her better. When the service was over, he took up his stand by the door but could not speak or murmur to her because when she left she was in the middle of a group of other ladies. He rushed back to his rooms. He was happy. He wanted to be alone with his thoughts. Next day was Easter Sunday and, just in case she should to go an earlier Mass, he was up early and sat through service after service and then, at long last, at the fashionable hour, she appeared. She was dressed in green and glittered with golden ornaments, he tells us in the *Ameto*. He claims he recognised in her in that moment the girl he had dreamed of when approaching Naples eight years before and he said to himself: "This is she who welcomed me to this city and promised me happiness." It is impossible to say how much of this is true though unlikely, how much of it is invention and a phantasy breeding conviction in a young lad's daydream.

Who was this lady? Thank goodness with Boccaccio we don't have to chase will o' the wisps as with Dante and Petrarch, Beatrice and Laura. Boccaccio tells us exactly who the lady was, and all details about her not just from the moment she was born but from the minute almost she was conceived. In Ameto he tells us that, at the Court of King Robert of Naples, there was a gentleman of the powerful House of Aquino, (the same family that had—in the previous century—given the great theologian, St Thomas, to the world.) This nobleman had married a young lady from Provence and lived with his wife in the royal palace. To cut a long story short, one day the King got into bed with her, but she, being wise, took care to sleep the same night also with her husband. When, nine months later, a little girl was born, the King and the husband were each convinced he was the father. The mother herself cannot have known whose child she was since the babe had the seraphic looks of the illustrious Father of the Church—Thomas Aquinas—but soon showed a wild disposition far more like King Robert's. Apparently the

infant's temperament finally convinced her mother that she could not
have a single drop of saintly blood and must be the King's daughter.
This was the Fiammetta of Boccaccio's dreams and her real name was
Maria. Her mother died after confiding her real father's name to her
daughter. The Aquino husband also died young, leaving Maria—as he
thought—an orphan. He left instructions that she be educated in a
convent: that of the Benedictine nuns of St Arcangelo da Baiano. As so
often happens in monasteries and convents, she became convinced she
should become a nun. Her vocation did not last long as the struggle in
her heart between her resolution to take the veil and her natural
feminine vanity gradually subsided. Vanity won and she grew to long for
the world and the world's men. The nuns fought hard to keep her when
the fame of her beauty spread and young suitors came offering marriage. Despite all obstacles, she was married to a young boy whose name
has remained unknown.

Boccaccio went to superhuman lengths to conceal from posterity the
name of the man whom he—and not he alone by far—cuckolded. As for
the girl she had no such qualms. She betrayed her husband practically
on their wedding night; certainly and often in their marriage bed. In
Boccaccio's work, entitled *Fiammetta*, the name he called Maria
Aquino by not to conceal her identity but to relive forever the delicious
palpitations of her burning blood and recall the light in her glittering
eyes, we read the tale of how and how much he and she yearned and
lusted for each other. In Boccaccio's case, it was love.

Fiammetta took a long time to choose him from among the many who
courted and won her favours. Boccaccio makes her say in his "Elegy to
Madonna Fiammetta" (generally called "Fiamenetia" for short) that
she had many lovers and "laughed at them, choosing those who took my
fancy at the moment and would be apt to give me liveliest pleasure. But,
once the fire was spent, I broke the vase and flung away the pieces."

It is remarkable that Boccaccio should have shrouded with delicacy
the husband's name from future generations, seeing how Fiammetta
dragged it in dishonour in her day. One of the reasons for Boccaccio's
generosity may have been that he himself suffered long the pangs of
jealousy where "Fiammetta" was concerned. He saw her surrounded by
adorers, richer, of more noble birth and with better opportunities than
he had himself. According to Della Torre, Maria's stupendous beauty
triumphed wherever she went; in church, at Court, along the beaches.
Lasciviousness was the core of her nature. Not that she didn't love her
husband, but she delighted in the added thrill of the 'secret fruit'.[6] Was
all this true? Or was it Boccaccio's day-dreaming? Strangely it is the

tightlaced older school of experts that believes practically every word of the tale, while the professors of our times, more lax times, are doubtful.

Going by what Boccaccio says, he again met Fiammetta of the flaming eyes twelve days later and, this time, she spoke to him at once. She was well known for always getting something out of her admirers and, on this occasion too, her words were words of command. She told Boccaccio to write a love story in her honour. He rushed home and immediately applied himself to writing *Filocolo*, which begins by portraying a young man's bliss in the dawn of love.

It proved to be the piece of writing that Boccaccio worked on longest. No wonder. From that day, April 12, 1331—when Fiammetta was barely seventeen—he had to wait five interminable years, before he could savour at long last the delights of his beloved's naked body. Some authors say he waited three months only but it is known that their days of enchantment ended in 1339, after three years of ardent passion, so that would place their first meeting in 1336, when Boccaccio was twenty-three. Now we know that Fiammetta, when she first set eyes on Boccaccio, thought she perceived some "lanuggine" some "soft down", on his chin. The day she asked him to begin writing "*Filocolo*", she became sure of it. This makes sense in 1331 when Boccaccio was barely eighteen. It would not make sense in 1336 when he would surely have had good strong whiskers. All this points to his having had to wait five years before he could physically possess Fiammetta, unless we are to take it he lay with her during eight years, a supposition that is not borne out by any document and most certainly would have been absolutely contrary to Fiammetta's flighty character. Till 1336 she played with him and he wrote *Filocolo* to please her and numberless letters in an attempt to win her.

At last, halfway through November 1336, Boccaccio arranged with the servant girl who had mounted guard on their secret and innocent trysts and had carried letters between them that he be introduced by stealth into his beloved's bedroom and hide there. Della Torre says: "The girl took him straight to her own quarters and went out locking the door. When night came, he heard the key turn and the girl led him to Fiammetta's chamber and told him to hide and not reveal himself". When Fiammetta arrived, the maid helped her to undress and Boccaccio, jittery and burning with desire, heard the servant girl weeping and giggling in turn and never asked himself nor wondered why his Fiammetta was not the least surprised. He managed to control his trepidation when Fiammetta's dress slipped from her shoulders revealing the shapely breasts, whose beauty he had long imagined and then the

magnificence of her thighs and legs that her skirts—long and wide—had
for so long hidden from him. She got into bed and he held his breath that
she should not hear him. When he judged she must be asleep at last, he
stepped out, approached and ran his fingers on the breasts he had so
long imagined and adored. Then his hand travelled down her body and
Fiammetta at this point, thought it was time to wake.

She cried out as if she had really been roused from slumber and was
alarmed. But he was on her, speaking in soft tones she recognized at
once!! Boccaccio himself tells us in the *Ameto* that he said: "I did not
come here to rob you of your virtue against your will; but have pity. I
am burnt with desire and can stand it no longer. If I can't have you, I
must die." And he drew a stiletto saying he would drive it in his own
heart there and then if there was no hope for him. Boccaccio says
Fiammetta made a leap for the knife, flung it far away and, covering him
with passionate kisses, cried: "This and not the sight of knives is what
Fiammetta needs and wants and must have." And Boccaccio had what
they both had wanted for so long and their love lasted close on three
years. Boccaccio followed her when she, with other Neapolitan beauties,
went to the sea at Baia near Pozzuoli in the summer and was requited
for the long time he had been compelled to watch Fiammetta from afar,
as she waded in skirts and petticoats held only high enough to reveal her
ankles, nothing more but enough to send his heart racing.

Then, in the summer of 1338, Fiammmetta suddenly began to tire of
him. She forbade him to follow her for the summer bathing. Boccaccio,
gnawed with jealousy at the thought of her among the coxcombs of the
Court, out on the rocks, among the waves and in the woods, tried to
console himself reading Ovid's *Ars Amatoria*, which he knew she read
incessantly ever since she had left the convent.

When she returned to Naples, he noticed, with dismay, a great
change in her. For once we can be completely certain that what he wrote
was pure fantasy: a philippic against the town of Baia, guilty of having
"corrupted the most chaste mind of his woman." Despite his humiliation
and his understandable rage, he still hoped and still loved her and was
to love her all his life. All his works, including parts of the *Decameron*,
are a hymn to her beauty, a cry against her fickleness, a groan for her
disregard of him. Then in January 1339, he knew it was the end.

As if the loss of Fiammetta were not enough, as he sat brooding
trying to think up ways to win her back, knowing all the while it was a
hopeless quest and that never, never, never any more would he revel in
her charms, financial disaster struck both him and his father. The Bardi
had gone bankrupt and drawn down with them the Boccaccio family.

Young Giovanni had to leave his house in Naples where he had lived in style and move out of the city. He found that now the portals of the Court were now firmly closed in his face and his erstwhile friends seemed volatilized. It was for Boccaccio a moment of bitter disillusion but he proved himself resilient. In a small house at Posillipo, he at last digested the classics. He also began to savour that endearing characteristic— better termed a quality or a virtue—of the poorest Neapolitans: their readiness to deprive themselves of their last crumbs to help someone when they are sure he is destitute save to get the better of him and his purse should he ever become rich. It was in this company that Boccaccio drank in the facts which he would later weave in some of the best short stories of all time.

But Boccaccio's Neapolitan period which had given him so much happiness and such dejection, so much love and so much disillusion,—in short so much life,—so much real life, came to an end in 1341, when his father, now a widower, summoned him to Florence. Life with father proved not to be easy for young Giovanni. The old man, melancholy and soured, chided him continually for having abandoned business, for lacking the experience in trade, which now might have helped them both in their straits. Knowing full well he did not have a merchant's mind, Giovanni threw himself into writing and the four years from 1341 to 1345—during which he stayed in Florence—were his most productive. He wrote the *Ameto* and hopelessly, desperately, as if to hurt himself with his own pen, he dedicated it passionately to Fiammetta, his only love. Then he set himself to write the *Amorosa Visione* "Amorous visions" of which Fiammetta, faithless but adorable, living in his thoughts as he lay with eyes closed and in the dark with other girls, is the soul that breathes in every line.

He then put the finishing touches to his "*Fiammetta*". The family of Aquino (perhaps at last aware she was the King's issue and not theirs) struck Maria's name from the list of its members, and she would have been forgotten but for Boccaccio's love, devotion, desperate writing of her, of her face, of her body, her breasts, her thighs, of all he missed so sorely.

Fiammetta appears on every plausible occasion in all of Boccaccio's youthful literary output. There are visions of her in some of the tales of the *Decameron*, the work that secured Boccaccio's fame and lives on to the present day. Her constant coming to light in his writing may well be taken to indicate that his love affair with her was no fantasy, as some authors claim, for surely someone with so rich an imagination as Boccaccio's most undoubtedly was, would, after not seeing her for eleven

years—from 1339 to 1351—have thought up some other voluptuous
wench to dream of. Meanwhile where had he lived? After the *"Amorous
Vision"*, the *"Elegy to Madonna Fiammetta"*, he had composed, between 1344 and 1346, the *"Ninfale Fiesolano"* in which he told of the
love of the shepherd Affrico and the nymph Mensola,—the per-
sonifications as we said earlier—of the two streams that run through or
near Corbignano. Did he draw from memories of childhood or did he
live there when he composed the tale? We know that Giovanni's father
had remarried and that his second wife, Bice de Bostichi, had bought
Giovanni a house so that he would remove himself and leave the veteran
newlyweds to live in peace without the eternal arguments and bickering
between father and son as to whether trade or culture were preferable.
Did she buy him the house at Corbignano? Or, as seems more likely, did
she not buy a house in town for her husband and herself, making
Giovanni a present of the Corbignano house with all its memories of
Boccaccio's father's former wife? Boccaccio's exact description through
the years of Fiesole, its gardens, its hillocks and its slopes, definitely lead
one to think he must have lived close to Fiesole or gone there very
frequently. And Corbignano is the scene not only of the *Ninfale
Fiesolano* but partly of the *Decameron* itself. The ten young people,
seven girls and three young men, who tell each other amorous and
adventurous tales in Boccaccio's masterpiece are described by him as
spending the first three days of their enforced sojourn in the country at
Corbignano, and the following week, on the other side of Fiesole, not far
from the Mugnone river in a villa along the road that is now the Via
Boccaccio, while the villa with its still trecentesque entrance is today the
gorgeous Villa Palmieri. The lower slopes of Fiesole, are not too far from
Florence to have prevented Boccaccio taking time off from his writing
for a series of minor jobs in the service of the Florentine Republic he
loved and was proud of.

He is known to have paid another flying visit to Naples, to have gone
there from Ravenna and then to Forlí, but if, in these travels, he acted
as emissary of the Florentines, he personally gained little from it all. We
find him back in Florence, or near it, a very poor man beset by financial
difficulties. His father had died. So had his second stepmother, the
comparatively wealthy Bice. Fiammetta too had gone to her grave. Boccaccio found himself alone in the world with his father's and Bice's
infant son, Jacopo, to look after. But he must have been renowned for
his trustworthiness because in 1350, when the Republic of Florence
finally decided in tardy acknowledgement of Dante's greatness, to grant
a payment of ten gold florins to Beatrice Alighieri, the nun who was the

Poet's daughter, it was Boccaccio and none other who was chosen to carry the gift to the convent in Ravenna where she lived. Perhaps it was this errand that gave Boccaccio the idea to try and persuade the Florentines to pay homage to Petrarch too and restore to the poet the fortune that the Republic had confiscated from his father. He succeeded and, this time too, he made nothing out of it,—at least not for a quarter of a century,—until Petrarch, dying in 1474, left him in his Will ... an old and much worn cloak! By then Boccaccio was not far off death himself. But in 1350 that was in the future and, meantime, Boccaccio's name appears as one of the official witnesses of the Florentine Republic's purchase of the town of Prato in 1351. He was later despatched on a mission to Ludwig of Bavaria, Marquis of Brandenburg, to secure his help, in case of need, against the Milanese. But Branca tells us "these missions and these honours did not lift him out of the straitened economic circumstances the Bardi bankruptcy had thrown him into." Nor did a mission to the Pope at Avignon in 1354 and—in April 1355— we find him eking out a living of a sort in Florence in a dull office for controlling the pay and absences from duty of the Republic's mercenary soldiers. In 1362—63 he got a job at the Neapolitan Court where he was badly treated both socially and financially. He tried to reach Petrarch in Venice, hoping for some help, but the Poet Laureate was away on one of his perpetual jaunts and poor penniless Boccaccio accepted the hospitality of Petrarch's son in law, the Milanese Franceschino da Brossano. He writes that "on the eve of my departure," (Franceschino) "knowing me to be poor and the hour being late, led me into a corner and, no one seeing, forced me to accept his liberality to my great embarrassment". But how else could he get home to Florence? Another journey in 1370 did not end so well. He had been invited to stay by the Abbot of the Certosa of Santo Stefano in Calabria. Then the Abbot, dismayed his invitation had been taken literally, left Calabria and disappeared before Boccaccio arrived. Boccaccio somehow made his way back to Naples and from there he wrote the Abbot a furious letter complaining of the treatment meted out "to a man you knew to be poor and old and infirm". We don't know how he got back to Florence. But he could no longer stay in the city, so he repaired to where he had spent a part of his youth at dates that are uncertain: his father's native village of Certaldo not far from Florence.

He was all alone. Despite his adoration of women, he had never married. He had loved deeply and lastingly his Neapolitan princess Fiammetta and had suffered cruelly from her flightiness. It had bred in him a profound distrust of women. Yet without women he knew he could

not live, and, at one time, as old age approached, he had—rather
naively—planned to marry a rich widow. She accepted his advances and
encouraged him to write to her. She turned out to be more cruel than
Fiammetta, viciously malevolent where the flighty Fiammetta had been
lighthearted. This widow, when she had collected a number of letters in
which the aged admirer she despised opened his heart to her and avowed
his passion, made a bundle of them and gave them to read to her real
lover, who, laughing at his wrinkled rival, scattered them all over Florence. Boccaccio, mad with rage, sat down to write *Il Corbaccio* with
the purpose to make her name mud for all posterity. Koerting says that
it is: "traced with a pen that has been dipped in poison; a venom such as
only one who has it within him could produce."[7]

But in old age, in 1373, despite his distrust and unhappy experiences
with women, he must have painfully regretted not having married any of
the several who had given illegitimate children who had not survived.

On 25 August 1373, he was offered a chair at the University of
Florence, possibly the Republic's parsimonious way of providing him
with a little money. He taught there for sixty days. He was already
affected by scab. He complains in his writing of "perpetual agony of the
veins, a swelling of the spleen and more ills than I can enumerate." A
doctor, called in to cure him, "to let the evil out", slashed him all over
his body with a razor. Despite this lunatic treatment, he survived till 21
December 1375.

He is buried in the church of San Michele and San Jacopo right close
to his Certaldo home, now magnificently restored. On the wall, to the left
of his tomb, hangs a tablet, with a laudatory tablet by Coluccio Salutati.
Boccaccio had earned scant recognition during his life—had died in
want—but he had heralded in the new era of enlightenment that through
the Florentine Chancellors and, Aeneas Silvio Piccolomini, was to lead
to the Medicean Golden Age.

Notes

CHAPTER ONE

¹ E. L. S. Horsburg—*Lorenzo The Magnificent and Florence in the Golden Age*—Methuen—1908

² Leon Battista Alberti—*Libri Familiae*—originally written in 1432—1434 NUE (Nuova Universale Einaudi) Torino 1969

³ Vittore Branca—*Dante, L'Umanesimo e il Rinascimento* in "Il convegno Italia Venezia e Polonia," Neeilorov—Tursan Zamosk 1965—Republished by Mieczyslaw Brakmen Wroclaw—Warsaw—Krakow, (to be found in Angelia Library, Rome).

⁴ Alfred von Reumont—*Lorenzo de'Medici Il Magnifico*—Verlag von Duncker & Humblot Leipzig 1883. "If we want to prove the value of our tongue we simply have to consider whether it renders with ease each of our thoughts and describes faithfully our sensations and feelings. There can be no more satisfactory answer to this question than what our own countrymen have found out. Dante, Petrarca and Boccaccio have demonstrated in their serious and graceful verses and way of speaking that all that is felt can be expressed lightly and naturally in our language. He who reads the Divine Comedy discovers that numerous theological problems and many concerning nature are discussed with the same degree of ease and exactness. (In our language as in Latin or Greek).

⁵ More closely resembling Pitt and his contemporaries than many Ministers in several countries today, particularly Italy where eloquence, save a few exceptions, took on the

form either of bombast with little relation to reality or the mouthing of lengthy ambiguous and obscure academical phrases meant to hide, at first hearing, what the speaker actually means.

[6] Maurice Andrieux—*Les Medicis*—Librairie Plon—Paris 1958 Andrieux writes: "This initiative was all the more generous in that Giovanni de'Medici, the wealthiest man in Florence, was the one upon whom the rigour of the law weighed heaviest. It has been malignantly insinuated that Giovanni was not displeased to let his co-citizens know—through the Catasto—how rich he was. "But" says Andrieux "whatever Giovanni's most intimate thoughts may have been, there is no doubt that it was patriotic and civic sentiment that drove him to enact the law and abide by it."

CHAPTER TWO

[1] The first to use the term 'Golden Age' was Marsilio Ficino, the neo-platonist, in a letter written in 1492. He used the term in contrast to Savonarola's appraisal of Il Magnifico's period. According to the bigoted fanatic monk, Lorenzo's Era had been a time of pagan adoration of the heathen gods, degradation of learning from Christian wisdom to pantheistic phantasy, lewd art (the friar insisted that some of Botticelli's paintings be burnt and Botticelli himself was made victim of such scruples that all his later work suffered in consequence.)

[2] Alfred von Reumont—*Lorenzo de'Medici Il Magnifico* Verlag von Dunker & Humblot—Leipzig 1883: "From his earliest youth, Lorenzo meditated on the existence and history of the common tongue".

[3] Ibid.

[4] Nicolai Rubinstein—*The Government of Florence under the Medici*. The only book extant that explains, in full detail, the Constitution and basic laws of the Florentine Republic. It embodies the most recent research and findings concerning the ways Lorenzo manipulated the Constitution particularly in times of national emergency.

[5] Ibid.

[6] Andre' Chastel—*Art et Humanisme à Florence au temps de Laurent Le Magnifique*: Einaudi Turin 1964 or Jonathan Griffin London 1965. Lorenzo loved to be in contact with intelligence and talent. One has the impression he was more interested in authors than in their works. He was a contemplative more than a builder.

[7] Letter written to Lucrezia Tornabuoni, Lorenzo's mother, herself a poetess. The date is 18 November 1478.

[8] Poliziano was not altogether wrong. Piero was to cause in 1494 the downfall of Medici rule in Florence by his shameful surrender of the Republic's fortresses to Charles VIII of France without a fight in 1494.

[9] Reumont hints at the possibility that rumous of homosexual leanings in Poliziano had reached Clarice. This does not seem altogether likely because in her letter from Cafaggiolo and in subsequent missives she clearly says she is willing to take Poliziano back into the household as preceptor of her children, should it be her husband's wish. In a deeply religious and even bigoted woman, this would appear surprising. Poliziano was destined to have a fearful row born of jealousy with Marullo, teacher and lover of Alessandra della Scala, with whom Poliziano was very much in love. Concerning Poliziano's homosexuality however, he is reputed to have died in 1494 either by being thrown down the stairs or slipping down the stairs which he had climbed in the dark to serenade a Greek boy with whom he had become thoroughly infatuated.

[10] Renaissance philosophers saw a close connection between Socratic, Platonic, Homeric thought, that of Vergil as well as with Christianity. While to the men of the

Middle Ages Vergil had been a poet endowed with great imagination, to Renaissance men he formed with Homer and Dante a trio of adepts to "Sacred Theology" the continuous theology having the Universal God as its subject. To Poliziano it was absolutely clear that Moses was perhaps the foremost expounder of this same theology which, in his view, he shared with Socrates and the others. To Clarice this concept was absolutely unintelligible. She saw in it only a danger to her children's catholic orthodoxy. To Poliziano it seemed as clear as day. Incidentally it was equally clear to Lorenzo, who despite his hourly preoccupation with the epidemic and the war with the Pope and the Neapolitans, did not find it in himself to punish Poliziano for holding to a notion that was so clear to both of them.

[11] To Poliziano it appeared that Clarice was—unwittingly—putting blinkers over her children's eyes. In his view (and in Lorenzo's) genius could only be compounded of inspiration coupled with a knowledge of the universal mystery. Take away either of them and there could be no genius such as he intended that any pupil of his and particularly any son of Lorenzo de'Medici should become.

[12] It was Lorenzo's villa at Careggi and Poliziano stayed there, safe from the plague and provided with all comforts for many months. He was not re-instated as Piero's and Giovanni's teacher for something like a year and a few months that is not until 1481. Even then, he was not the children's sole teacher but shared the post with a theologian, Giorgio Benigno, whose knowledge Lorenzo trusted implicitly. It was not as broad in its views as Poliziano's but sufficiently orthodox for the children's religious instruction. (When Pico della Mirandola elaborated his contentions which Rome judged heretical, Lorenzo had them looked over by Giorgio Benigno.) Besides, Benigno, Bishop Giovanni da Prato and another teacher of Theology, Antonio Barberini, were also called upon to teach the two boys. So it looks as if, in the end, Clarice won her point and removed all religious education of her children from Poliziano. But the poet continued to teach the boys classics.

[13] Actes du XXVIII ème Congrès International de l'Art, Amsterdam 1952. The letter was discovered by E. Gombrich.

[14] Andre Chastel—*Art et Humanisme à Florence au temps de Laurent Le Magnifique*—Librairie Plon—Paris—1958 Chastel writes, contrary to Rinuccini's view: "Lorenzo had a prae-ordained plan of artistic renewal. It was his great ambition to foster excellent painters and sculptors." Quoting Vasari, Chastel continues "Lorenzo loved with a great love both sculpture and painting, regretted that, in his time, there were no celebrated sculptors and decided to create a school to foster young talent." Vasari speaks of "The Garden of St. Mark" a sort of Academy where artists (among them Leonardo da Vinci and Michelangelo) developed their natural talent." They did so by studying the models of ancient art rather than by the study of nature and this may be the reason why Alamanno Rinuccini judged Lorenzo insufficiently "modern." Another reason that may have induced Alamanno Rinuccini to consider Lorenzo a not sufficient renovator of the arts, was that Il Magnifico did not commission large architectural works or sculptures. Chastel says: "Through a confidence that may appear excessive, Lorenzo was at pains to convey the inexhaustible flow of Florentine artists to other cities and so spread the glory of Florence through the world." In 1485 Lorenzo sent Leonardo, after his training in the Garden of St. Mark, to Ludovico il Moro in Milan and one of the results is "The Last Supper." In the same year, Verrocchio is sent to Venice, where he fashions Colleoni's statue.

In 1489 Lorenzo recommends Antonio Pollaiolo to Ludovico il Moro who is in need of a diligent artist to substitute the wayward Leonardo who is late in fulfilling his commitments. Lorenzo also sent Andrea Sansovino to the King of Portugal to build a four-towered palace that has no equal in Florence.

[15] Alfred von Reumont in his *Lorenzo de'Medici* says of Rinuccini: "A Party supporter of the Medici of long standing, he suddenly attacked Lorenzo, whose intellectual gifts

he fully recognised, with a judgement, whose severity brings to light how in what sense the aristocrats interpreted the equality of rights and how difficult it was for the Medici to secure their benevolence, even when they granted them favours. (Rinuccini's) heavy accusations against the system of government, represented by Lorenzo throw a singular light on the character of a man, who does not hesitate to make use of punishment which he himself condemns." For Rinuccini's favourable apparaisal of the Pazzi conspiracy see Chapter IX. Notes 2, 3, 7, 8.

[16] Alfred von Reumont says of Alessandra: "Like many ladies of her century she dedicated herself in her youth to greek studies and Demetrius Chalkondolas and John Lascaris were her teachers."

[17] Marullo's poems were published in Florence in 1497.

[18] Alberti—Four Books I Libri della Famiglia reprinted 1969 by Einaudi, Torino.

CHAPTER THREE

[1] A youthful poem which includes a dispute that Lorenzo really had with Ficino, in the Medicean villa at Careggi near Fiesole about the year 1474. It forms part of a collection of poems reprinted in 1969 by Sansoni Editore of Florence with the title of "Il Poliziano—Il Magnifico—Lirice del 400"—arranged and with commentary by Massimo Bontempelli.

[2] Gemäldegalerie—Berlin—Staatliche Museen Preussischer Kulturbesitz Kat. No. 106A. Picture gallery—Berlin—National Museum of Prussian culture— Catalogue number 106A.

[3] Probably the star Arcturus.

[4] Massimo Bontempelli *Il Poliziano, il Magnifico, Lirici del Quattrocento* Sansoni Ed. Firenze 1969.

[5] It was revealed by Poliziano in a poem, though Poliziano omits her family name.

[6] A contemporary likeness of Lorenzo—Ghirlandajo's work—appears in a group represented in a fresco in the Sasselli Chapel in the Church of Santa Trìnita in Florence.

[7] Botticelli was to paint a similar standard for Giuliano Medici, Lorenzo's brother in 1575.

[8] Roscoe—*Life of Lorenzo de' Medici called the Magnificent*. London 1799—Many later editions.

[9] Roland was one of Charlemagne's knights. According to French legend—sung in the Chansons de geste—legend taken up by Luigi Pulci in *Il Morgante* and repeated by Ariosto, Roland died making a last stand to prevent the Arabs from crossing the Pyrenees at Roncevaux. He did actually meet his end at Roncevaux but not fighting Arabs. He was crushed by large rocks rolled down on him from the heights by the Navarrese, whose time-honoured autonomous rights, Charlemagne had refused to guarantee.

[10] Pastor, in his *"History of the Popes"* finds fault with Lorenzo winning first prize at the tournament. He writes of him: "Eaten up with pride ... even in games, he would always be first." However it would appear difficult to imagine a young man in love taking part in a contest in front of his loved one and wanting to lose. Translation edited by Frederick Ignatius Antrobus—Routledge Kegan Paul London 1950 32 Vols also St Louis Missouri) B Merdez Book Co 15-17 South Broadway 32 Vols.

[11] A miniature of Cristoforo Landino—standing in front of Florence Cathedral is in the collection of Italian Illuminated Manuscripts in the Bodleian Library at Oxford (n.83).

[12] Indro Montanelli in his *Italia dei Secoli d'oro* Rizzoli Ed. Milano 1967 comments they didn't seem to realize "where there are no national soldiers in the end there are no free citizens."

[13] Ralph Roeder in the chapter on Lorenzo de' Medici that he contributes to J. H. Plumb's *"The Penguin Book of the Renaissance"* Penguin editions 1972 first published by the American Heritage Publishers Co. Inc. 1961, disregards this part of the contract between the Orsini and the Medici and writes: "Malcontents complained that the ambition of the rising bourgeois was unbounded, the Medici were satisfied with nothing less than a foreign baronial alliance. Actually there were several Florentine families of ancient lineage such as della Gherardesca, Pucci and others, though not all of them could claim a nobleman's title because Florence was a Republic."

[14] Horsburg—*Lorenzo the Magnificent*—Methuen—London and *Florence in the Golden Age*.

[15] Pope Leo Medici was as much annoyed with Tetzel for not devising better ways of collecting money as with Luther for raising theological questions. He despised the former's meanness and had a sneaking admiration for Luther's freedom of conscience, but he was much too taken with his dream of rebuilding St. Peter's to prevent the Curia and particularly the mean Cardinal Caetan from persecuting Luther.

CHAPTER FOUR

[1] Nicolai Rubinstein—*The Government of Florence under the Medici*—the only book that explains fully the intricacies of the Florentine Constitution. In it, Rubinstein points out that Lorenzo's election to Leading Citizen of the State did not—juridically—take place by normal constitutional means. Those who should have elected him according to the law were merely called upon to ratify a choice that had already been made by a restricted group of citizens. Rubinstein says—on the basis of three letters written at the time by Sacromoro, Milanese representative in Florence, to his lord the Duke of Milan—that a group, 700 citizens in all, some of them prominent, others ordinary citizens took the initiative in designating Lorenzo First Citizen, before the Government of the Republic, the Signoria, had had time to assemble. "The gravity of the situation" says Rubinstein "was felt to warrant exceptional measures, even if they had no constitutional standing."

[2] William Roscoe—*The Life of Lorenzo de'Medici called The Magnificent*.

[3] Josef Finkenzeller—*Glaube ohne Dogma?—Schriften der Katholischen Akademie in Bayern*—Patmos Verlag Düsseldorf 1972. On page 62, Finkenzeller points out that all dogmas so far proclaimed by the Popes through the Ages are expressed in terms of "Abendlandischen Philosophie" that is in terms of Western Philosophy. He argues that, if the Church wishes to fulfil her missionary task in the pluralistic Society of today, she must not prevent the unfolding of a Theology or of several theological systems, capable of explaining dogmas in forms of speech more understandable to the peoples of Africa and Asia." If what Finkenzeller—a most prominent professor of Catholic theology at Munich University—says is true, then it was equally true in the days of Paul II—only the Catholic Church was not then called upon to address herself to Asians and Africans, but to the men of the Renaissance. Paul II utterly failed to see that the old Early Christian and medieval enmity to the classical gods of antiquity was no longer applicable to the men of the Renaissance. What had been a necessary rule for preventing the Christians of the Roman world from slipping back into paganism, was utter folly in the Renaissance, when men didn't read the classics and spoke of the gods of classical times not because they were tempted to adore and serve them, but because the study of them was a release

and brought freedom from the superstitious and fears that had gradually accumulated during the Middle Ages.

⁴ The *Dictionnaire de Théologie Catholique contenant l'expose' des doctrines— commence' sous la direction* de A. Vacant, Professeur du Grand Séminaire de Nancy et de E. Mangenot, Professeur a L'Institut Catholique de Paris et continue' sous celle de E. Amanñ, Professeur de Theologie Catholique de l'Universite' de Strasbourg avec le concours d'un grand nombre de Collaborateurs. Paris 1923. In the seventh volume of this comprehensive work, we read that even before the Second Vatican Council, it was held true that "Pontifical infallability ... in the fullness of apostolic power *is met with only in acts which effectively emanate from the Pope and are manifested as such ... in order that there really be infallability it is required* that the truth put before the faithful *should already 1) have been proclaimed on a previous occasion or 2) is something that the Church has already admitted or believes in or 3) enjoy the unanimous and constant consent of theologians.* "It is astounding that Paul II should have thought he satisfied these three conditions when he persecuted the Literati. The acceptance of his measures against them and of the cruelty of those measures can only be explained by the existence of a servile, uncritical attitude concerning the Pope's claims to infallibility. It may have been due to ignorance but, in larger part, it stemmed from unwarranted Papal claims to infallibility in matters in which the Popes are not infallible.

⁵ Hans Küng—*Unfehlbar? Eine Ànfrage.* (Zürich, Einsiedeln, Köln 1970) and Karl Rahner—*Zum Problem Unfehlbarkeit. Antworten auf die Anfrage von Hans Küng.* (*Quaestio disputata 54*) Freiburg, Basel, Wein 1971.

⁶ See note 3.

⁷ Pastor—writes: "Paul II was devising means for recovering monarchical power."

CHAPTER FIVE

¹ According to some sources, it was not the tiara that cost most but a *"sedia gestatoria"* in which Popes are lifted so that the crowds can see them.

² William Roscoe—*The Life of Lorenzo de'Medici called The Magnificent.*

³ Donatello is credited with creating the Medicean Collection. Under Lorenzo the care of it had passed to Bertoldo, the sculptor. Bertoldo was later to be also Head and Instructor of the Garden of Saint Mark's—the Academy founded by Lorenzo—where, among many others, Leonardo and Michelangelo studied sculpture.

CHAPTER SIX

¹ Eugenio Garin—*Medioevo e Rinascimento.*—Editore Laterza—Bari and his *Scienza e Vita civile nel Rinascimento* idem translated into English with title "*Italian Humanism, Philosophy and Civic life of the Renaissance* by Peter Munz, Blackwell, Oxford 1965.

² Lucio Lombardo Radice—*L'Uomo del Rinascimento*—Editori Riuniti.

³ Lauro Martinez—*The Social World of the Florentine Humanists.* Princeton University Press, Princeton J. J. 1263 also Routledge and Kegan Paul, London.

⁴ See contemporary lifelike fresco by Ghirlandaio in the Sassetta Chapel in the church of Santa Trinita in Florence.

⁵ Giovanni Battista Picotti—*Ricerche Umanistiche* in *Studi, Lettere, Storia e Filosofia*—edited by Upper Normal School, Pisa.

[6] Juliana Hill Cotton—*Poliziano and Medicine*.

[7] Robert Weiss—Lecture delivered at *IV Convegno internazionale di Studi sul Rinascimento in Florence* from 23 to 26 September 1954.

[8] Strangely when, years later, Lorenzo's younger son Giovanni, the future Pope Leo X, became prior of the same church of St. Paul, the income he declared from the emolument he drew was 150 not 100 florins. Either Poliziano had been very prudent in his tax declaration and understated his income or the Priory had meanwhile been endowed with bequests of wealthy citizens.

[9] It is believed it was one—the most important—of the documents Soccino tried to steal when.he attempted to leave Pisa for Venice and was apprehended. See Chapter Five.

CHAPTER SEVEN

[1] William Roscoe—*Life of Lorenzo de'Medici called The Magnificent*. Roscoe is the most penetrating researcher of the Laurentian period and subsequent discoveries, many of them brilliant, have brought to light that most of those who are not in accord with Roscoe's interpretation did not realize that the enemies of the Medici at the time either had a grudge against them or were their downright enemies. In a few cases, such as that of Alamanno Rinuccini, they were visionaries who had no grasp of the very real dangers to Florence at the moment when they wrote. Rinuccini failed to realize that a return to the Pazzi, whom he praises as tyrannicides would have meant Florence falling under papal oppression.

[2] Politianus—*De conjuratione Pactiana Commentarius* (1478) also in *Opera Politiana*—(Basle 1553) and *Politiani Prose volgari*—ed. Adimari, (Naples 1769). Even the inveterate apologist of the Popes, Ludwig Pastor, states in his *History of the Popes* that Poliziano's was "A contemporary work substantially true but written with great bitterness."

[3] Luca Landucci—a Florentine Pharmacist (Speziale) wrote his Florentine *Diary* between 1450 and 1516 year of his death.

[4] Letter from Albertinus, Prior of San Martino to Marchioness Barbara of Mantua 28 April 1478. (Gonzaga Archives, Mantua).

[5] Report also dated 28 April 1478 (State Archives—Milan).

[6] Gregorovius *History of Rome in the Middle Ages* places attack at moment of Elevation and responsibility for crime on Sixtus IV.

[7] Nicolai Rubinstein—*The Government of Florence under the Medici*. Clarendon Press, Oxford pp. 196-7.

[8] Eugenio Garin in *Umanesimo Italiano*—Laterza, Zari (It appeared first time in German in 1947) quotes Alamanno Rinuccini's *De Libertade* ("Of freedom") and draws the conclusion that Rinuccini living a life apart from the politics in the country and in solitary meditation, looked upon culture, not as a participation in the active life of the State, as other Literati did. He considered that such participation was impossible for an honest man under Medici rule and held culture to be merely a refuge for the philosopher. This explains why Rinuccini, estranged from the society of his time, had no impact upon it. He defined the Pazzi conspiracy as "a just and honest undertaking to free the country".

[10] Nicolai Rubinstein—In *Italia Medievale e Umanistica* Ed Antenore Padua 1958. Rubinstein discovered a letter written by Jacopo to Sacromoro, Milanese Envoy in Florence, for delivery to the Duke of Milan. In it, Jacopo attempts to persuade the Duke to send a scholar to Germany to recover classical documents that Poggio Bracciolini had

collected, particularly during the Council of Constance. The discovery of one of these documents had wrongly been credited to Petrarch, Jacopo maintained.

CHAPTER EIGHT

[1] Among the Literati, apart from Jacopo Bracciolini who physically took part in the plot, the only known one was Alamanno Rinuccini, who saw in the conspiracy an attempt to restore republican liberties and, in his place of retirement in the country and detached from politics, completely failed to realise that a success of the conspiracy would have meant, at best, a return to the old aristocratic oligarchy and, at its very probable worst, the fall of Tuscany under Papal domination.

[2] The choice of ringing of bells as a signal to the conspirators in the Palazzo della Signoria to lay hands on the members of the Florentine Government definitely lends authority to Roscoe's version, supported by other testimony, that the attack on the Medici brothers in the cathedral took place at the moment of the Elevation of the Host. The Milanese Envoy's statement in his letter to Galeazzo Sforza dated 28 April 1478, that the assault on the Medici brothers took place about the Agnus Dei takes no account of the fact that no bells are rung at that moment.

[3] De Conjuratione Pactiana Commentarius.

[4] Lauro Martinez—*The Social World of the Florentine Humanists*—Routledge, and Kegan Paul, London and Princeton University Press, Princeton N.J.

[5] It would seem impossible since Jacopo Bracciolini was a member of Ficino's Academy and corresponded regularly with Ficino. Why he received no financial help from Il Magnifico remains a mystery. If he were indeed a squanderer and full of debts such as Poliziano hints, that might be a reason, since Lorenzo, though always ready to overspend for ancient documents and for the city's good, was not one to waste money foolishly nor to countenance idle spending in others. On the other hand, there is no evidence showing him to have been a violent anti-Medicean before his participation in the Pazzi conspiracy. Poliziano, by his description of him, strongly hints he did it for money but, given Poliziano's possible jealousy of Jacopo, who lived in the halo of his father's fame, we cannot accept without some misgiving Poliziano's appraisal of him. On the face of it, Jacopo may have been dazzled by the prospect of personal fame, distinct from his father's, at being the one actually to unseat the government of Florence and physically take possession of Palazzo della Signoria.

[6] Conjuratione Pactianae Commentarium.

CHAPTER NINE

[1] They were found to be neither Florentine nor Tuscan but people brought expressly from Perugia, whose inhabitants were often in the service of the Papal States either recruited or as mercenaries. It is a sad commentary to the claim made by the conspirators that "half Florence" would rise to their support, that—when the moment came—they could not muster a sufficient number of Florentines (not even twenty as the Perugini were) to carry out the main action of the uprising: that of unseating the government.

[2] According to Alamanno Rinuccini's account In Memorie Storiche dal 1282 al 1460 con la continuazione di Alamanno e Neri suoi figli, fino al 1506—Archivio di Stato and

reprinted 1841—Piatti-Firenze, the Archbishop personally tried to lay hands on Petrucci, but the Gonfaloniere 'noticed it.' Rinuccini writes literally "Gli volle porre le mani addosso, di che il Gonfaloniere si avvide." This account definitely clashes with all other narratives in which the Archbishop is constantly represented as the prime mover in schemes but never as a man of action. His attempt to lay hands on Petrucci, putting him on the alert, is all the more improbable in that a young and lusty young man, Jacopo Bracciolini, was just outside the door. Rinuccini ignores Bracciolini's part altogether, except he is mentioned among those hanged later. We do not know whether this was because Rinuccini did not have his facts straight or through jealousy of Bracciolini, another man of letters.

[3] Rinuccini gives the rather improbable detail that before hanging Bracciolini and the Archbishop, Petrucci sat down to a meal. "Dopo mangiare, lo impiccorno." This account seems in strident contrast with Rinuccini's own assertions a few lines earlier when he says that Jacopo de'Pazzi arrived in the piazza della Signoria with about sixty followers to capture the door of Palazzo della Signoria which he found defended by some volunteers, but they were so few that, had they not been helped by volleys of stones from the palace, they would have been the losers. Messer Jacopo, seeing that the Palace was firmly held by the Signoria, "si avvili" lost heart and abandoned the square in which he had arrived to the cry of freedom.

[4] Eugenio Garin in *L'Umanesimo Italiano*—Laterza Bari writes: "When in 1478, the crowd, wild with indignation, tore the Pazzi and their followers limb from limb for their attempt to overthrow the Medici, to the cry of liberty of the conspirators the people significantly opposed the motto: 'Long lives Lorenzo who gives us bread.' ". Evidently il Magnifico took care not only of the Literati but also of the poor to whom he assured 'Freedom from want.' unlike the old aristocratic oligarchy.

A. Fabroni in his *Laurentii de Medicis Magnificis Vita* Pisa 1784 had written the same as Garin. Both authors indicate that the people of Florence preferred the security, personal and economic, of the Medicean Era to the factional strife and exploitation of the earlier oligarchical times.

[5] Pactianae Coniurationis Commentarium.

[6] According to Rinuccini, Jacopo de'Pazzi and a few followers were set upon by the entire population of San Godenzo, a remote village, high up in the Apennines above the Casentino. This does not exclude that first it was a single shepherd personally to attack him and capture him and keep him captive despite his offers of gold.

[7] Alamanno Rinuccini ends his account of the Pazzi conspiracy saying: "Though it was a just and honest attempt to free their country, it had little success." Later Rinuccini, who had already glorified the killers of Galeazzo, tyrant of Milan, in his De Libertade implies that the Pazzis too were out to free Florence from a tyrant. He also claims he can take no part in politics but must retire into solitude, having culture as his only comfort "because there is no freedom." Garin says (Umanesimo italiano) that for Rinuccini "With no freedom on a political level, man turns inwardly on himself, seeks the freedom of the sage." It may be noted in passing that Rinuccini's appraisal of the assassination of a man and the wounding of another as 'just and honest' would have been prosecutable in modern democratic Italy as 'apologia di reato' which means 'Justification of a punishable offence' and an encouragement to others to commit the same offence. In Medicean Florence—except for his self imposed retirement—Rinuccini suffered no annoyance.

[8] Synodus Florentina Contra Sixtus IV in favorem Laurenti de Medici et domus ejus in occasione conjuration Familiae de Pazzi. Rospigliosi Collection now donated to Vatican Library IV 213.

CHAPTER TEN

¹ Gino Capponi—*Storia della Repubblica di Firenze* vol. ɪɪ Firenze, Barbera 1875. Referring to the Confession of Montesecco—the captain at arms who should have killed Lorenzo de'Medici (see previous chapter) Capponi writes: "Scala admits to having suppressed 'for good reasons' certain passages of (Montesecco's) confession. The original manuscript does have blank spaces". Caponni suggests that the words left out "might be words that, contrary to Lorenzo's intentions, might have irritated King Ferrante [of Naples.] Capponi draws the conclusion that this is very probably so, particularly with regard to that point in Montesecco's confession where the captain tries to draw Jacopo de'Pazzi into the conspiracy by relating to him all the powerful support the plot could claim. In other words, the mighty King of Naples was secretly favourable to it—possibly as a means of strengthening his position in the Republic of Siena. Capponi says that the other deletions too would concur with this interpretation, namely that Lorenzo wanted to avoid in any way offending the Neapolitan King, whom he had learnt from Montesecco, was adverse to him but was not yet an open enemy.

² Boccaccio began his career in the Bardi Bank at Naples and his Fiammetta was Neapolitan. Since then, Florentine bankers had been the financial prop of the Kingdom of Naples.

³ They were mostly ecclesiastical works. 26 Volumes of St. Chrysostom, 28 of St. Ambrose; 31 of St. Gregory; 81 of St. Augustine; 57 of St. Jerome; 51 of St. Thomas; 41 of Canon Law; 51 Records of Councils; 59 volumes of Old and New Testament; 98 Interpretation of Scriptures and Scriptural texts; 116 volumes by lesser known Greek writers on religious subjects; 109 by more celebrated Greek authors on religious subjects.

Though not so numerous there was also a large number of works by classical authors: 14 volumes of Seneca; 53 of Latin Poets; 125 of Roman History; 19 Latin Writers on Astrology and Geometry; 55 Latin works on Medicine; 103 Latin Philosophers. Most remarkable is the Greek collection on profane subjects: 70 volumes of Greek poetry; 59 of Greek History; 49 by Greek Astrologers; 14 Greek works on Medicine.

CHAPTER ELEVEN

¹ Pastor—*History of the Popes*.

² William Boulting—*Aeneas Silvius—Orator—Man of Letters—Statesman and Pope*—Archibald and Constable Ltd. London 1904.

³ Der Briefwechsel Aeneas Silvi Piccolomini. Correspondence of Aeneas Silvio Piccolomini—Wolkan Collection in Vienna—Letter n.99 written 5 December 1443.

⁴ All the quotes from Piccolomini's *Commentaries* in the present and the following chapters are taken from either the remarkably excellent translation into Italian by Professor Giuseppe Bernetti, undertaken at the request of Monsignor Mario Ismael Castellano, Archbishop of Siena, Edizioni Cantagalli, 1976. or the translation into English by Florence Alden Gragg with historical introduction and notes by Leona G. Gabel, Smith College in History, Northampton (Mass) or again from one of the following original texts of the Commentarii. The very first manuscript, partially written in Aeneas Silvius's own hand and often annotated in the margin by him is the *Codice Cartaceo Reginense*, preserved in the Vatican. It was looked over on Pius II's personal instruction by Gianantonio Campano. A second copy of the *Commentarii* is an exact and faithful transcription of the first by the German copyist, John Gobelin of Linz am Rhein, not far from Cologne. It is called the *Corsiniano* copy and is in the Biblioteca dei Lincei in

Rome, adorned with charming miniatures and is the one that Professor Bernetti consulted most. The first copy of the *Commentaries* to have been printed is believed to be that in the University Library at Basle (Falk 818—Bs 21—Frey Gryn D.III 14) *Commentarium Aenae Silvii De Concilio Basilae celebratus—Libri duo—Olim primum scripti nunc vero primum impressi, cummultis aliis numquam antehoc impressi.* Andreas Cratanda, Basle 1524. This book includes pages on the Basle Council which are absent in the other Commentarii neither the Reginense nor the Corsiniano. These pages may have been removed or corrected at the wish of Aeneas Silvius once he had become Pope or may have been erased by ecclesiastic censors after the Pope's death. Many other works of Aeneas Silvius suffered correction after he had died. In the Basle University Library there is the document: *Aeneas Sylvii Piccolomini Senensis—qui Pius Secundus appellatus est, opera quae extant omnia, castigata et in unum corpus redacta.* Dating from 1667, that is from after the Countereformation. This may explain the term *"castigata"* 'censored' and would entail some censorship of Pius's works long after he had died.

Published by Espasa Calpe S. A. Madrid 1975—originally published by Editorial Sudamericana, Buenos Aires, 1940—42—44—47—52—59. Also in 1955 by Editorial Mexico. Also in English by Hodder and Stoughton, London in 1939 and Hollis and Carter, London 1949 and by Macmillan in New York in 1939. In it De Madariaga says that Christopher Columbus mentions facts described by Pius II and names Pius II as the source of these facts in a letter which De Madariaga includes in Chapter XXX of his book. It is in the nature of a report by Columbus to the King and Queen of Spain (Carta que escribio' Don Cristobal Colon, Virey y Almirante de la Indias a los cristianissimos e muy poderosos Rey y Reyna de Espana.)

De Madariaga in a note in the Fourth Edition of his book on Columbus (Espasa-Calpe Madrid Ed) quoting other authors and arguing with those who raise doubts as to Columbus's Jewish origin writes:

"We have here (in a note by Columbus on the margin of one of Pius's astronomical books) a clear indication that Columbus makes use of phrases and adopts attitudes characteristic of Hebrews". De Madariaga also points out that—according to Jewish tradition and Hebrew chronology, the "destruction of the second House" took place in A. D. 68 and not in A. D. 70 when it occurred according to Christian reckoning. When Columbus says it occurred 1413 years and 1411 years before the moment he makes his annotation on the margin of Pius's book, he is adopting the Jewish reckoning and not the Christian.

CHAPTER TWELVE

[1] Aeneas wrote a vivid description of the election—with amusing incidents and entertaining details—it is in *"De Gestis Concilii Basilensis"* preserved in the Basle University Library. Many editions of it have been published of it, notably the translation into English by Denis Hay and W. K. Smith—Clarendon Press Oxford 1967.

[2] Frederick was not the only one. In fact there was a race among European sovereigns to sell their official recognition and allegiance to the Pope who might be ready to offer most. The King of France asked Felix V for 300,000 ducats. Felix, the stern hermit, though commanding vast wealth, wished his Pontificate to rest on the Council's decision not on simony and refused the King's demands. The King of France promptly swore his obedience to Eugene IV. His Most Catholic Majesty, Alfonso of Aragon too granted his recognition to "the One true Pope, Eugene IV" but not before the Pontiff had proclaimed him sovereign of the Kingdom of Naples, a territory the Popes claimed they could bestow on whom they liked.

[3] The ceremony of crowning Aeneas, took place on 27 July 1442 and is depicted by Pinturicchio in a painting in the Piccolomini Library in Siena.

[4] *Commentaries* (Chapter 11). Aeneas also found time to compose a pentalogue, a political dissertation supposedly taking place between him, Frederick III, Kaspar Schlich and two other individuals. The dispute is intended to show that the introduction of humanism into a state strengthens the nation. The argument fell on deaf ears. The uncultured Frederick was chiefly interested in horses and hounds. The versatile Aeneas promptly came up with a Latin treatise "De Natura et Cura Equorum." "Of the nature and care of horses."

[5] Charinus is meant to represent Aeneas himself.

[6] Sedullio is meant to represent a close friend of Aeneas: John von Eich.

[7] In the letter of apology, written by Aeneas to his friend Pfullendorf, who had complained of what he termed "the immorality of the play" and that one of the characters in it was too much like himself and exposed him to ridicule Piccolomini claimed he had been inspired by Plautus. The resemblance of the play to some of Plautus's writings is also stressed by Professor Giuseppe Bernetti—*Saggi sugli Scritti di Enea Silvio Piccolonin—Papa Pio II* Tipografia S T A A V—Florence 1971. Bernetti says: "It is clear that Piccolomini intended to write above all a comedy that would renew the arguments of those Latin authors who—in the years immediately preceding the time when Piccolomini wrote *Chrysis*—had aroused passionate enthusiasm and great intellectual curiosity as a result of the discovery of twelve unknown comedies by Plautus.

[8] One of the best translations is that by Wilfrid P. Mustard—The Johns Hopkins Press—Baltimore also the Oxford University Press 1928.

CHAPTER THIRTEEN

[1] See note 2 Chapter 12.

[2] Besides Felix was related with several of the Electors.

[3] See Chapter 11.

[4] Gioacchino Papparelli in his *Enea Silvio Piccolomini*—Editor Laterza—Bari 1950 p. 173: "Frederick made Eugene pay a high price for his recognition of him. He not only insisted that the Pope should crown him in public and with much ceremony but made Eugene give him 221,000 ducats to cover all the expenses of the journey to Rome and moreover restore to the Germans important benefices and lucrative rights. All this was the work of Piccolomini."

[5] Monsignor (later cardinal) Domenico Tardini and State Secretary to John XXIII, invariably told his secretaries when they came into his office with a problem marked "very urgent" to put the relative folder at the bottom of the pile saying: "By the time we come to it, it will probably have solved itself." It often did but not always. Tardini was imposed as Secretary of State on Pope John as a condition of John's election to the Papacy and was an attempt to put a brake on the Pope's impetuosity because he was known to be anxious for change and renewal. Tardini tried his best but did not succeed and Pope John will be forever the Pope of the Catholic Church's twentieth century renewal.

[6] It was essential to get the Pope's signature before his death because a new Pope, treading his first steps amid the difficulties of his incipient reign would not have wanted to offend his entourage and set it against himself at the very beginning of his pontificate and might even, to please the Romans, have rejected the agreement altogether. It would not have been the only time such a thing happened. Most instances when it occurred have been kept a closely guarded secret but when Pope Pius XI died on 10 February

1939, he had written out and was about to sign a document against Fascism in Italy. He was not able to affix his signature to it before dying. He died in the night, strangely quite alone. Cardinal Pacelli (three weeks later he became Pope Pius XII) in the morning, in his rank of Cardinal Camerlengo, ruler of the Church while the See was vacant, found the document of indictment against fascism and tore it up as valueless because it did not carry the dead Pope's signature.

[7] See Chapter IV on Paul II.

[8] See chronological table of life and works of Aeneas Silvius Piccolomini in Giuseppe Bernetti's translation of the *Commentaries*, vol. I (Edizioni Cantagalli, Siena 1972).

[9] The Liri runs in a valley in the mountains that bar some of the approaches between Rome and Naples. The Liri, together with the river Rapido, not far from it, was the site of an ill-timed and disastrous attack by the American Fifth Army in World War II. Had the General commanding (Mark W. Clark) or the other Generals read Piccolomini's *Commentaries*, they would have been aware of the dangers the two rivers presented and Aeneas the Writer would have had a beneficent influence not only on the society of his time but on many American families of the twentieth century, deprived of sons, fathers and husbands in an onslaught that might have been avoided.

[10] See Chapter XII Aeneas's poem "Rumperis invidia" verse extract.

[11] For Leon Battista Alberti see Chapter I.

CHAPTER FOURTEEN

[1] Santa Reparata—*La Cattedrale risorta* by Guido Morozzi—Piero Bargellini—Giorgio Batini—Bonechi Editore Firenze—June 1970.

CHAPTER FIFTEEN

[1] Hans Baron—*The Crisis of the early Italian Renaissance*. Princeton University Library—published in cooperation with the Newberry Library—Princeton N. J. 1966

[2] Gene A. Brucker—*Renaissance Florence*—John Wiley and Sons Inc. New York, London, Sydney, Toronto 1969.

[3] Berthold Louis Ullman—*The Humanism of Coluccio Salutati*—Editrice Antenore —Padua 1963.

[4] George Voigt—*Risorgimento dell'Antichita'* (Translated from the German by Professor Valbusa)—Sansoni Editor—Florence.

[5] Alfred von Martin—*Coluccio Salutati und das Humanistisches Lebensideal* Taubnitz 1916 (Coluccio Salutati and the humanist ideal of life).

[6] Lauro Martinez—*The Social World of the Florentine Humanists*. Routledge and Kegan Paul Ltd., London—Also Princeton University 1963.

[7] Daniela De Rosa—Coluccio Salutati—Istituto di Storia—Facolta' di Lettere— Firenze—1978.

[8] Demetrio Marzi—La Cancelleria della Repubblica Fiorentina. Editor Licinio Cappelli—Rocca San Casciano—1910.

[9] The renowned Professor Eugenio Garin in *Scienza e Vita civile nel Rinascimento Italiano*—Laterza Editor, Bari, 1972. See also *'Italian Humanism'* by Eugenio Garin, translated by Peter Muir, Basil Blackwell Ed. Oxford 1965 also *Medioevo e Rinascimento* by Eugenio Garin, Laterza Ed. Bari also *"I Cancellieri umanisti della Repubblica Fiorentina* by Eugenio Garin in Studi Fiorentini.

[10] Nicolai Rubinstein—*Politics and Society in Renaissance Florence* Faber and Faber Ltd. 1965.

[11] N. Rubinstein's is the most comprehensive and up to date study of these epigrams and their background.

[12] Other works consulted: *The development of Florentine Humanism* by Donald Wilcox—Harvard University Press—1969. *I Cancellieri Umanisti della Repubblica Fiorentina* by Eugenio Garin in Studi Fiorentini—Firenze 1963.

CHAPTER SIXTEEN

[1] Lauro Martinez—*The Social World of the Florentine Humanists*. Routledge and Kegan Paul—London.

[2] Donald J. Wilcox—*The Development of Florentine Humanist Historiography*—Harvard University Press—1969.

[3] Hans Baron—*The Crisis of the Early Renaissance*.

[4] Donato Acciaiuoli is the same person who, as Florentine ambassador to Rome, became the target of Sixtus IVth's animosity following the failure of the Pazzi conspiracy.

[5] Demetrio Marzi—*La Cancelleria della Repubblica Fiorentina*. Editor Licinio Cappelli—Rocca San Casciano—1910.

[6] Leonardo Bruni—*Difesa di Leonardo Bruni contro i riprensori del Popolo di Firenze nella impresa di Lucca*—Leonardo Bruni in Vatican Library.

CHAPTER SEVENTEEN

[1] Eugenio Garin describes Chancellor Bracciolini as "a solemn ornamental figure."

[2] All letters quoted are taken from Poggio's Epistolarium.

[3] It will be recalled that the details of the plot should have been carried to Piccinino by Aeneas Silvius Piccolomini, who was unaware that the document, entrusted him by the Bishop of Novara, contained such treasonable instructions.

CHAPTER EIGHTEEN

[1] Giovanni Papini—Dante vivo—Libreria Ed. Fiorentina 1957.

[2] Nicola Zingarelli—La vita di Dante—Zanichelli Bologna 1903.

[3] Translation Charles Norton—Boston—1867.

[4] Bruno Nardi in his "*Dante and Guido Cavalcanti*" Ed. De Luca, Rome 1965—confirms that the first poetical encounter between the two arose out of Dante's second meeting with Beatrice in 1283.

[5] Giovanni Papini in his *Dante vivo* (see note 1) writes: "one does not see in Beatrice the least return of Dante's loving admiration. There is no evidence at all of it whether she greets or whether she doesn't." Her pique, when he wrote verses for another, is not a demonstration of love but merely a show of annoyance at not being flattered herself.

[6] Giovanni Papini says that also Jacopone da Todi, who had been imprisoned under

an accusation of heresy by Boniface because he had preached poverty and a return to the spirit of Saint Francis—wrote verse against Boniface VIII.

7 Count Carlo Troya—*Veltro Allegorico di Dante*—Ed. Moline Florence 1826. Troya was an ardent Dantologist and, he set out to visit every place Dante was supposed to have been. Troya collected documents, word of mouth tradition and every evidence he could lay his hands on. From his findings, it is clear that Dante travelled over most of central and northern Italy. The claim that he visited England and Germany is unsubstantiated. Those who say he went to England base their assertion on two things: that he writes in detail on the philosophy of the then Archbishop of Canterbury but—to do this—he doesn't necessarily have to have visited the town of Canterbury or England. Equally flimsy is the assertion of the Reverend E. H. Plumtree DD, Dean of Wells, who in his *Life of Dante*—Isbister and Co., Ltd.—15—16 Tavistock Street, Covent Garden—1900, says that Dante's ample description of the city port of Wissant in Belgium, the port from which many sailed from the Continent to England, proves that he must have gone to England because "Whatever else would one go to Wissant for?" The fact is that Dante's knowledge of branches of English philosophy and places leading to England doesn't prove that he was necessarily in England.

8 The present day owner of Romena castle is the knowledgeable Count Luca Goretti, rigorously exact in all that concerns his ancient castle. That Dante did reside there either in 1304 or in 1310, there is no doubt.

CHAPTER NINETEEN

1 Susanna Dobson—*The Life of Petrarch*—printed by John Beatty Dublin 1777. Dobson tells of a letter Francesco Petrarch wrote to his brother in which he says: "Remember the time when we wore white habits on which the least spot or a plait displaced would have been the subject of grief; when our shoes were so tight we suffered martyrdom in them. When we walked the streets what care we took to avoid the puffs of wind that might have disordered our hair and the splashes of water that might have tarnished the gloss of our cloaks."

2 Umberto Bosco—*Francesco Petrarca*—Ed Laterza 1961.

3 Arnaldo Della Torre—*Storia interiore del Petrarca avanti l'innamoramento con donna Laura*—S. Lapi Ed. Citta di Castello (Florence) 1906.

4 Enrico Sicardi—*Cortesie galanti et amorose imprese di Francesco Petrarca* in the Italian review "*Rivista d'Italia* no. of January 1907.

5 Henry Cochin—*Sur le Socrate de Petrarque*—Imprimerie Caggiani Rome 1918.

6 Berlière Ursmer—a Benedictine—believed the place to be the Benedictine Abbey of St. Jacques in Liège. Ursmer revealed this on 12 December 1904 in the Inaugural speech of the Belgian Institute in Rome that day. The text of the speech—printed by the Institut Historique Belge may be consulted in the Vatican Library.

7 Ursmer asks the question in the speech mentioned in note 6.

8 Julius Caesar was practically the only one of the great "Roman" authors to have been born in Rome itself.

9 Count Cipolla—*Motivi del ritorno di Francesco Petrarca in Italia nel 1347*. 1906 Book in Vatican Library.

10 Other works consulted: Ernest Hatch Wilkins—*Life of Petrarch* University of Chicago Press—Chicago 1961.
Petrarch's "*Coronation Oration* in *Publications of the Modern Language Association of America*—P M L A LXVIII 1241—50.
Edizione nazionale delle Opere di Francesco Petrarca a cura di Giuseppe Billanovich—Sansoni Editore—Florence (many editions.)

Thomas Campbell—*Life of Petrarch*—Henry Colburn Ed.—Great Marlborough Street—London 1841.

[11] Edward Hutton—*Giovanni Boccaccio*—a biographical study—J. Lane, London and New York. 1910.

CHAPTER TWENTY

[1] Vittore Branca—*Giovanni Boccaccio* in *La Letteratura Italiana*. Carlo Marzorati Editor, Milan 1956.

[2] Henry Hauvette—*Literature Italienne*—Prix Halplen, Paris 1914 and his Etudes de Bocace—Bottega d'Erasmo—Turin 1968.

[3] Vittore Branca—*Schemi letterari e schemi autobiografici nelle Opere di Giovanni Boccaccio*—Florence, 1944 and his "*Studi su Boccaccio* (7 vols) Florence, 1973.

[4] Giuseppe Billanovich—*Restauri boccacceschi*—Rome 1946.

[5] Edward Hutton (who had a villa near Corbignano) *Giovanni Boccaccio A biographical study*. J. Lane—London and New York 1910.

[6] Arnaldo Della Torre—*La gioveinezza di Giovanni Boccaccio* S. Lapi Editor—Cittá di Castello—1905.

[7] Gustav Koerting—*Boccaccio's Leben und Werke*—Leipzig 1880 Life and Work of Boccaccio.

Index

ABOUT THE BOOK

A comprehensive exquisitely written and constructed history of the literature of the Italian Renaissance, the cradle of modern civilization.

Humanist writers succeeded in creating the profession of writer with all its now familiar social and economic power. Prince Rospigliosi shows that it was these pioneer professional writers who created the Renaissance, and not, as is often supposed, that they were its product. They dealt lethal blows to rigid hierarchical medieval authoritarianism, thereby transforming society into the modern world.

Prince Rospigliosi has elaborated a colourful tapestry about the rich and extraordinary lives led by the Italian Humanists. Michelangelo, Lorenzo de' Medici, Ariosto, Machiavelli were not only original geniuses, but also great individual characters, who come to life throughout this refreshingly lively history. This is an indispensable book for both layman and scholar.

ABOUT THE AUTHOR

Prince William Rospigliosi descends from the Tuscan family to which Pope Clement IX and the great Rospigliosi Cardinals belonged. During the Renaissance, his ancestors were notaries in Pistoia and themselves contributed to Humanist literature. Educated at Cambridge University, he spent much of his early career in broadcasting and journalism. He was Vatican correspondent for Time and Life for seventeen years, while contributing regularly to Italian newspapers and magazines. He has written a number of outstanding stories including *A Clock for Fiumiciono* (subsequently made into a film) and a book about his experiences in Rhodesia.